Conservative but Not Republican

Conservative but Not Republican provides a clear and comprehensive framework for understanding the formation and structure of ideological self-identification and its relationship to party identification in the United States. This book bridges the literature from a number of different research areas to paint a detailed portrait of African-American ideological self-identification. It also provides insight into a contemporary electoral puzzle facing party strategists, while addressing gaps in the current literature on public opinion and voting behavior.

Tasha S. Philpot is Associate Professor of Government at the University of Texas at Austin. She specializes in American Politics, with a particular interest in African-American Politics, Political Psychology, and Political Behavior. Her book *Race, Republicans, and the Return of the Party of Lincoln* (2007) received the 2008 WEB DuBois Outstanding Book Award, and her work has been published in journals including *The American Journal of Political Science, Journal of Black Studies, PS: Political Science and Politics,* and *Political Behavior.*

Conservative but Not Republican

The Paradox of Party Identification and Ideology among African Americans

TASHA S. PHILPOT

University of Texas at Austin

CAMBRIDGE
UNIVERSITY PRESS

CAMBRIDGE
UNIVERSITY PRESS

University Printing House, Cambridge CB2 8BS, United Kingdom

One Liberty Plaza, 20th Floor, New York, NY 10006, USA

477 Williamstown Road, Port Melbourne, VIC 3207, Australia

314-321, 3rd Floor, Plot 3, Splendor Forum, Jasola District Centre, New Delhi - 110025, India

79 Anson Road, #06-04/06, Singapore 079906

Cambridge University Press is part of the University of Cambridge.

It furthers the University's mission by disseminating knowledge in the pursuit of education, learning and research at the highest international levels of excellence.

www.cambridge.org
Information on this title: www.cambridge.org/9781316615959
10.1017/9781316687185

First published 2017
First paperback edition 2018

A catalogue record for this publication is available from the British Library

Library of Congress Cataloging in Publication data
NAMES: Philpot, Tasha S., author.
TITLE: Conservative but not Republican : the paradox of party identification and ideology among African Americans / Tasha S. Philpot.
DESCRIPTION: New York : Cambridge University Press, 2016. |
Includes bibliographical references and index.
IDENTIFIERS: LCCN 2016040380 | ISBN 9781107164383 (hardback : alk. paper)
SUBJECTS: LCSH: African Americans–Political activity–United States. |
African Americans–Politics and government. | Identity politics–United States. |
Democratic Party (U.S.)–Membership. | Republican Party (U.S. : 1854-)–Membership.
CLASSIFICATION: LCC E185.615 .P47 2016 | DDC 324.2734089/96073–dc23 LC record available at https://lccn.loc.gov/2016040380

ISBN 978-1-107-16438-3 Hardback
ISBN 978-1-316-61595-9 Paperback

To Hanes Walton, Jr.

Contents

Contents

Figures

Tables

Acknowledgments

There are many people to whom I owe a great debt of gratitude and without whom this project would not have been completed. First, I wish to thank the person to whom this book is dedicated, Professor Hanes Walton, Jr. Even though he is no longer of this Earth, he continues to inspire me to be a better teacher, mentor, researcher, and scholar. There are not enough words to express how much of an impact he has had on my life. He is truly missed.

I also wish to express my gratitude to a number of other scholars who have aided in the development of this project. First, I would like to thank Larry Bartels and the Center for the Study of Democratic Politics at Princeton University, who provided me the physical and intellectual space to grow this project during its early stages. Second, I wish to thank the Project for Equity, Representation, and Governance at Texas A&M University, the Colloquium on Race, Ethnicity and Immigration at the University of California at Berkeley, the Inter-University Consortium for Political and Social Research at the University of Michigan, the Distinguished Visiting Scholars Program at Washington University, and Georgetown University's Department of Government for allowing me present and receive helpful feedback on earlier versions of this project. I also wish to thank Ernest McGowen, Nadia Brown, Chima Nwachukwu, and John Iadarola for their research assistance. Finally, this book benefited greatly from financial support from the National Science Foundation (SES-0840550; SES-0610267), the University of Texas at Austin's Department of Government, and the Irma Rangel Public Policy Institute.

I am extremely grateful for the support and friendship of a number of colleagues. I am particularly thankful to Jessica Trounstine, D. Sunshine Hillygus, and Maggie Penn (a/k/a L.I.P.S.) for being my political science sister circle. I am also indebted to my colleagues and advocates at the University of Texas at Austin: Terri Givens, Daron Shaw, Paula Newberg, and Bryan Jones. I also wish to thank Paula McClain, Karen Kaufmann, Vincent Hutchings, and Nicholas Valentino for their continued friendship, love, and mentorship. Attending the University of Michigan was one of the best decisions I ever made and I don't know what I would do or where I would be if it weren't for the "Michigan Mafia." I especially owe a huge thank you to Andrea Benjamin for a "hookup" during the eleventh hour of completing this book. Lastly, I would like to thank members of "Team Tasha" who reside outside of the academy – Joya Hayes, Vikki Andrews, RoShana Adamson, Kendra Gaither, Geri Stewart, Jacquie Jones, and the members of the Beta Psi Omega Chapter of Alpha Kappa Alpha, Sorority, Inc.

I owe the greatest debt of gratitude to my family for supporting me through the years as this book neared completion. First, a special thank you to the light of my life, Natalie McDaniel, for providing much needed perspective when completing this book became overwhelming. Thank you to my mother, Marcia Philpot, and my mother-in-law, Nedra McDaniel, for providing reinforcement when Natalie's "perspective" became overwhelming. Finally, I wish to thank my partner in crime, Eric McDaniel, who keeps me going when the road gets too burdensome to bear.

Introduction

> Most Black people don't think alike, but most Black people vote alike.
> – Representative J.C. Watts (R-OK)

On April 15, 2013, Herman Cain held a press conference to announce the convening of a new organization, the American Black Conservatives (ABCs). The ABCs are a group of about a dozen Black conservatives, including neurosurgeon Ben Carson. The purpose of the group is to unite Black conservatives and create a separate Black conservative "brand" (Travis 2013). Although he previously ran for the Republican presidential nomination in 2012, Herman Cain has since advocated for the distinction between conservatism and Republicanism. In an effort to attract more African Americans to the conservative movement, Cain wants to distance himself and other Black conservatives from the negative perception Blacks have of the Republican Party. Furthermore, in contrast to the contemporary Republican Party and other conservative groups, Cain and the ABCs are interested in explicitly bringing a Black perspective to solving the nation's economic problems, suggesting a unique brand of conservatism experienced through a racialized lens (Travis 2013).

Arguably, Herman Cain's political views do not represent those of the average African American. Yet, the tension between Black ideology and Black party identification can be observed among members of the rank-in-file Black electorate. As former Member of Congress J.C. Watts notes in the opening quotation, most Black people vote alike. To be sure, contemporary American politics is marked by Blacks' overwhelming support for the Democratic Party and its candidates. Roughly three-quarters or more of Blacks have identified with the Democratic Party since the 1960s. Over this same period, Democratic congressional and presidential candidates have benefited from no less than 85 percent of the Black vote (Bositis 2008). Despite repeated attempts to cut into the Democratic Party's stronghold on the African-American electorate, GOP outreach efforts have fallen on deaf ears (Philpot 2007).

Representative Watts is also correct in noting that there is quite a bit of heterogeneity in the political thinking of African Americans, certainly more diversity than their voting behavior would suggest. In particular, in the Black community there is a long history of conservatism that pre-dates Emancipation. This conservatism is thought to be based on a shared tradition of "being churchgoers, of building cohesive family units through [Blacks'] reliance on extended family and kinship networks, and of adher-ing to other principles that have been identified as conservative" (Watson 1998, 75). Thus, African Americans' religiosity and subsequent conserva-tive position on moral issues suggest that Blacks should be more receptive to the Republican Party.

This, however, is not the case. Take, for instance, the debate sur-rounding whether homosexual couples should be legally allowed to marry. During the general election in November 2004, 11 states held ballot referenda calling for the banning of same-sex marriages, domes-tic partnerships, and/or civil unions. Supporters of gay marriage bans condemned the union of same-sex couples along moral grounds. Those in opposition heralded same-sex marriage as a civil rights issue (Clemetson 2004). Because of its size and cohesion, the Black voting bloc could determine victory or defeat in many states (Walton and Smith 2010). But, *a priori*, the Black vote could have gone either way:

> The fact that many black Christians are both politically liberal and socially conservative makes them frustratingly difficult to pigeonhole in a political envir-onment in which, many pundits contend, voters are cleanly split along ideological lines. Many blacks opposed to gay marriage, for example, support equal benefits for gays as a matter of economic justice (Clemetson 2004, A1).

Prior to the election, those on both sides of the debate made appeals to Black clergy and their congregations, with conservative groups like the Family Research Council courting conservative denominations and liberal groups such as the National Black Justice Coalition reaching out to the more liberal factions of the Black church (Clemetson 2004). Ultimately, however, framing same-sex marriage as a civil rights issue did not reson-ate with many Black voters and Black religious groups. For example, in

TABLE I.I *Percent voting for same-sex marriage ban and George W. Bush in 2004, by state*

	White Support for Same-Sex Marriage Ban	Black Support for Same-Sex Marriage Ban	Bush Vote among White Supporters of Ban	Bush Vote among Black Supporters of Ban
Arkansas	76	64	74	8
Georgia	75	78	88	15
Kentucky	75	68	76	15
Michigan	58	57	71	12
Mississippi	88	72	89	10
Ohio	62	57	73	19
Oklahoma	76	72	80	34

Note: Figures are weighted values.
Source: National Election Pool General Election Exit Polls, 2004.

response to the larger political culture bringing the issue of gay marriage to the forefront, delegates to the African Methodist Episcopal Church, with a membership of 2.5 million, voted at their 2004 General Conference to ban the performance or blessing of gay marriage in the church (Chang 2004).

Ultimately, the exit poll data presented in Table I.I show that in seven of the eleven states in which the gay marriage ban appeared on the ballot,[1] a majority of Blacks voted for ballot measures defining marriage as a union between one man and one woman (National Election Pool, Edison Media Research, and Mitofsky 2005). Black support for the ballot referenda was on par with that of Whites. Levels of support for the same-sex marriage ban were lowest among Blacks in states like Michigan and Ohio, where overall support for the ban was closer to the 50 percent threshold. In the Deep South states of Georgia and Mississippi, where voters convincingly passed these ballot initiatives, about three-quarters of Blacks voted in favor of excluding homosexual couples from the institution of marriage. Even in states like Arkansas and Kentucky, where Black support lagged behind White support, nearly two-thirds of Blacks voted in favor of a same-sex marriage ban.

If opposition to homosexual marriage is any indication of the conservative nature of voters in these states, then Black voters should have been

---

[1] Montana, North Dakota, Oregon, and Utah are excluded because of too few Black observations.

ripe for the picking for the Republican Party. The link between ideology and party identification is well established, even if the strength of the relationship is debatable (Abramowitz and Saunders 1998; Carmines and Stimson 1989; Rapoport 1997; Box-Steffensmeier and De Boef 2001; Levitin and Miller 1979). Decades of empirical research documents that ideological conservatism is positively correlated with support for the Republican Party and its candidates. This relationship can be observed by looking at George W. Bush's vote share among Whites who voted in favor of the same-sex marriage ban in 2004. Regardless of state, no less than 70 percent of this group voted for Bush. Despite their overwhelming support of it, however, the gay marriage ban did not become a defining issue for Blacks in the 2004 presidential election. As noted at the time by Reverend Gene Rivers, president of the National Ten-Point Leadership Foundation, "Most of the same people who believe fundamentally that marriage is between a man and a woman and who will stand up and support that with conservatives voted for Al Gore in 2000 and oppose tax cuts for the rich and cutting social services in 2004" (Clemetson 2004, A12). Consequently, no more than 20 percent of Blacks who voted in favor of banning same-sex marriage voted for the incumbent Republican president, with Oklahoma being the exception. In Arkansas, the Bush vote share among Black supporters of the gay marriage ban did not even reach 10 percent (see Table I.1).

By 2012, a majority of Americans indicated that they supported gay marriage, including President Obama. During a radio interview in 2004 while running for the U.S. Senate, President Obama stated that, based on his faith as a Christian, he believed that marriage was "something sanctified between a man and a woman" (Healy 2008, A1). Eight years later, President Obama revised his position and announced his support for same sex marriage during an interview with co-anchor of "Good Morning America" Robin Roberts (Obama 2012). President Obama's "evolving" ideas about gay marriage matched the general trend on this topic. A recent study by Pew Research Center indicated that there was a 17 percentage point increase in support for same sex marriage – from 31 percent in 2004 to 48 percent in 2012. And although there was a 34 percentage point difference between Democrats and Republicans in their support of gay marriage (66 percent of Democrats in support, compared to 32 percent of Republicans), the percentage of Republicans supporting gay marriage had also increased from 2004 to 2012 ("Changing attitudes on gay marriage" 2015). Nevertheless, the gap between Democrats and Republicans on this issue indicated that it was still a good predictor of partisan support in 2012. But was this true for both Blacks *and* Whites? Using the 2012 ANES, we are able to gauge support for gay marriage as well as support for political parties. The results suggest that despite the heightened saliency that came with President Obama declaring his support for gay marriage, this issue failed to become a deciding factor in Blacks' partisanship. Overall, 29 percent of Blacks and 25 percent of Whites opposed gay marriage.[2] Among Blacks who opposed gay marriage in 2012, less than 3 percent reported voting for Republican presidential candidate Mitt Romney, compared to 87 percent of Whites. Likewise, less than 2 percent of Blacks who opposed gay marriage self-identified with the Republican Party.[3] The rest either identified as Democrat (75 percent) or Independent (24 percent). Of the Whites who opposed gay marriage, 55 percent identified as Republican, 33 percent identified as Independent, and 12 percent identified as Democrat.

Why doesn't ideology predict party identification and candidate support the same way among Blacks as it does for Whites? This question serves as the impetus of this book. *Conservative but Not Republican* explores the ways citizens make sense of ideological labels. More specifically, the central aim of *Conservative but Not Republican* is to examine the factors that influence both the predictors of Black ideology and the applicability of ideology to Blacks' partisan evaluations. I argue that we cannot fully understand the relationship between Blacks' ideology and party identification unless we take into account the mix of considerations – including Blacks' attitudes about religious, social welfare, racial, military, and moral issues – used to determine whether African Americans will ultimately label themselves as liberal or conservative. Furthermore, we must also consider how racial considerations can often supplant the expression Blacks' ideology when it comes to choosing with which political party to identify. Taking into account the unique conceptualization and conditional applicability of the liberal–conservative continuum offers a more comprehensive understanding of the structure and function of ideology in American public opinion.

---

[2] Respondents were asked which answer choice came closest to their view: 1) Gay and lesbian couples should be allowed to legally marry; 2) Gay and lesbian couples should be allowed to form civil unions but not legally marry; or 3) There should be no legal recognition of a gay or lesbian couple's relationship. For these analyses, opposition to gay marriage denotes respondents' selection of the third answer choice.

[3] Party identification here is measured using the 3-point pid_self variable provided in the 2012 ANES time series study. The category "Independent" included respondents who specified they had no preference or another party preference.

IDEOLOGICAL TRENDS IN BLACK AMERICA

Evidence of conservative thought in the Black community dates as far back as the eighteenth century (Eisenstadt 1999). In addition to well-known historical Black conservative figures such as Booker T. Washington, Black leaders from W.E.B. DuBois and Frederick Douglass to A. Philip Randolph and Louis Farrakhan have incorporated conservative thinking into their advocacy of a more equal America. Most commonly, Black conservatism has manifested in the tension between the pursuit of government response to racial injustice versus the desire to pursue a strategy of Black political and economic autonomy (Eisenstadt 1999). Thus, strains of conservatism have, to some extent, always permeated Black politics – from the elite level on downward.

Recent work has demonstrated that there are actually a multitude of ideological strains within the Black community (Dawson 2001; Harris-Lacewell 2004). Dawson (2001), for instance, describes six Black ideologies – radical egalitarianism, disillusioned liberalism, Black Marxism, Black nationalism, Black feminism, and Black conservatism – that serve as trends in Black political thought.[4] Of these six ideologies, Dawson argues that Black conservatism has the least grassroots support within the Black community, although his conceptualization is much narrower than that considered here and in the broader research on ideology in American politics.[5] For instance, Lewis (2013) argues that Black conservativism is not only defined by anti-government attitudes, but also religiosity and support for traditional family values. Further, when we use this broader definition, Black conservatism is not as far out in the margins of Black political thought as previously conceived.

---

[4] Dawson (2001) does not examine Blacks' placement on the liberal–conservative continuum. From his perspective, that is not to say that Blacks do not organize their politics along this dimension. Rather, Dawson argues that there have been "dramatically divisive conflicts within the black community," such as the Anita Hill-Clarence Thomas hearings, which did not fall neatly along the liberal–conservative continuum (45). In these cases, alternative ideologies, which developed out of Black counterpublics, better explain those cleavages.

[5] Dawson's measure of Black conservatism is based on a narrow set of racial and economic issues that do not fully encapsulate the nature of Black conservatism. He finds support for this claim using an additive index of four measures that conceptualize Black conservatism and radical egalitarianism as polar opposites of each other. Moreover, Dawson's radical egalitarianism/Black conservatism scale's reliability coefficient is only 0.28, suggesting that this conceptualization of Black conservatism is not an internally consistent measure.

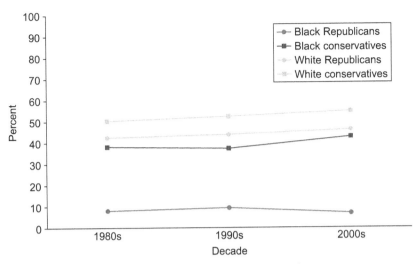

FIGURE I.I Percentage of conservatives and republicans, by race
Note: Figures are weighted values. Republicans include strong and weak Republicans, as well as Independents who lean Republican. Conservatives include extremely conservative, conservative, and slightly conservative.
Source: American National Election Study Cumulative Data File, 1948–2012.

Moreover, scholars have actually noted the growing conservative nature of the African-American electorate over the last few decades (Watson 1998; Tate 2010). Generally speaking, Whites tend to be more conservative than Blacks in any given decade. Nevertheless, a significant percentage of Blacks self-identify as conservative. For instance, during the 1980s, 50 percent of Whites and 38 percent of Blacks self-identified as conservative (see Figure I.1). Two decades later, that number is 55 percent for Whites and 43 percent for Blacks (American National Election Studies and Stanford University 2015).[6] Yet, the rate at which Blacks identify as

---

[6] These numbers were generated using the summary liberal–conservative scale provided in the ANES cumulative data file. Originally, respondents were asked to place themselves on a seven-point scale, ranging from extremely liberal to extremely conservative. The "conservative" category is comprised of those respondents who indicated that they were either extremely conservative, conservative, or slightly conservative. Included in these figures are responses to the follow-up "choice" question whereby respondents who initially indicated that they didn't know or hadn't that much about their ideological self-identification were asked "If you had to choose, would you consider yourself a liberal or a conservative?"

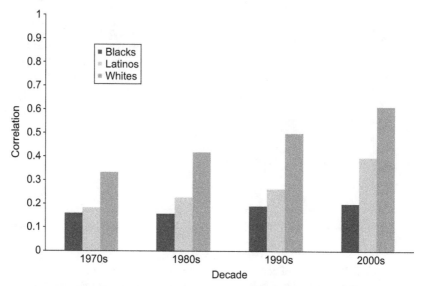

FIGURE I.2 Correlation between party identification and ideology by race and decade

Note: Values are Pearson product–moment correlations. Party identification is a seven-point scale ranging from strong Democrat (0) to strong Republican (1). Ideology is a seven-point scale ranging from extremely liberal (0) to extremely conservative (1).

Source: American National Election Study Cumulative Data File, 1948–2012.

Republican lags considerably, especially when compared to Whites.[7] The percentage of Black Republicans never reaches beyond 10 percent, regardless of decade. The percentage of White Republicans, on the other hand, moderately increases from 42 in the 1980s to 46 in the 2000s (American National Election Studies and Stanford University 2015).

Figure I.2 provides a longitudinal look at the correlation between ideological self-identification and party identification.[8] Among Whites, the relationship between party identification and ideological self-identification has been growing stronger over the last four decades. During the 1970s, the correlation between these two constructs was 0.33. Since then, the correlation has increased from 0.42 in the 1980s,

[7] Party identification here is measured using the Party ID Summary provided in the ANES cumulative data file. The category "Republican" includes both strong and weak Republicans, as well as those Independents who lean Republican.

[8] The full seven-point party identification and ideological self-identification scales are used for these analyses.

0.50 in the 1990s, to 0.61 in the 2000s. The correlation between party identification and ideological self-identification has remained consistently low among Blacks over the same time period, hitting its lowest point in the 1970s and 80s ($r = 0.16$). Currently, the correlation among Blacks is 0.20, one-third that of Whites. As a comparison, Figure I.2 also indicates that the correlation between Latinos' party identification and ideological self-identification had been consistently low and on par with that of Blacks throughout the 1970s and 80s. But by the 2000s, that correlation had increased to 0.40, 20 percentage points higher than Blacks. This evidence suggests that Blacks truly are the exception to the rule when it comes to the American electorate's recent alignment of their partisanship with their ideological self-identification.

Not only does Blacks' ideological self-identification weakly correlate with party identification, Black conservatives behave more like Black liberals than they do White conservatives when it comes to vote choice. In 2012, for instance, 96 percent of Black liberals and 78 percent of Black conservatives identified with the Democratic Party (see Figure I.3). In contrast, 81 percent of White liberals identified as Democrats while only 13 percent of White conservatives did so.[9] We see a similar pattern emerge when we look at presidential vote choice in 2012. Among Whites, we observe the expected relationship. Eighty-six percent of liberals voted for Obama, the Democratic Party's presidential candidate, while only 14 percent of conservatives voted for him. Nearly all of Black liberals reported voting for Obama and 89 percent of Black conservatives reported voting for the incumbent Democratic president (ANES 2012). Note that this is not just an artifact of the 2012 election. There is strong support for the Democratic presidential candidate among Black conservatives, even when that space is not occupied by an African-American candidate. In 2004, 83 percent of Black conservatives voted for Kerry, compared to 97 percent of Black liberals. Compare this to Whites, where 82 percent of liberals and just 18 percent of conservatives voted for Kerry in 2004 (University of Michigan 2006). So while fewer Black conservatives voted for Kerry than Black liberals, the difference between the two is nowhere near as stark as it is among Whites. Thus, Black conservatives lean toward the Democratic Party and its candidates significantly more so than their White counterparts.

---

[9] The same variable construction described in footnotes 6 and 7 were applied to the 2004 and 2012 data.

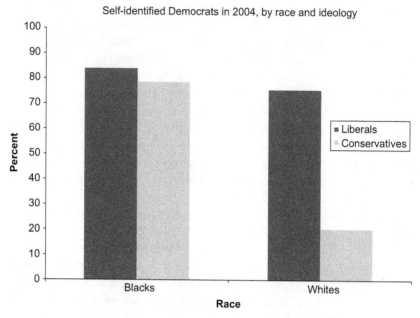

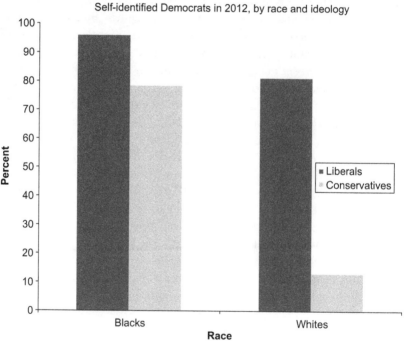

FIGURE I.3 Party and candidate support, 2004 and 2012
Note: Figures are weighted values. Democrats include strong and weak Democrats, as well as Independents who lean Democrat. Conservatives include extremely conservative, conservative, and slightly conservative. Liberals include extremely liberal, liberal, and slightly liberal.
Source: American National Election Studies, 2004 and 2012.

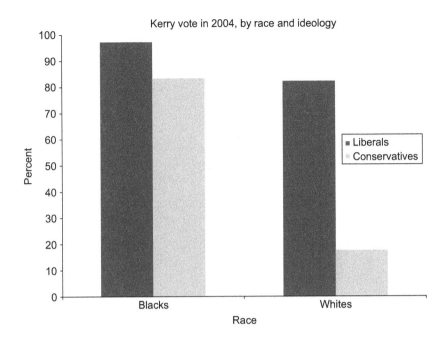

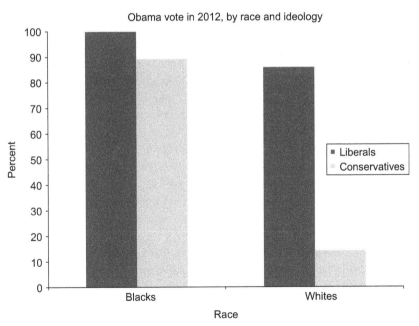

FIGURE I.3 (*cont.*)

TABLE I.2 *Demographic profile of Republicans and conservatives, by race*

	Black Conservatives	Black Republicans	White Conservatives	White Republicans
% Married	39	49	65	67
% Female	46	29	48	49
% Living in the South	60	53	32	34
% Home Owners	49	64	82	83
% Employed	46	55	53	56
Mean Age	44	38	51	50
Median Income	$32,500	$62,500	$57,500	$62,500
% College Degree	12	19	32	35
Median Church Attendance	Almost every week	Almost every week	Almost every week	Almost every week

Note: Figures are weighted values.
Source: American National Election Study, 2012.

Furthermore, it appears as if Black conservatives and Black Republicans are two different groups of people. Table I.2 provides a demographic profile of conservatives vs. Republicans by race. Beyond the noticeable differences between Blacks and Whites, there are noteworthy differences between Black Republicans and Black conservatives that do not exist between White Republicans and White conservatives. Nearly across the board, White Republicans and White conservatives look demographically similar. In contrast, there are often large differences in the characteristics of Black Republicans and Black conservatives. Black Republicans are more likely to have college degrees and tend to be younger on average than Black conservatives. Black conservatives are also less likely than Black Republicans to be married, employed, and own homes. Finally, Black conservatives are more likely to be female and live in a southern state than Black Republicans.

Why is there such little overlap between Black conservatives and Black Republicans? Extant work on Black conservatives has primarily focused on the increasing number of Black conservative elites (Sigelman and Todd 1992; Kilson 1993; Watson 1998; Tate and Randolph 2002). Personalities such as Shelby Steele, Thomas Sowell, Alan Keyes, Ward Connerly, and Clarence Thomas have risen to prominence as a result of their alliances with conservative organizations, including the Republican Party

(Watson 1998). Scholars, for instance, have explored how different these leaders are from the average Black American. In an examination of how Clarence Thomas differed from mainstream Black America, Sigelman and Todd (1992) found that there was considerable distance between Thomas and Blacks in general in their perceptions of the proper role of the federal government in ensuring equality. Whereas Thomas believed that it was the responsibility of Blacks to improve their own position in life without government intervention, 77.9 percent of Blacks in 1991 believed that the federal government was doing too little to help Blacks in the United States and 75.1 percent of Blacks believed that more legislation was needed to improve the condition of Blacks (Sigelman and Todd 1992, 240–1). Less work, however, has been devoted to examining the contours of Black conservatism within the general electorate.

Conservative but Not Republican begins to fill this gap in the literature. I argue that Black party identification is not driven by or reflective of Blacks' extremely liberal policy positions. This is evident by Blacks' position on gay marriage described above. In fact, Blacks' placement on issues varies considerably (Tate 2010; Seltzer and Smith 1985), despite earlier studies that predicted that conservatism would not find support in the Black community (Hamilton 1982). As a result, a growing number of Blacks self-identify as conservative. Rather, I argue that the correlation between Black party identification and Black ideology is a function of two phenomena. First, I argue that Blacks have developed a unique conceptualization of the liberal–conservative continuum, which has grown out of their distinct position in American society. This argument is predicated on the notion that ideology is multidimensional and that ideological self-identification is determined by one's position within a number of policy domains. Not all of these dimensions are equally salient across different races. The relevancy of each policy domain to Blacks' ideological self-identification is shaped by the historical relationship Blacks have had with government and politics in that area. Because Whites have not been privy to these experiences, they use a different set of dimensions in determining their ideological self-identification. Furthermore, because of their unique position in American society, Blacks' conceptualization of the liberal–conservative continuum does not neatly overlap with that of the broader electorate, causing a weaker correlation between Blacks' party identification and ideological self-identification than observed among other racial groups.

Second, I argue that the expression of Blacks' ideology is conditional on their level of group consciousness. Racial considerations continue to weigh heavily in the political thinking of African Americans, regardless of political ideology. This we know from previous research (Dawson 1994; Gurin, Hatchett, and Jackson 1989). I offer an additional layer to our understanding of the relationship between race and party identification by examining the moderating role of racial group consciousness on political predispositions. Specifically, I contend that the relationship between party identification and ideological self-identification for Blacks is contingent on racial group consciousness. When group consciousness is high, Blacks regardless of ideology will identify with the Democratic Party. I argue, however, that Democratic Party identification is most likely to weaken among Blacks with low levels of group consciousness. A unique conceptualization and conditional applicability of the liberal–conservative continuum, I posit, are the reasons why there are not more Black Republicans in the American electorate. The remainder of the book is dedicated to empirically evaluating these claims.

Much as *Romeo and Juliet* is not just a story about Italians but of a tumultuous love affair, the main characters of this book are African American but this is not a story solely about Black politics. At its heart, *Conservative but Not Republican* is a book about how individuals and groups, who simultaneously hold competing considerations, manage this complexity. Hence, this theoretical framework is applicable to more than just Blacks. Conceptualizing ideology as both multidimensional and hierarchical helps us to think about the inherent tensions between ideology and voter decision making for many different groups in the electorate. There are other so-called issue publics in American society for whom one issue overrides all others (see Hutchings 2003, for instance). And despite being liberal or conservative on other issues, that one issue will be the most salient when determining that group's ideological self-identification. Understanding the ranking of ideological dimensions for different groups in society enables us to discern the difference between citizens who are ordering ideological information versus those who are ideologically innocent.

Likewise, Blacks are not the only group in American society who must negotiate through multiple and often competing identities. In politics, members of other affinity groups – for instance, those oriented around gender, sexuality, or religion – may also find themselves in conflict with their partisan attachments or ideological ideals. Thus, it is helpful to think about how one's avowed identity might mute the observable relationship between ideological self-identification and party identification as it is predicted to in the case of African Americans. In doing so, we must consider the political context in which that group has operated and what relationship that group has had with the two major parties. For example, one of the reasons why group consciousness is such a strong predictor of party identification among Blacks is because of the legacy of race and the two-party system in the United States (Carmines and Stimson 1989; Philpot 2007; Frymer 1999; Gurin et al. 1989). For some Blacks, this creates a tension between an ideological self-identification that pulls them towards the Republican Party and a sense of group consciousness that pushes them away from the Republican Party. Replicating the moderating effect of group consciousness on ideological self-identification across issue publics would require finding another group that experiences a similar tension with one or both of the two parties and has a high level of group consciousness. Such groups are hard to come by; but if these conditions are met, the theoretical proposition should still hold.

PLAN OF THE BOOK

Addressing the central question of why the growing number of Black conservatives has not yielded a comparable rise in the number of Black Republicans requires a two-part story. Part One sets out to demonstrate that Blacks have a unique conceptualization of the liberal–conservative continuum, which has implications for the correlation between party identification and ideological self-identification. Specifically, my argument is that (1) the liberal–conservative continuum is multidimensional; (2) not every dimension is universally relevant to ideological self-identification; and (3) the dimensions most relevant to Blacks' ideological self-identification are those where African Americans' have historically had the most experience with respect to politics and government.

The inquiry into the unique relationship between Blacks' ideological self-identification and party identification begins in Chapter 1, which makes the case for conceptualizing ideology as multidimensional. In particular, Chapter 1 provides the foundational evidence to support the argument that the low correlation between Blacks' ideology and party identification stems from the way African Americans conceptualize the liberal–conservative continuum. First, it briefly chronicles the literature on political sophistication and ideological thinking and demonstrates that a lack of political sophistication does not fully account for the weak correlation between Blacks' ideological self-identification and party identification. Chapter 1 then provides evidence for the multidimensional use of the terms *liberal* and *conservative* across six policy realms – laissez-faire, racial, military, social welfare, religious, and moral – and traces the use of these ideological dimensions over time. This is done through a content analysis of the *New York Times* over a 150-year period and the *New York Amsterdam News* over an 80-year period. Using survey data and data collected from semi-structured qualitative interviews, this chapter then goes on to show that the same ideological labels found in the newspaper coverage parallel that in public opinion.

With the six policy domains in mind, Chapter 2 develops a set of theoretical expectations regarding the particular policy dimensions that should be relevant to Blacks' ideological self-identification. I hypothesize that only those issue areas in which African Americans have had the most experience with politics and government will be pertinent to their ideological self-identifications. Furthermore, because of these same experiences, Blacks will have a unique packaging of these ideological dimensions that does not neatly fit with that of the broader electorate. Consequently, the relationship between party identification and ideological self-identification is much weaker for Blacks than it is for Whites. I challenge the current literature that suggests that Blacks' attitudes about the appropriateness of government in addressing racial disparities constitute the dividing line between Black liberals and Black conservatives. That is not to say that race is not important. Rather, I argue, race has implications for the way Blacks have interacted within the other domains. Chapter 2 provides support for this argument by drawing upon extant research in psychology and political science to lay out a framework for how individuals develop their ideological self-identification and ideological constraint. With this framework in mind, Chapter 2 then traces the historical relationship between Blacks and the six policy domains discussed in Chapter 1.

Chapter 3 sets out to empirically test the theory presented in Chapter 2. In this chapter, I examine which issue areas African Americans use when determining whether to label themselves liberal or conservative and how these domains are bundled together to form a constrained ideology. Chapter 3 introduces survey data from the 2010 Post-Midterm Election Study. Using an 18-item battery of questions that attempts to measure each dimension of ideology, these data confirm that racial issues do not define what it means to be a Black liberal vs. a Black conservative. Rather, religious and social welfare issues are the strongest dimensions predicting Black ideological self-identification. The importance of race, however, manifests in how the relevance of specific policy dimensions varies by race, reflecting different experiences that Blacks and Whites have had in their interactions with politics and government. I augment the survey results with qualitative data in order to provide a "thick description" of why and to what extent Blacks consider themselves liberal or conservative.

Part II of *Conservative but Not Republican* continues to examine if and how racial group considerations shape whether ideology is translated into partisan attachments and political behavior. In Chapter 4, I argue that group-relevant considerations moderate the correlation between ideology and support for a political party and its candidates. To be sure, African Americans possess unrivaled levels of group consciousness. It is this group consciousness, I argue, that supersedes ideology when Blacks evaluate political parties. As foundational support for these claims, Chapter 4 investigates the roots of Black group consciousness and how prevalent it currently is in the Black community. Chapter 4 begins with a general explanation of how group consciousness is formed. It then provides a brief history of group consciousness in the Black community and the psychological mechanisms that led to its development. Lastly, the chapter examines the contemporary predictors of group consciousness using data from the qualitative interviews and survey data from the 2010 Post-Midterm Election Study and the 2012 Religious Worldview Study.

Chapter 5 continues to provide theoretical and empirical justification for arguing that the relationship between party identification and ideological self-identification is conditional on levels of group consciousness. I argue that when group consciousness is high, Blacks regardless of ideology will identify with the Democratic Party. As levels of group consciousness decrease, however, I contend that attachment to the Democratic Party will also weaken. Chapter 5 begins with a review of the scholarly research on the relative importance of ideology versus social groups in predicting party identification and vote choice, pointing out that research in this area has yet to examine how group considerations and ideology might work in tandem with one another. This chapter then provides empirical evidence derived from the 2010 Post-Midterm Election Study and the 2012 Religious Worldview Study, along with qualitative data, to support the argument that group considerations and ideology can have both independent and joint effects on candidate and party support.

Chapter 6 expands the analyses presented in Chapter 5 to explore how group consciousness moderates ideology's effect on other political attitudes and behaviors. This chapter focuses primarily on how Afrocentric Black conservatives – those Black conservatives with high levels of group consciousness – negotiate the tension they experience between their ideology and their racial consciousness. Using the 2010 Post-Midterm Election Study and the 2012 Religious Worldview Study, this chapter demonstrates that many Black conservatives are often caught between a rock and a hard place when it comes to navigating between their sense of racial solidarity and conservative ideals. Consequently, Afrocentric Black conservatives' reported turnout in presidential elections, their presidential approval, and their evaluations of Republican public figures will more closely mirror that of Black liberals than they will Black conservatives with low group consciousness.

Chapter 7 concludes the discussion of race, ideological self-identification and party identification by summarizing key findings and discussing their implications. In this chapter, I speculate about the potential for Blacks functioning in a two-party system in light of the results presented in the earlier chapters. I also make predictions regarding the nature of Black partisan support given current events in Black politics, including voter suppression, the candidacy of Dr. Ben Carson, and the modern civil rights movement. Chapter 7 ends with a roadmap of avenues for future research.

PART I

I

Peeling Back the Layers

The Multidimensionality of the Liberal–Conservative
Continuum

I work with the welfare system so to see it suck us up and break families
up, once again it's about the whole population and not just about an
individual group of people and so for that reason I think that I see that as
liberalism ... I think conservative means ... have the belief of the Bible, it
kind of guides you.

— Respondent 49

One of the premises of this book is that Blacks have a unique conceptualization of the liberal–conservative continuum, which has implications
for the correlation between their party identification and ideological self-
identification. In exploring this premise, our first step is to discern what
people mean when they use the terms *liberal* and *conservative* and how
that has changed over time. Chapter 1 does this by first demonstrating
that a lack of political sophistication cannot be the sole explanation for
the idiosyncratic relationship between Blacks' party identification and
ideological self-identification. Second, Chapter 1 defines six distinctive
policy dimensions in which the terms *liberal* and *conservative* have been
applied. Next, by using a content analysis of the *New York Times* over a
150-year period and the *New York Amsterdam News* over an 80-year
period, this chapter illustrates how the definition of ideological labels has
grown increasingly more policy-oriented. Lastly, using survey data and
data collected from semi-structured qualitative interviews, this chapter
goes on to demonstrate how the uses of ideological labels found in the
New York Times and the *New York Amsterdam News* parallel that in
public opinion.

POLITICAL SOPHISTICATION AND IDEOLOGY

African Americans constitute the most cohesive voting bloc in American politics. Since 1964, Blacks have reported voting overwhelmingly for the Democratic Party. As Figure 1.1 indicates, Black support for Democratic presidential candidates has not dropped below 80 percent since the 1970s. Furthermore, these levels of support are unmatched by other racial groups. Among Whites, Democratic presidential candidates struggle to receive more than 50 percent of the vote, and not since Carter in 1976 has a Democratic presidential candidate received more than 45 percent of the White vote. Latino support for the Democratic Party waxes and wanes. In 1976, 82 percent of Latinos voted for Carter, which was a level of support comparable to that among Black voters. Only 53 percent of Latinos, however, voted for Kerry in 2004, which indicated that their support for the Democratic presidential candidate more closely mirrored that of White voters.

Given the strong link between Blacks and the Democratic Party, scholarly research on American political behavior has largely ignored

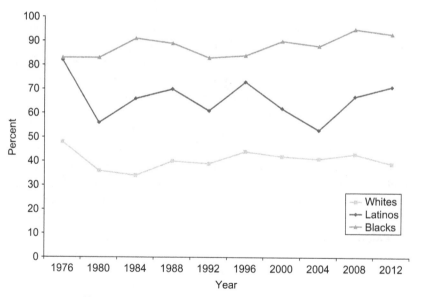

FIGURE 1.1 Self-reported Democratic presidential vote, by race and year
Note: Values are percentage of self-reported Democratic presidential vote for each election year.
Source: The Roper Center for Public Opinion Research.

variation in the policy attitudes or ideological preferences of African Americans. Models of partisanship and voting behavior simply include a dummy variable for Black, thereby assuming racial category is all that is needed to explain Blacks' attachment to political parties. Consequently, previous literature does little to help explain the puzzle of why there are a significant number of Black conservatives but very few Black Republicans.

One explanation for the disconnect between Black conservatives and Black Republicans comes from the broader research on American political behavior, which highlights the lack of political sophistication in the electorate. Decades of empirical research have cast doubt on the basic ability of the mass public to understand what it means to be liberal or conservative (Kinder 1983; Converse 1964). The most consistent finding is that those with high levels of political sophistication – that is, with higher levels of political interest, political knowledge, and education levels – are more likely to think along ideological lines (Converse 1964). For instance, Knight (1985) found that ideological conceptualization was highly correlated with cognitive ability and political motivation; ideologues had higher levels of education and political interest than non-ideologues. With respect to ideological self-identification, Jacoby (1991) found that there was greater congruence between placement on the liberal–conservative continuum and individuals' policy positions among those with higher levels of education. Previous studies have shown Blacks to have, on average, lower levels of political knowledge than Whites (Delli Carpini and Keeter 1996). Given what we know about the relationship between political sophistication and ideology, Blacks' lower levels of political knowledge might account for the idiosyncratic relationship between their ideological self-identification and party identification. In other words, because they do not truly understand the meaning behind ideological labels, some Blacks are mistakenly labeling themselves conservative even though their policy preferences would suggest otherwise. As predicted by Campbell et al. (1960), however, party identification serves as a less complex means of evaluating the political world, allowing Blacks with liberal policy preferences to connect with the Democratic Party and its candidates.

Evidence dispels the notion, however, that political sophistication is the explanation for Black conservatives' identification with the Democratic Party. Using the 2012 American National Election Study (ANES), Table 1.1 examines respondents' mean placement on four standard

TABLE 1.1 *Levels of political knowledge, by race and ideological self-identification*

	Blacks	Whites	Difference
Liberals	1.44	1.90	−0.46*
	(1.08)	(1.27)	
	N = 239	N = 979	
Conservatives	1.45	1.80	−0.35*
	(1.19)	(1.19)	
	N = 243	N = 1901	
Difference	−0.01	0.10*	

Note: Values are weighted means. Standard deviations appear in parentheses. Starred differences are statistically significant at the $p < 0.10$ level (two-tailed test).
Source: American National Election Studies, 2012.

political knowledge questions as a cumulative test of political sophistication.[1] Specifically, respondents were asked if they could identify which political office John Boehner, Dick Cheney, David Cameron, and John Roberts currently occupied.[2] Respondents, regardless of race, on average, respondents answered less than two of the questions correctly (mean for total sample = 1.62; standard deviation = 1.20). If we look at levels of political sophistication by race and ideological self-identification, the differences appear to be substantively small. Among Blacks, the difference between liberals and conservatives is negligible. Among conservatives, the difference between Blacks and Whites is statistically significant but substantively the equivalent of less than half of a correct answer (ANES 2012). The results presented in Table 1.1 suggest that there is nothing particularly unusual about Blacks' level of political knowledge that could account for the distinctive relationship between

[1] These are commonly used measures of political knowledge. A version of these four questions have been asked as part of the American National Election Studies (ANES) for over twenty-five years.

[2] For these analyses, the summary political knowledge measure ranged from zero (indicating that the respondents were unable to correctly identify any of the names presented) to four (indicating that respondents correctly identified all four of the names presented). Ideological self-identification was generated using the summary liberal–conservative scale provided in the 2012 ANES. Originally, respondents were asked to place themselves on a seven-point scale, ranging from extremely liberal to extremely conservative. The *conservative* category is comprised of those respondents who indicated that they were either extremely conservative, conservative, or slightly conservative. The *liberal* category is composed of respondents who responded that they were either extremely liberal, liberal, or slightly liberal.

their ideological self-identification and their party identification. Furthermore, even if the small difference between Black and White political knowledge could explain some of why Black conservatives do not identify as Republican, it would not be able to explain the full discrepancy.

Instead, I argue that the idiosyncratic nature of the relationship between Blacks' ideological self-identification and party identification is better understood not as a function of Blacks' lack of political sophistication, but as the way Blacks conceptualize what it means to be liberal and conservative along distinct policy dimensions – with some more or less relevant to their ideological self-identification. The opening quotation at the beginning of this chapter is a perfect representation of this point. Respondent 49, a Black female from Alabama, defines liberalism in terms of social welfare, but thinks about "conservative" as being defined by one's adherence to the Bible. Presumably, a similar pattern exists when we look at ideological self-identification. Namely, (1) there are a host of realms in which individuals apply ideological labels, and (2) the relevance and applicability of these realms is not universal. More specifically, when individuals are placing themselves on the liberal–conservative continuum, the relevance and applicability of each of the policy dimensions is primarily rooted in America's race relations and Blacks' historic interactions with government and politics.

IDEOLOGICAL THINKING?

An ideology, as it is defined by Campbell et al. in *The American Voter* (1960), is a "particularly elaborate, close-woven, and far-ranging structure of attitudes" (192). It is the glue that binds attitudes together and provides a sense of internal consistency across a range of ideas and issues. According to Jost (2006), "ideology helps to explain why people do what they do; it organizes their values and beliefs and leads to political behavior" (653). Ideology provides a lens through which individuals interpret the world in which they function (Campbell et al. 1960). This lens provides meaning and context to all the social, political, and economic phenomena that one might encounter over the course of a lifetime.

The dominant paradigm in the study of political ideology has been that the American public is unable to conceptualize politics at a level of abstraction high enough to be rendered "ideologues" (Campbell et al. 1960). Moreover, scholars believe there is very little stability across political attitudes (Converse 1964). In other words, "most Americans approach the political world innocent of ideology: indifferent to standard ideological concepts, lacking a consistent perspective on public policy, and with authentic opinions on only a handful of policy questions" (Kinder 1983, 393).

Subsequent studies in this area have sought to challenge this notion, examining which subgroups of the American populace have organized sets of belief systems and what psychological, political, and environmental circumstances have led Americans to have more stability in their attitudes. Some argue that once you use a less restrictive means of defining and measuring what it means to be an ideologue, ideological thinking is quite widespread (Brown 1970). For instance, Lane's set of lengthy, in-depth interviews with working-class men revealed that although they may not elegantly articulate them, all citizens possess belief systems. These political orientations are acquired early in life and reflect an individual's interaction with the socio-political world (Lane 1962). Further, Achen (1975) revealed that a source of observed instability in citizens' attitudes was low reliability in survey questions. He found that "When the correlations among attitudes were corrected for this unreliability, the result was a sharply increased estimate of the stability and coherence of voters' political thinking" (1229).

The most common retort, however, is related to political polarization in American politics. Namely, over the last five decades, the parties have grown more ideologically polarized, with the Republican Party moving further to the right and the Democratic Party moving further to the left (Aldrich 1995; Rohde 1991; Poole and Rosenthal 1997). For instance, Zschirnt (2011) explains:

As conservatives have increasingly wielded political power and as symbols of conservatism have acquired newfound cultural prominence, affect toward both has become an increasingly important determinant of ideological self-identification. Specifically, research conducted subsequent to the rise of the New Right in the 1980s has suggested that negative affect toward certain symbols of the new Republican Party has become an increasingly important component of liberal identity

(690).

Because the political parties have become ideologically homogenous, citizens have been able to take cues from both their preferred and their ill-favored parties on how to ideologically identify (Levendusky 2010; Carmines, Ensley, and Wagner 2012).

Consequently, many more Americans are able to express themselves in terms of *liberal* and *conservative*. As Figure 1.2 illustrates, the number of people unable to place themselves on the liberal–conservative continuum

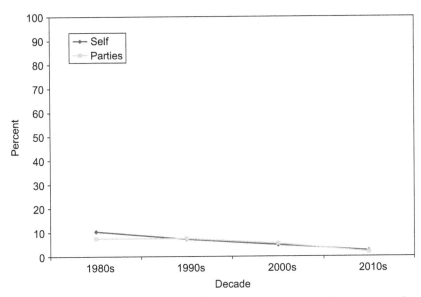

FIGURE 1.2 Percentage of people unable to place themselves or the parties on the liberal–conservative continuum

Note: Values are weighted percentages of "Don't knows" in response to assessments of ideological self-identification and ideological party placements.

Source: American National Election Studies Cumulative Date File, 1948–2012.

has steadily decreased over time.[3] Whereas 10 percent of respondents during the 1980s did not know whether they were liberal or conservative, only 2 percent in the 2010s did not know where to place themselves on the liberal–conservative continuum (American National Election Studies and Stanford University 2015). Furthermore, scholars have found that the internal consistency between ideological self-identification and respondents' issue positions has steadily increased over time (Abramowitz and Saunders 2006). Figure 1.2 indicates that there has been a recent increase

---

[3] These numbers were generated using the summary liberal–conservative scale provided in the ANES cumulative data file. Originally, respondents were asked to place themselves on a seven-point scale, ranging from extremely liberal to extremely conservative. The category presented are those respondents who replied "Don't know" even after they received the follow-up "choice" question whereby respondents who initially indicated that they did not know or had not thought that much about their ideological self-identification were asked "If you had to choose, would you consider yourself a liberal or a conservative?"

in the ability of survey respondents to recognize ideological differences between the two major parties. The percentage of respondents not knowing if one party is more conservative than the other has decreased from 8 percent in the 1980s to 2 percent in the 2010s (American National Election Studies and Stanford University 2015).[4] So while the American electorate as a whole may not be ideologues, levels of ideological constraint are not as low as once thought.

The use of ideological considerations in political evaluations has also become more pervasive among members of the electorate. In an examination of the 2008 election, Jacoby (2010) found evidence that ideological self-identification had both an indirect and direct effect on vote choice. As an indirect effect, citizens' placement on the liberal–conservative continuum served as a mechanism by which to make sense of political issues. These issues were then used in determining for whom to vote. As a direct effect, ideological labels served as a cue to match voters with the candidate that best served their interests. Furthermore, "liberal-conservative ideology seems to be disseminated throughout the entire electorate, rather than isolated within the most knowledgeable, attentive, and active segments of the mass public, as it has been in previous years" (567).

DIMENSIONS OF THE LIBERAL–CONSERVATIVE CONTINUUM

The definitions of *liberal* and *conservative* vary across time and context (Muller 1997; Erikson, Luttbeg, and Tedin 1991). For the most part, however, modern American liberalism has come to denote the belief that everyone is equal and that there should be diversity and equality in deliberation and governance. Liberals emphasize individual freedom and "positive government action to remedy social deficiencies and to improve human welfare" (Kerlinger 1984, 15). Conservatism, in contrast, "begins with the belief that the greatest good for the greatest number will emerge in both the economic and political marketplaces if competition in those arenas can be kept as unimpeded as possible" (Pohlmann 1999, 12). Conservatives believe that individuals are inherently unequal and thus do not believe in popular rule. Conservatism emphasizes liberty, especially with regard to private property, and opposes government intervention (Tedin 1987). While liberals advocate

---

[4] Responses represent those who indicated "Don't know" to the following question: "Would you say that either one of the parties is more conservative than the other at the national level?"

for social change, conservatives believe in maintaining the status quo and protecting traditional religious and moral values (Kerlinger 1984).

There is mounting evidence to suggest that people's ideas about ideology are structured multidimensionally (Kerlinger 1967; Conover and Feldman 1981; Brown and Taylor 1972; Treier and Hillygus 2009; Feldman and Johnston 2014). There are a host of realms in which individuals apply ideological labels and the applicability of these realms is not universal. In their book, *Ideology in America*, Christopher Ellis and James Stimson aptly note:

> "Liberal," "liberalism," "conservative," "conservatism": Few conversations about politics in the United States can avoid at some point using these words. The big picture of American politics is often a struggle between liberal and conservative sentiments over symbols, over policy, over even culture. But what do the words mean?...The meanings of the terms themselves, even among elites and political sophisticates, are not immutable. And many citizens clearly bring different connotations to the terms than we do (Ellis and Stimson 2012, 2).

For instance, Knoke (1979) identified three dimensions underlying liberalism and conservatism: social, economic, and racial. In examining ideological constraint, Jackson and Marcus (1975) discovered seven respondent-identified dimensions underlying ideology, including social order vs. dissent, minority rights vs. majority rule, and patriotism vs. violence. Using open-ended survey responses, Sanders (1986) divided reflections on the meaning of liberal and conservative into four categories – general philosophical positions, economic, social, and foreign policy. More recently, scholars have used the social and economic dimensions of political ideology to explain support for other ideologies, such as social dominance orientation and right-wing authoritarianism (see Jost, Federico, and Napier 2008 for a review). While each of these dimensions are not completely unrelated, they are distinct realms that people use to classify political entities (Jost et al. 2008).

While other scholars have recognized the multidimensional nature of ideology, this chapter contributes to this literature by evaluating the nature and meaning of ideological labels in the Black community. Abramowitz (2010) argues that the increased ideological consistency witnessed in the American populace is a result of the growing polarization between the two major parties. That is, Americans are better able to sort themselves as liberals and conservatives as the ideological line between Republicans and Democrats becomes more defined. This explanation, however, cannot account for why Black conservatives still identify as Democrats. Based on Abramowitz's argument, we would either expect Black conservatives to be increasingly supportive of the Republican Party or the number of Black conservatives to be decreasing as support for the Democratic Party continues to remain high so that Blacks' ideological self-identification and party identification comes into alignment.

I argue that, in addition to the parties becoming more clearly defined as liberal and conservative in recent years, ideological labels have increasingly become attached to various policy domains. This has allowed citizens to not only think of themselves generally as liberal and conservative, but also to conceptualize themselves along the liberal–conservative continuum with respect to specific issue areas. Having policy-specific ideological referents allows citizens to develop a more nuanced interpretation of their ideological self-identification. A more nuanced ideological self-identification where individuals can compartmentalize their policy preferences within ideological domains could help explain how one could identify as a conservative but still identify as a Democrat.

Scholars recognize the importance of the way ideological labels are used in public discourse but there does not exist a comprehensive breakdown of the uses of *liberal* or *conservative* over time by different issue domains. Yet, this information is critical to understanding how these ideological labels have been connected to various public policies and whether it has fluctuated over time. To address this omission, a content analysis of the *New York Times* over a 150-year period was conducted. the *New York Times* was selected because of its prominence among news sources. Not only is it one of the most widely circulated newspapers in the United States, it is considered an elite media outlet and an inter-media agenda setter for other news sources (Izadi and Saghaye-Biria 2007; Golan 2006). Its reputation for being the "newspaper of record" in the United States makes it a suitable source for analyzing the general usage of these terms.

Determining how Blacks use these labels in political debate requires capturing the dual nature of Black politics. In 1903, W.E.B. DuBois published his famous work, *Souls of Black Folk*, in which he describes the "double-consciousness" of African Americans. More specifically, DuBois argues that African Americans experience a "twoness—an American, a Negro; two souls, two thoughts, two unreconciled strivings; two warring ideals in one dark body, whose dogged strength keeps it from being torn asunder" (DuBois 2013 [1903], 13). One consequence of this twoness has been the formation of alternative information networks (Harris-Lacewell 2004), most notably the Black press (Wolseley 1990). The first Black newspaper, the *Freedom's Journal*, was founded in 1927. Since then, Black newspapers have augmented African Americans' understanding of the social, economic, and political world with a uniquely Black perspective that challenges the status quo in a way that mainstream newspapers do not (Wolseley 1990). Note, however, that Blacks do not read Black newspapers at the expense of mainstream newspapers. Rather, African Americans vacillate between both information sources ("Black America today: General media fact sheet" 2008). Therefore, in order to examine the origins and usage of ideological labels in Black political discourse it is not only necessary to examine what the nature of the mainstream political debate has been, but also what the nature of the political debate has been in Black newspapers as well.

To this end, a content analysis of the *New York Amsterdam News* was conducted over an 80-year period. The *New York Amsterdam News* was selected because of its comparability to the *New York Times*. Both newspapers are based in New York but are nationally circulated (Gibbons and Ulloth 1982). Since its founding in 1909, the *New York Amsterdam News* has been one of the premier Black newspapers, along with the likes of the *Chicago Defender* and the *Pittsburgh Courier* (Pride and Wilson 1997). Furthermore, one study found that New York residents believed that the *New York Amsterdam News* did a better job covering the Black community and was a more reliable source of news than mainstream newspapers (Gibbons and Ulloth 1982). Note, however, that the *New York Amsterdam News* is a weekly (rather than a daily) newspaper.

Selecting which policy domains to look for was based on the existing literature on the multidimensionality of ideological self-identification. For instance, Herzon (1980) identified three factors underlying lawyers' self-placement on the liberal–conservative continuum – tougher constraints vs. removal of constraints, government monitoring of dissident behavior, and government welfare activity. Stimson (1975) used nine issues to represent the five dimensions – economic, foreign affairs, racial, civil liberties, and social aspects of politics – that gave meaning to the liberal–conservative continuum. In this project, I use six categories – laissez-faire, racial, military, social, religious, and moral – as the overarching belief systems used to organize discrete political information. These categories represent a comprehensive, yet parsimonious, list of issue areas. Thus, articles were coded for their discussion of *liberal* and *conservative* in conjunction with laissez-faire, racial, military, social welfare, religious, and moral issues (see Appendix for article selection and coding methodology).

Within the *New York Times,* *liberal* and *conservative* are most commonly used to describe preferences for the size of government, dubbed here as *laissez-faire* (see Table 1.2). This category represents the default and most general usage of the ideological labels. *Laissez-faire,* a term used to describe limited government, was originally associated with classic liberalism and emphasized the importance of private property, rule of law, capitalism, and individual rights (Kerlinger 1984). As Dewey (1935) explains, however, "[g]radually a change came over the spirit and meaning of liberalism. It came surely, if gradually, to be disassociated from the *laissez faire* creed and to be associated with the use of governmental action for aid to those at economic disadvantage and for alleviation of their conditions" (21, *emphasis* in original). Hence, support for free markets and limited government intervention are now associated with modern conservatism (Pohlmann 1999). In the early decades of the sample frame, laissez-faire usage of *liberal* and *conservative* is dominated by coverage of British politics. Specifically, the terms refer to the Conservative and Liberal Parties, whose names are derived from their stance on free trade, the strength of the monarchy, and free enterprise. Similar usage emerges in 1877 to include French, Nicaraguan, and Canadian politics and later Spanish, Russian, and German politics. The increased use of ideological labels in this context during 1947 results from coverage of foreign governments as they rebuild and reorganize in the aftermath of World War II. Within the United States, the use of *liberal* and *conservative* with respect to party labels is a lot less frequent and mostly refers to local, rather than national, party politics. For instance, articles that mention Liberal and Conservative Parties in the United States during 1967, 1977, and 1987 focus on New York City and State elections.[5] In the early 1900s, ideological labels were more often applied to debates about

---

[5] Articles that reference New York's Liberal and Conservative Parties are coded as "social welfare" rather than "laissez-faire." The political party system in New York is unique to its system of machine politics. As Bernheim (1888:100) explains: "Political institutions are the outgrowth of political conditions. The New York party organizations and their method of nominations to public office are clearly the result of the number and the importance of the elective offices; and they have no counterpart in London, Paris or Berlin." Third parties in New York emerge as a representation of various clubs, interests, and citizen groups. Candidates running for office in New York can simultaneously run under more than one party label or a fusion of two or more parties (Bone 1946). News coverage of New York's political parties focuses primarily on the representation of the parties' various constituency groups in the form of patronage and/or public policy.

TABLE 1.2 Prevalence of ideological dimensions, by year

New York Times

	1857	1867	1877	1887	1897	1907	1917	1927	1937	1947	1957	1967	1977	1987	1997	2007
Laissez-faire	49	29	58	66	60	65	49	49	49	66	54	39	58	62	38	35
Racial	33	47	9	2	2	0	0	3	4	0	10	11	12	4	10	3
Military	4	17	10	0	10	0	27	25	15	12	13	8	6	8	7	14
Social Welfare	6	4	11	19	17	16	13	17	28	18	18	28	12	10	27	33
Religious	6	1	9	8	6	4	5	3	3	3	5	9	4	7	10	11
Moral	2	1	4	6	4	14	6	2	2	1	1	7	10	10	8	5
N	49	75	71	67	48	49	63	59	69	76	80	91	87	84	84	80

New York Amsterdam News

	1857	1867	1877	1887	1897	1907	1917	1927	1937	1947	1957	1967	1977	1987	1997	2007
Laissez-faire								15	8	8	9	7	14	19	6	16
Racial								33	43	40	40	41	32	47	46	45
Military								15	6	2	0	6	4	4	4	6
Social Welfare								12	30	39	36	37	34	23	31	21
Religious								9	13	4	7	12	3	7	6	10
Moral								15	6	12	9	6	11	4	18	10
N								33	63	52	55	81	90	74	55	67

Note: Values represent the percentage of articles characterized by each dimension during a sample year. In some cases, columns exceed 100 percent because articles were coded as using more than one dimension.
Source: New York Times, 1857–2007 and *New York Amsterdam News*, 1927–2007.

33

government regulation of monopolies, utilities, and railways. By 1977 and continuing through present day, coverage of laissez-faire issues incorporated the discussion of U.S. foreign trade policy and whether the country should place restrictions on imports from other countries. Nevertheless, just over half (55 percent) of the use of *liberal* and *conservative* to talk about laissez-faire ideology is within international news coverage.

As Table 1.2 illustrates, the laissez-faire dimension is a lot less commonly used in the *New York Amsterdam News*. This difference can be attributed to the greater prominence the *New York Times* gave to foreign affairs relative to the *New York Amsterdam News*; only 15.2 percent of articles in the *New York Amsterdam News* that were coded as laissez-faire focused on international news, compared to 55 percent in the *New York Times*. Of the laissez-faire issue articles that appeared in the *New York Amsterdam News*, most used ideological terms as a non-specific way of labeling particular candidates and politicians. Throughout the sample frame, ideological labels were also used to describe banking and investment policy. In the 1940s, almost all of the laissez-faire issue articles dealt with price control, particularly in the wake of the dissolution of the Office of Price Administration. For instance, one article, which discussed the impact of inflation for wage earners, describes an economic plan proposed by future President Eisenhower:

The Eisenhower plan is important for several reasons. Firstly, it makes sense, real down to earth common sense. It is nonsense to try to stop inflation simply by limited controls over prices and wages and by allocating some critical materials – which is President Truman's so-called plan. Eisenhower is the first influential American in the conservative ranks to call attention to the fact that profits have been higher this year than ever before in the history of the nation. Inflation cannot be checked until some of these extraordinary profits can return to circulation in terms of the purchasing power of masses of people

(Weston 1947, 10).

In the 1940s, there was also an article that featured the "liberal" and "conservative" sides of the debate over the Marshall Plan. Overall, however, this was not a commonly used dimension in the *New York Amsterdam News*.

The second policy area in which the use of ideological labels is examined is within the context of racial issues. In principle, Americans overwhelmingly support racial equality. There is considerable less endorsement, however, for government policies aimed at addressing racial disparities (Kinder and Sanders 1996). In this respect, racial ideology does not equal racist attitudes, per se, but rather attitudes about racial policies (Carmines and

Stimson 1981). Thus, racial conservatism is defined as opposition to policies that target racial disparities and racial liberalism is categorized by support for government efforts to ensure racial equality. This is largely how the *New York Times* employs these terms. In 1857, ideological labels indicated the sides of the slavery debate. Many of the articles recounted the violent battle between abolitionists and conservatives over whether to admit Kansas as a free state or a slave state. Ten years later, the discussion shifted to Reconstruction policies. For instance, in describing a candidate for Congress, the *New York Times* reported:

Col. Williams has been bitterly opposed to the Civil Rights Bill and the Negro Franchise Law. He will be opposed by the negroes, but be supported by many conservative Radicals, and all of the late Secessionists who can vote

("The flood in Tennessee" 1867, 2).

By 1877, there is a considerable drop-off in the use of ideological labels with respect to racial issues, although the racial domain becomes modestly more prominent during the Civil Rights Movement. During this time, the *New York Times* described the friction that emerged among liberal and conservative Democrats over civil rights legislation introduced in Congress, with conservative Southern Democrats in opposition. As the Civil Rights Movement progressed, coverage followed how the division among Democrats widened as Southern Democratic candidates ran for office on segregationist platforms. From 1977 to 1987, the use of ideological labels in the discussion of race was expanded to detail the conservative and liberal views of South African Apartheid. Most recently, ideological labels have been used to describe positions on urban poverty, drugs, and affirmative action.

Not surprisingly, the racial dimension is the most commonly employed in the *New York Amsterdam News*. To be sure, Black newspapers "began in the context of the abolitionist movement and their continuance has been dependent on their presentation of the situation of Black people, and advocacy of changes in the oppressive aspects of that situation" (O'Kelly 1982, 1). From 1927 to 1947, using ideological labels in conjunction with the discussion of race relations was dominated by stories of Jim Crow and the fight for desegregation, with the terms *liberal* and *conservative* denoting one's stance on these issues. As an example, one article described the experiences of college professors who were traveling through the Midwest: "Even in a state of such liberal tradition as Wisconsin, Negro professors ran against Jim-Crowism and discrimination in a hotel last week" ("Weekly topics" 1937, 6). In 1957, the *New York Amsterdam*

News usage of ideological labels in the race domain was fairly singular in focus as it closely followed the debate over legislation that would eventually become the Civil Rights Act of 1957. Liberals worked to pass this legislation by year's end, while conservatives tried to delay or prevent the bill from passing.[6] By 1967, this discussion widened to include the implications of Black support for the Republican Party should conservative Ronald Reagan become the presidential nominee in 1968, Representative Adam Clayton Powell's struggle to keep his congressional seat without the support of his liberal colleagues in Congress, and the future of Black coalitions with liberal Whites. As the *Regents of the University of California* v. *Allan Bakke* case was argued in the Supreme Court in 1977, affirmative action became prominent in the *New York Amsterdam News*, with ideological labels being used in the racial domain to describe one's posture toward this issue. Most of the 1987 articles in the racial domain discussed the negative impact the Reagan Administration's decisions and policies had on Black America. The main focus of several articles was President Reagan's nomination of conservative Robert Bork for the Supreme Court and how it would mean a reversal of the civil rights gains attained just a few decades earlier. In the more recent years of the sample frame, articles in the *New York Amsterdam News* used ideological terms to describe liberal vs. conservative racial attitudes, the immigration debate (with liberals supporting amnesty and conservatives supporting increased border patrol), and Obama's possible electoral coalition with liberal Whites within the racial dimension.

The military dimension captures attitudes about the military and national defense. Military liberalism is characterized by opposition to "large-scale defense spending, military aid, military intervention, and CIA subterfuge" while military conservatives "endorse military priorities in the name of national security" (Mandelbaum and Schneider 1978, 82). Table 1.2 tracks the use of the terms *liberal* and *conservative* within the discussion of military issues throughout the sample period in the *New York Times*. From 1857 to 1887, we see a rise in the use of these terms in military coverage. The dominant usage was to describe two sides of a military conflict, e.g., the 1867 coverage of the Reform War between

---

[6] In an effort to prevent the Senate from voting on 1957 Civil Rights Act, Senator Strom Thurmond of South Carolina, who was then a Democrat, launched a 24–hour and 18–minute filibuster. This was the longest filibuster in the Senate's history and the record still stands (Higginbotham 1991).

Liberal and Conservative forces in Mexico. In 1897, we see the term conservative first used in the *New York Times* to describe politicians' approach to foreign affairs:

Several influential Senators who previously were regarded as "jingoes," since their visit to Canton have become very conservative, and no one on the Republican side of the chamber is now urging action of any kind with respect to the war in Cuba ("This week in Congress" 1897).

Conservative, in this instance, denotes caution rather than a pro-military stance. Not until the increased prevalence of this dimension in 1917, during World War I, do the terms *liberal* and *conservative* take on anti- vs. pro-military meanings, respectively, in this sample of articles. In 1927, these terms are primarily used to describe a power struggle among liberal, conservative, and progressive factions in Nicaragua. The return to its contemporary use occurs during the pre–World War II era, with discussions about how to contain communism, fascism, and Nazism. This framework for using *liberal* and *conservative* continues throughout the rest of the sample frame in the *New York Times* and is applied to other U.S. foreign policy concerns as they emerge. For instance, an article about the planning of the 1968 Democratic platform describes a proposed liberal peace plank that would call for a cease-fire in South Vietnam and end American air raids in North Vietnam (Ayres 1967). Similarly, in a 1987 letter to the editor, Representative Connie Mack (R-FL) contrasts President Reagan's conservative approach to U.S. Central American policy of providing assistance to contra forces in Nicaragua to the liberal policy of "appeasement" (Mack 1987).

In the early decades of the *New York Amsterdam News*, ideological labels within the military domain are applied to the same issues covered by the *New York Times*. *Liberal* and *conservative* were used to describe the various factions involved in the Nicaraguan Revolution. Additionally, the *New York Amsterdam News* used ideological labels to describe the competing sides of the civil unrest occurring in Cuba, Brazil, and Haiti – nations with significant Black populations. Unlike the *New York Times*, the number of articles within the military domain in the *New York Amsterdam News* is nearly negligible throughout 1947 and 1957 (see Table 1.2). Coverage of the Vietnam War, however, reverses this trend. Interestingly, the articles in the *New York Amsterdam News* discussing the Vietnam War were racialized, creating a unique perspective of what it means to be liberal or conservative on military issues.

In one article, dated August 12, 1967, the *New York Amsterdam News* published a quote from a speech James Meredith gave to students at the Mary Holmes College in Mississippi. The famed civil rights figure and U.S. Air Force veteran advised the students to volunteer for the armed services and the War in Vietnam because they made the Black man "realize he's a man and he won't come back and let his kids be beat up" ("News of the week" 1967, 2). When the students hissed at him in response to his statement, Meredith retorted "those liberals have really been working on you all" ("News of the week" 1967, 2). In this context, Meredith was arguing that being a military conservative not only meant supporting the war effort, but developing the strength and pride necessary to fight the racial injustices in the United States. After 1967, there is a decline in the number of articles in the *New York Amsterdam News* that applied ideological labels in the military dimension. In the remaining sample years, ideological terms are used to describe U.S. foreign policy toward African nations, the War in Iran, and various insurgencies in African and Caribbean countries.

One of the most consistent uses of the terms *liberal* and *conservative* in the *New York Times* occurs within discussions of social welfare issues. The social welfare domain represents attitudes about the federal government's involvement in addressing disparities in citizens' standard of living (Bennett 1973). The realm of social welfare policies can range from education spending to government-sponsored job creation (Kinder and Winter 2001). Those liberal on social welfare issues believe it appropriate for the federal government to provide a safety net for disadvantaged groups. They differ philosophically from conservatives, who believe in individualism, self-reliance, and minimal government intervention in a free market economy (Feldman and Zaller 1992). Early uses of these terms in the *New York Times* occur in debates about the working class and issues related to fair wages, both in the United States and in Europe, although social welfare constitutes a small percentage of articles from 1857 to 1877 (see Table 1.2). In 1887, the percentage of articles using *liberal* and *conservative* with respect to social welfare increases as organizations like the Knights of Labor and the American Federation of Labor become active in the political environment. There is another increase in the use of ideological labels within social welfare debates in 1937 as divisions arise among Democratic Party elites over President Roosevelt's New Deal policies. For instance, one article described tension between Roosevelt and Southern Democrats:

The President barely concealed a note of triumph yesterday when he said he would not consent to a renewal of crop loans unless conditioned on the kind of Federal production control which the New Deal has sponsored. It seemed clear to many Mr. Roosevelt believed that, in this vital matter, he has the upper hand of the conservative Southern members of Congress who have been balking his program, and intends to use it (Krock 1937, 22).

The period between 1947 and 1957 is marked by coverage of liberal vs. conservative debates over social welfare issues in other countries such as England, France, and Canada. By 1967, coverage shifts back to domestic policy in the United States as the Johnson Administration's Great Society programs are scrutinized and conservative Southern Democrats transition into the Republican Party. The most recent use of ideological labels in the area of social welfare is a lot more varied; issues range from public school funding to extending welfare benefits to immigrants.

After race, the social welfare dimension is the most prevalent construct in the *New York Amsterdam News*. As Table 1.2 indicates, the percentage of social welfare articles in a given year ranged from 12.1 percent in 1927 to 38.5 percent in 1947. Similar to the *New York Times*, the discussion of social welfare in conjunction with ideological terms in the *New York Amsterdam News* increased in 1937 as disagreement arose over Roosevelt's New Deal policies. A crucial difference between the two news sources, however, is that the *New York Amsterdam News* framed the New Deal policies in terms of how they affected African Americans. On October 23, 1937, Adam Clayton Powell, Jr., wrote a column condemning the discriminatory behavior of Frank Merlin, who headed New York's Vaudeville Division of the Federal Theatre Project sponsored by the Works Progress Administration (WPA). Specifically, Powell argued that:

Frank Marlin is a Negro hater. The whole WPA official set-up ranks as the same as long as they condone this and other discriminatory practices. The WPA cut Negroes wholesale in the counsellors' division. They have closed many projects to Negroes and have a special domestic project for Negroes only. How the "Little Flower" [Mayor Fiorello LaGuardia] has allowed this without at least uttering a word of condemnation is beyond my idea of the leadership of a liberal man (Powell 1937b, 13).

For Powell, being a liberal not only meant supporting the WPA and its related projects, but making sure that Blacks could fully benefit from them as well. In 1937, the *New York Amsterdam News* also focused heavily on the connection between the labor movement and African Americans, taking a decidedly pro-labor stance. For instance, when the Committee of Industrial Organizations led a sit-down strike against General Motors in 1936–37, Roy Wilkins wrote that:

Negroes should be following these events with more than passing attention because our future as a race is bound up with the struggle for a decent life for the worker ... For that reason, anything that concerns labor generally should concern us. We must not be deceived by the conservatives of the race or by the propaganda of the White capitalists. Any thinking Negro can recognize the arguments against labor as the same old arguments against Negroe (Wilkins 1937, 13).

Within this context, being liberal not only meant being pro-labor but it also meant being pro-Black. The discussion of labor in conjunction with race would dominate the social welfare coverage throughout 1947. From 1957 through 1997, ideological labels were primarily used to distinguish between New York's political parties. The *New York Amsterdam News* did return, however, to linking race and social welfare in its discussion of support and opposition of President Johnson's War on Poverty. Opposition to anti-poverty measures is framed as Congressional conservatives' backlash in response to the urban riots in cities like Detroit and Watts. Alternatively, support for anti-poverty measures is framed as an appeal to liberals in Congress to help alleviate the abject poverty and devastation facing many Black neighborhoods. Ideological labels were also used in 1997 to describe the deleterious effect of Mayor Rudy Giuliani's conservative crime policies on the Black community and liberals' concern for the future of poverty and homelessness in the wake of the 1996 Personal Responsibility and Work Opportunity Reconciliation Act. In 2007, the usage of the terms *liberal* and *conservative* in the social welfare dimension was broader in focus, ranging from a discussion of income inequality to speculating about how well Hillary Clinton would represent African Americans if she were to become president of the United States. The common thread throughout, however, was that each side of the liberal vs. conservative debate of social welfare issues was translated into which side was pro- vs. anti-Black.

Religion is another area in which people use ideological labels. Although, as Table 1.2 indicates, discussions of religious ideology is not one of the more common uses of *liberal* and *conservative* in the *New York Times*. Traditionally, religious ideology denotes one's degree of orthodoxy and commitment, with religious conservatives attending religious services more frequently and holding more fundamentalist beliefs (Hempel and Bartkowski 2008). Religious liberals are those that are "anti-dogmatic, favorable to spiritual freedom and innovation" (Collins 1993, 131). An illustration of this can be seen in a 1907 movement to repeal a New York law that prohibited Sunday performances in its theater and opera houses. In a number of articles covering this debate, the *New York Times* reported the arguments of conservative Jewish and Christian groups on the City's enforcement of the Fourth Commandment. Additionally, one's religious ideology is defined by levels of support for traditional family values and gender roles (Glass and Jacobs 2005). For example, an 1877 article uses *liberal* to describe support for female clergy:

In order to obviate such an erroneous impression, would it not be advisable for divines to withdraw all opposition; to help, in place of hindering, every good, faithful, capable woman who feels moved to aid them in teaching divine truths and enforcing the lessons of Christianity? That would seem to be the only liberal and commendable course ("Clergywomen" 1877, 6).

More recently, the *New York Times* has applied ideological labels to religious organizations' stance on homosexuality, as reported in the following article about the Episcopal Church:

Responding to an ultimatum from leaders of the worldwide Anglican Communion, bishops of the Episcopal Church have rejected a key demand to create a parallel leadership structure to serve the conservative minority of Episcopalians who oppose their church's liberal stand on homosexuality (Goodstein 2007, 16).

Note also that the debate over gay marriage is the impetus behind a modest increase in the contemporary use of ideological labels within a religious context.

The religious dimension was slightly more salient in the *New York Amsterdam News*. Overall, *liberal* and *conservative* are used much the same way as they were in the *New York Times*. Beginning in 1937, religious conservatism was also juxtaposed with racial liberalism. Take, for instance, the following passage written by Adam Clayton Powell, Jr., in which he specifically questions what it means to be a liberal:

Christianity will never mean anything until White people admit the brotherhood of all other groups ... No man in my estimation is a liberal as long as he fails to recognize and to do something tangible about the position of the Negro in America (Powell 1937a, 11).

In other words, Powell suggests that it is hypocritical to claim to hold a strong adherence to Judeo-Christian beliefs while simultaneously holding racially conservative ideals; the two are orthogonal to one another. The *New York Amsterdam News* continues to connect race and religion during its 1960s coverage of the Civil Rights Movement. The rise in the number of articles using ideological labels to discuss religious issues in 1967 can largely be attributed to this racialization of ideology as the *New York Amsterdam News* discussed whether liberal religious groups would join Blacks in the fight for racial equality. Thus, ideological labels within the religious dimension have taken on the dual role of not only denoting the degree of orthodoxy but also one's degree of racial liberalism and conservatism as a religious entity.

Finally, ideological labels are applied within the discussion of moral issues. Moral issues are those that appeal to an absolute sense of what is right and wrong. Moral conservatives believe that "there is a privileged moral principle or cluster of moral principles, prescribing determinate actions, with which it would always be wrong not to act in accordance no matter what the consequences" (Nielsen 1972, 219). Moral liberalism, in contrast, allows for multiple interpretations of the moral good and the freedom to act as one chooses as long as others are not harmed (Reiman 1997). The expression of moral conservatism resembles religious conservatism although it need not be associated with a particular dogma. The dominant use of ideological labels here denotes whether someone is acting in a just and law-abiding fashion. Additionally, from 1887 to 1917 *liberal* described those who were anti-Prohibitionists, while conservative described support for the Temperance Movement. In 1977, moral conservatives and liberals were those on either side of the abortion, euthanasia, and pornography debates. Beginning in 1987 and continuing to 2007, ideological labels are used to describe reactions to the emergence of HIV/AIDS. For instance, one article describes conservatives as those "who saw the epidemic as retribution for perversion" (Kevles 1997, BR8). More recent uses of the term *liberal* in the moral context refer to condoning drug use and dishonesty while "conservative" is equated with integrity and upholding traditional family values.

With respect to the *New York Amsterdam News*, the application of ideological labels in the moral dimension was most often featured in discussions of the proper way to conduct one's self. Several articles designated conservative as being refined, reserved, and having good manners. For example, a 1947 article discussed the Negro National

League's (NNL) desire to clean up its image. The "conservative elements of the NNL" elected the Reverend John H. Johnson as their president, who would hopefully eliminate "the practice of cussing out loud at their powwows" (Burley 1947, 10). Other usages for conservative included holding traditional values. Take for instance a 1957 article which discussed the alarming rate of divorce:

> We can never be accused of being a super-conservative ... but somehow we have just enough southern blood running through our veins to hold fast to some of those old-fashioned ideas about love ... and marriage ... and home ties. But these day-by-day reports of divorces and marital separations are enough to make even the most crass and unbelieving sort of individual look askance ... and sorta wonder what all the restlessness is all about (Granger 1957, 8).

Finally, ideological labels were used to describe one's manner of dress as either respectable (conservative) or outlandish, sexualized, or otherwise nontraditional (liberal). In a discussion of a Mariah Carey video, one reporter notes, "Her more conservative fans must have busted their Bible belts viewing her salaciously gyrating in the 'Honey' video, changing clothes on camera from a skin-tight wetsuit, into a fierce flesh-revealing bikini" (Rogers 1997, 23). And while there were a few articles that discussed actual public policies (e.g. the conservative vs. liberal side of disciplining children, sexual education, and abortion), the vast majority of articles in the moral dimension in the *New York Amsterdam News* dealt with the proper etiquette of Black life.

The above analyses allow us anecdotally to see how ideological labels have become attached to various issue domains over time. This content analysis, however, can also demonstrate quantitatively the increasingly nuanced usage of ideological labels. Figure 1.3 graphs the use of ideological labels over time by summing the total number of articles by year across the issue areas.[7] By imposing a trend line over the data, we can see an upward trajectory, indicating that the use of the terms *liberal* and *conservative* have become more specialized over the sample years. This indicates that the use of ideological labels within elite discourse has grown increasingly more policy-specific. If not for the single outlier in 1857, representing the increased discussion of race as the battle over slavery came to an apex, the slope of the trend line would be steeper in the *New York Times*.

---

[7] Since laissez-faire represents the more general use of ideological labels, this category was omitted from Figure 1.3.

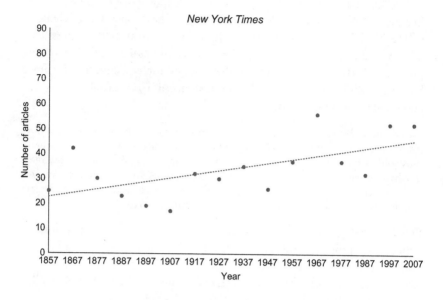

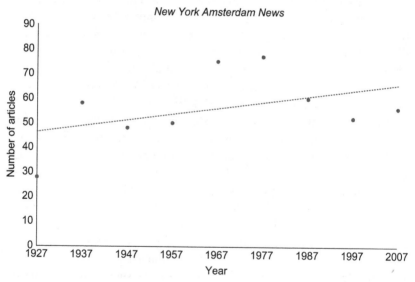

FIGURE 1.3 The prevalence of issue-related ideological discussions in elite discourse

Note: Values represent the number of articles across dimensions during a sample year.
Source: New York Times, 1857–2007 and *New York Amsterdam News,* 1927–2007.

In summary, the content analysis of the *New York Times* and the *New York Amsterdam News* reveals that there are many policy dimensions in which the terms *liberal* and *conservative* have been defined and applied. Not all of these dimensions are equally salient. Further, the relevance of each dimension varies over time based on the politics of the day. Nevertheless, these dimensions represent independent arenas where ideological thinking can be employed.

Thinking about public opinion, there is an assumption that the weight the newspapers place on the various ideological domains will have an impact on the saliency of these dimensions in individuals' overall definitions of liberal–conservative continuum. Based on the content analyses, we should expect the racial, social welfare, religious, and moral dimensions to weigh most heavily in ideological thinking of African Americans given their relative prevalence in elite discourse, particularly in the *New York Amsterdam News*. The analysis of the *New York Amsterdam News* also demonstrated that ideological labels took on racialized meaning within the issue domains, fundamentally altering what it means to be *liberal* and *conservative* in these areas. Thus, there is an expectation that this too will resonate in Black public opinion.

Beyond serving as the foundation for establishing the dimensions of ideology, this content analysis is also important in its own right. By demonstrating ideological labels have been increasingly linked to issue domains, it extends public opinion research by providing individual policy dimensions as an additional source of ideological information beyond party polarization. From this standpoint, citizens not only formulate their ideological self-identification through partisan cues, but also through individualized conceptualizations of the liberal–conservative continuum.

PUBLIC OPINION AND THE DIMENSIONS OF IDEOLOGY

While the *New York Times* and *New York Amsterdam News* content analysis was useful in allowing us to see whether various dimensions of ideology existed in elite discourse, it does not tell us whether and how the mass public utilizes these dimensions in its assessments of politics. Generally speaking, there are many factors that contribute to the formation of one's ideology. Taken together, all of these components in their entirety constitute an individual's total ideology, defined as a person's "ideology with respect to different areas of social life: politics, economics, religion, minority groups, and so forth" (Adorno, Frenkel-Brunswik, Levinson, and Sanford 1950, 2). Thus, the goal of this section is to explore individuals' total ideologies. More specifically, this section of Chapter 1 is dedicated to examining whether the ideological dimensions discovered in the content analysis can be found in public opinion. Since there is sufficient evidence demonstrating that public opinion is influenced by elite discourse (see Zaller 1992 for instance), we would expect to see distinct dimensions emerge in public opinion, just as we did in the newspapers.

To test this empirical claim, I use survey data collected as part of the ANES. The ANES have repeatedly featured open-ended questions asking respondents what came to mind when they thought of people with either liberal or conservative political views. For the purpose of these analyses, responses were classified by ideological dimension and coded similar to the *New York Times* and *New York Amsterdam News* articles. See the Appendix for exact question wording and coding scheme). The top half of Table 1.3 presents the results for all of the respondents.

Looking first at the base line category, we see that 27.5 percent of responses fell along the general laissez-faire dimension in 1978. Beginning in 1978, we also see that social welfare was a commonly used dimension. Specifically, 24 percent of responses were coded as social welfare. Less than 5 percent of the responses fell into the categories of military, moral, and racial. Finally, none of the responses were coded as religious. In 1980, both social welfare and laissez-faire remained the most commonly used dimensions. The military and moral dimensions increased modestly in their use, however, while the racial dimension decreased slightly. Although social welfare and laissez-faire still remained the most common dimensions in 1984, the social welfare dimension increased by 6 percentage points, making it the most prevalent dimension that year. The military dimension also peaked that year at 7.1, while the racial dimension declined to 1.8, its lowest use of all the sample years. By 1988, we see a significant rise in the use of the moral dimension (10.5 percent, compared to 6.3 in 1984). All of the other dimensions declined in use, including social welfare, which returned to its pre-1984 level. In 1992, the moral dimension continued to increase in use. Also, it is only in 1992 that we see more than 2 percent of the responses falling within the religious dimension. While there is a considerable decrease in the military dimension, the remaining dimensions exhibit similar levels to the previous year.

The next part of the analysis seeks to explore how Blacks, in particular, use the different ideological dimensions. If we look at the bottom half of *Table 1.3, we see that Blacks tend to have a more specialized*

TABLE 1.3 *Use of ideological dimensions in public opinion, by race and year*

	1978			1980			1984			1988			1992		
	All	Blacks	Whites	All	Blacks	Whites	All	Blacks	Whites	All	Blacks	Whites	All	Blacks	Whites
Laissez-faire	28	11	29	29	19	30	25	12	25	26	18	27	24	15	25
Racial	4	6	4	3	4	2	2	1	2	2	5	2	2	2	2
Military	4	1	4	7	2	7	7	3	7	6	3	6	2	2	2
Social Welfare	24	33	24	27	42	26	33	47	31	23	29	23	22	37	21
Religious	0	0	0	0	0	0	1	0	1	1	2	1	2	0	2
Moral	4	0	5	5	3	6	6	2	7	11	8	11	15	7	15
Total Number of Responses	4,750	249	4,420	3,363	205	3,099	2,617	205	2,435	7,977	651	7,146	5,544	462	4,876
N	1,451	90	1,331	853	55	772	710	58	643	2,082	190	1,843	1,458	138	1,273

Note: Values represent the percentage of responses characterized by each dimension during a sample year.
Source: American National Election Studies, 1978, 1980, 1984, 1988, 1992.

conceptualization than Americans as a whole. That is, Blacks were much less likely to use the general laissez-faire category when explaining the meaning of ideological labels (11 to 19 percent of Black responses fell into this category). This is consistent to the comparison of the *New York Times* and the *New York Amsterdam News*. Instead, Blacks more often conceived of *liberal* and *conservative* using the other issue domains. The most commonly used dimension to describe *liberal* and *conservative* was social welfare. In any given year, no less than 28 percent of Black responses were related to aspects of social welfare. Social welfare was most commonly used in 1984, when 47 percent of Black responses fell into this category. Interestingly, Blacks' conceptualization of liberalism and conservatism was not heavily racialized. The highest percentage of race-related responses (5.6 percent) occurred in 1978. At its lowest in 1984, less than 1 percent of Black responses related to race.

As a comparison, Table 1.3 also includes similar analyses for Whites. The first notable difference between Blacks and Whites is how much more frequently Whites use the baseline laissez-faire category; Whites use this dimension 25 to 30 percent of the time. White responses were also two to four times more likely to fall within the military dimension, although it was not heavily employed by either group. Note, however, that even at its highest use in 1984, only 7 percent of White responses and 3.4 percent of Black responses fell into the military category. Likewise, the difference between Black and White moral responses ranged from 2.5 to 9 percentage points. Both groups experienced a considerable increase in the use of this dimension beginning in 1988, but Black usage decreased and White usage increased in 1992. Finally, the religious dimension did not receive prominent use by either group. Blacks did not describe liberals and conservatives in religious terms until 1988. Even then, less than 2 percent of Black responses were religious in 1988 and 1992. Similarly, the highest percentage of White responses in the religious dimension occurred in 1992, with 2.3 percent being classified as such.

Because the ANES data end at 1992, I incorporate a more recent data source to give a contemporary snapshot of Black and White assessments of the meaning of the terms *liberal* and *conservative*. Specifically, I conducted eighty-one semi-structured interviews between 2006 and 2008 wherein I asked respondents to define what it meant to be liberal and conservative, as well as what groups, people, and issues they associated with those labels. These data are derived from a non-random sample of respondents not associated with the ANES who were administered a series of open-ended questions related to ideology. (See Appendix for a

TABLE 1.4 *Use of ideological dimensions in public opinion, by race*

	All	Blacks	Whites
Laissez-faire	0.22	0.15	0.29
	(94)	(27)	(62)
Racial	0.08	0.09	0.08
	(49)	(24)	(22)
Military	0.05	0.03	0.06
	(20)	(5)	(12)
Social Welfare	0.36	0.36	0.34
	(190)	(73)	(98)
Religious	0.11	0.13	0.09
	(60)	(30)	(26)
Moral	0.17	0.20	0.14
	(95)	(49)	(38)
N	81	41	35

Note: Values represent the c-coefficient based on the co-occurrence of responses characterized by each dimension. The number of co-occurrences appears in parentheses.
Source: Qualitative Interviews.

detailed description of the sample.) While the qualitative sample and the ANES sample were not asked the same questions, the qualitative sample can help further illuminate ideas associated with ideological labels. For consistency's sake, responses were coded similar to the newspaper and ANES analyses to see which of the six ideological dimensions categorized them. (See Appendix for a more detailed methodological description.)

The first column in Table 1.4 indicates that social welfare was the most common dimension used when defining liberal and conservative. That is, when asked what it meant to be either liberal or conservative, a response that could be categorized as following within the social welfare domain occurred 190 times, yielding a c-coefficient of 0.36. For example, when Respondent 24, a White 64-year-old woman from New York, was asked what came to mind when she thought of *liberal*, she responded, "Someone that's more concerned with individual persons' problems I guess. How each person economically how they are, their job, healthcare and stuff like that." With respect to the term "conservative," Respondent 46, a 64-year-old White woman from California, defined it as:

Republican. My parents. Keeping the wealth just for the top. Definitely not willing to share the wealth. Really, definitely not Democratic. I think they're very selfish, self-centered people. For example, I can't imagine them being concerned about the environment. And I think it's taken a great deal of effort to get them to start looking at environmental needs.

Two other commonly used dimensions were laissez-faire and moral. The rate of co-occurrence for laissez-faire was 94, with a c-coefficient of 0.22, while for moral the rate of co-occurrence was 95, resulting in a c-coefficient of 0.17. Consistent with the *New York Times* and ANES findings, the religious, racial, and military dimensions were used, but not to a great extent.

While not presented in Table 1.4, respondents also listed exemplars of what it meant to be either liberal or conservative. These were people, groups, or organizations that transcended the boundaries of the ideological dimensions, such as the Republican Party, which was listed 39 times when respondents were asked to define the meaning of conservative and the Democratic Party, mentioned 28 times when respondents were defining what it meant to be liberal. Other conservative exemplars included George W. Bush (23), John McCain (9), Fox News (5), Rush Limbaugh (5), Bill O'Reilly (3), Dick Cheney (3), Ronald Reagan (3), William F. Buckley (3), Ann Coulter (2), and Michael Bloomberg (2). On the liberal side, Hilary Clinton was mentioned twelve times, followed by Bill Clinton (5), Ted Kennedy (3), Al Franken (2), John Edwards (2), Barbara Boxer (2), Howard Dean (2), John Kerry (2), Nancy Pelosi (2), the *New York Times* (2), Ralph Nader (2), and Ross Perot (2).[8]

If we look at Blacks and Whites separately, we see divergent uses in the ideological dimensions. (See columns 2 and 3 in Table 1.4.) For instance, Blacks were more likely than Whites to use the religious and moral dimension in defining liberal and conservative; the c-coefficients for those dimensions were 0.13 and 0.20, respectively. This is what we would expect, given the content analysis of the *New York Amsterdam News*. One Black respondent's simultaneous usage of these two constructs gives us an idea of how these dimensions get employed:

Actually, maybe more old fashioned in terms of their thinking. They don't believe in things like abortion and probably sex before marriage, those type of things. I'd say they more, they follow the Bible, they use the Bible as their guide in life (Respondent 23).

Like the *New York Amsterdam News*, this respondent described conservatism in terms of respectable behavior.

Whites, on the other hand, used the laissez-faire dimension more frequently than Blacks. The c-coefficient for laissez-faire for Whites was 0.29 (62 co-occurrences), compared to 0.15 (27 co-occurrences) for

---

[8] The number of times each exemplar is mentioned appears in parentheses.

Blacks. Again, this is consistent with the differences found in the newspaper content analyses. The following quote provides an example of how Whites, in this case a White female college student, used the laissez-faire dimension to define conservatism:

Generally this whole idea of personal responsibility and less government interference. That people need to take charge of their own life and that government, when it gets involved, it's going to be inefficient. That they tend to weigh interest of economic growth. Specific, like private property, individual rights more heavily than most general emotional stuff (Respondent 13).

Additionally, Whites were slightly more likely to use the military dimension, although its use was not very widespread among either group of respondents. This was surprising, considering how salient the military dimension was in both papers in recent years.

There was essentially no difference between the two racial groups with respect to the social welfare dimension or the racial dimension. As stated earlier, the social welfare dimension was a heavily used domain while the racial dimension was not. There was, however, a significant difference in how Blacks discussed the social welfare dimension. Blacks were four times more likely to associate what it meant to be liberal or conservative on social welfare issues with Black organizations, Black leaders, or other racialized constructs.[9] Commonly associated with being liberal on social welfare issues were President Barack Obama (who was a U.S. Senator at the time), Representative Charlie Rangel (D-NY), liberal Whites, the National Action Network, and the National Urban League; Republican White males were identified as being conservative on social welfare issues. Similar to the *New York Amsterdam News*, the Black public's understanding of social welfare has become intimately intertwined with race.

CONCLUSION

Chapter 1 has provided the necessary foundation for the next step in our inquiry. It has allowed us to view a dynamic picture of the conceptualization of ideological labels over time and how the definition of these labels has grown increasingly more policy-oriented. Through the content

---

[9] Sixteen Blacks used racialized responses when describing the social welfare dimension, compared to four Whites.

analysis of a mainstream and an African-American newspaper, this chapter has demonstrated that there are at least six distinctive dimensions in which the terms *liberal* and *conservative* can be employed. In doing so, it has demonstrated that there is real variation in the ideological understandings of Blacks (at both the elite- and mass public-level) and that a lack of political sophistication cannot be the sole explanation for the lack of Black Republicanism, especially among Black conservatives.

The comparison of the *New York Times* to the *New York Amsterdam News* has been particularly instructive in illustrating how issues on the national agenda are then transformed into items relevant to the Black agenda and what ramifications this has for Black ideology. As stated earlier, the purpose of Black newspapers is to provide an African-American perspective of the day's events. It should be no surprise, then, that a large portion of articles in the *New York Amsterdam News* fell along the racial dimension. More surprising was the racialization of the other ideological domains. By superimposing race over the military, social, and religious dimensions, ideological labels in the *New York Amsterdam News* took on a whole new meaning. Not only did they denote the liberal vs. conservative sides of policy debates, but they subsumed the racial aspects of those debates as well. Consequently, we see the usage of these ideological labels fundamentally altered. Indeed, we even witnessed two competing elements joined together as one. This was the case with the religious and military dimensions whereby being a pro-military or being a devout Christian (in both cases being conservative along the military and religious dimension, respectively) also meant being racially liberal.

The incorporation of race into the other policy domains helps to explain why race is not a salient construct when we examine public opinion. Race is operating on multiple levels. On one level, ideological labels are being applied to explicitly racial issues such as slavery, Jim Crow, affirmative action, etc. On another level, ideological labels are discussed within the context of ostensibly nonracial issues that have become racialized through elite debate. These issues – such as education, crime policy, income inequality – are viewed by Blacks as social welfare issues that nevertheless disproportionately affect African Americans. Blacks hear these same issues being discussed by civil rights organizations and Black leaders and associate them with the Black agenda. They may not be racial issues, per se, but they do have some racial impact. And relatively speaking, the relevance and prevalence of social welfare issues outweigh explicitly racial issues.

The multi-leveled impact of race on defining ideological labels is further explored in Chapter 2. With the results from the present chapter in mind, Chapter 2 explores the historical antecedents to Blacks' understanding of the liberal–conservative continuum. Now that Chapter 1 has examined Blacks' general definitions of ideological labels, these historical analyses will be used to gauge the saliency of the dimensions relative to one another when it comes to their ideological self-identification. The next step is to develop a set of testable hypotheses that predict which policy domains underlie the ideological self-identification of African Americans. If Blacks use multiple dimensions when defining the liberal–conservative continuum in general, then it makes sense that they would also apply these constructs to their own ideological self-identification. Understanding the mix of ingredients used to formulate Blacks' ideological self-identification and how these dimensions get bundled together into a constrained ideology is the goal of the next chapter.

2

From Whence We Came

The Historical Basis of Black Ideological Self-Identification

Chapter 1 demonstrated that both Black elites and Blacks in the mass public distinguish among six policy domains in their use of ideological labels in contemporary American politics. Although the racial, social welfare, religious, and moral dimensions were most salient among Black elites, the Black mass public used the racial dimension much less frequently when defining ideological labels. That is not to say that race is not important to Blacks' definition of the liberal–conservative continuum. As discussed in Chapter 1, not only are ideological labels applied to explicitly racial issues, but through the racialization of ostensibly nonracial issues, race operates through the other ideological dimensions as well. Presumably, this conceptualization of *liberal* and *conservative* based on public policy debates should also shape ideological self-identification. Therefore, we next turn to examining the nature of Blacks' ideological self-identification.

What differentiates a Black conservative from a Black liberal? Asumah and Perkins (2000) posit that: "Individualism, materialism, and limited government all serve as major tenets for American political ideology. Most conservatives wholeheartedly believe in these principles, and Black conservatives are no exception" (56). To the extent that previous literature has considered Black conservatives, however, it is most often with respect to explicitly racial policy preferences. That is, Black conservatives are narrowly defined as those who oppose government intervention in addressing racial inequalities. Unlike Black liberals who believe that racial differences are due to institutionalized and systemic barriers (both past and present), Black conservatives believe that individual deficiencies account for Blacks' unequal standing in American society (Smith 2002). Because of this, Black conservatives think that government intervention is unnecessary and trust that the free market and self-determination will address the gap between Blacks and Whites (Harris-Lacewell 2004). Similar to their White counterparts, Black conservatives advocate a strategy of self-reliance as a means of overcoming adversity and denounce government interventions designed to ameliorate inequality. Moreover, "claims that blacks have suffered special oppression and deserve special consideration are rejected for a number of reasons, including the view that blacks are one of several groups that have suffered disadvantage and therefore should receive no special consideration" (Dawson 2001, 20). But are attitudes about race all that defines Black conservatism? Although this has not previously been empirically tested, I argue that Black conservatives apply the tenets of individualism, materialism, and limited government to other issue areas. Not all of these areas, however, are relevant when determining Blacks' ideological self-identification. As stated earlier, only those issue areas in which African Americans have had the most experience with politics and government will be pertinent to their ideological self-identifications. Furthermore, because of these same experiences, Blacks have a unique packaging of these ideological dimensions that differs from the general electorate.

Thus, the goal of Chapter 2 is to develop a set of expectations regarding which policy domains should be relevant to Blacks' ideological self-identification and in what capacity. I begin by providing a theoretical framework for how individuals develop their ideological self-identification and ideological constraint. With this framework in place, Chapter 2 then traces the historical relationship between Blacks and the six policy domains discussed in Chapter 1. I argue that the role of race is much more complex than originally conceived as a defining determinant of Black ideological self-identification. As seen in Chapter 1, although explicitly racial issues were once important among Blacks, their relevance has declined in recent years. Currently, race has important implications for other policy domains, such as social welfare, military, and religious. It is these dimensions that better predict the difference between Black liberals and Black conservatives. Furthermore, race has shaped how Blacks constrain their ideological understandings.

THE FORMATION OF IDEOLOGICAL SELF-IDENTIFICATION

For the most part, scholars have treated ideological self-identification as an independent variable, examining the extent to which it could consistently predict vote choice (Holm and Robinson 1978; Knight

1985), issue positions (Levitin and Miller 1979; Popp and Rudolph 2011), and party identification (Box-Steffensmeier and De Boef 2001; Abramowitz and Saunders 2006). Studies treating ideological self-identification as a dependent variable have mostly focused on how the distribution of liberals, conservatives, and moderates has fluctuated over time (Robinson and Fleishman 1988). As a result, we know surprisingly little about the structure and content of individuals' ideological self-identification.

Still, though not their central purpose, several studies on ideology have been able to yield some insight into the underpinnings of self-placement on the liberal–conservative continuum. With regards to policy preferences, Levitin and Miller (1979) found modest correlations between ideological self-identification and nine issues: government's guaranteeing of jobs and standard of living, protecting the rights of the accused, busing, aid to minorities, government-provided health insurance, urban unrest, tax policy, equality for women, and the legalization of marijuana. The strength of the correlations was fairly consistent between 1972 and 1976, ranging between 0.20 (equality for women in 1972) and 0.38 (busing in 1972). Attitudes about tax policy and ideological self-identification yielded the weakest correlation (0.12 in 1972 and 0.16 in 1976). Feldman (1988) examined which core beliefs and values correlated with the liberal–conservative continuum. He found a modest correlation between individualism and egalitarianism and ideological self-identification in the expected direction. That is, liberals placed higher on the egalitarianism scale while conservatives were higher on the individualism scale. There was no relationship, however, between ideological self-identification and attitudes about free enterprise. Finally, in trying to account for the decline in self-identified liberals over time, Ellis and Stimson (2012) found that since the 1960s, liberal identity has become increasingly correlated with feelings towards Blacks and Black leaders, labor unions, and urban unrest. Further, they took this as evidence of a "changing in the dominant symbols of ideological liberalism from the white working-class American of FDR to the largely nonwhite underclass – as well as the counterculture movement – of the 1960s and beyond" (Ellis and Stimson 2012, 88). Ellis and Stimson also examined "extrapolitical" identities – those driven by "lifestyle, behavior, and religious preference" – that are expressed using ideological labels but, nevertheless, have no political meaning (116). They demonstrated that "lifestyle" variables, such as biblical literalism and attitudes about childrearing, were significant predictors of ideological self-identification, even after controlling for respondents' positions on cultural issues and economic and scope of government preferences.

While these studies have been able to tell us something about the content behind ideological self-identification, they are not able to speak to its structure and organization. We still do not know what socio-political referents people use to define liberalism and conservatism and why certain criteria are more salient than others. Therefore, I offer a theoretical framework for understanding the determinants of ideological self-identification, grounded in existing research in psychology and political science, which can speak to this hole in the current literature.

Ideological self-identification can be thought of as part of a self-schema. As Fiske and Taylor (1991) explain:

Self-schemas are cognitive-affective structures that represent one's experience in a given domain. They organize and direct the processing of information relevant to the self-schema. People who hold self-schemas for a particular domain...consider the domain to be personally important and typically have well-developed conceptions of themselves in these domains (182–3).

Once developed, the self-schema can then be used in future judgments, inferences, and decisions about the self (Markus 1977). Hence, a self-schema representing one's ideological self-identification embodies the way an individual sees oneself in relation to the rest of the political world. Based on encounters with political events, candidates, issues, and other political symbols, individuals develop a categorization of themselves relative to known and trusted guideposts.

This model is similar to one proposed by Conover and Feldman (1981), in their article "The Origins and Meaning of Liberal/Conservative Self-Identification." According to Conover and Feldman, individuals associate ideological labels with both cognitive factors, such as issue-preferences, and emotional factors, such as political symbols. Then, based on the evaluative meaning of ideological labels, individuals determine their ideological self-identification.[1]

I expand their model, however, in two important ways. First, I argue that people organize information compartmentally. That is, individuals are able to categorize political information into larger repositories that

---

[1] Conover and Feldman, however, do not believe that ideology is bipolar; a positive evaluation of liberals does not necessitate and negative evaluation of conservatives and vice versa (but see Zschirnt 2011).

help structure and make sense of loose bits of otherwise unrelated knowledge.[2] From this standpoint, there are many realms within which individuals can identify themselves as *liberal* or *conservative* (Kerr 1952). Second, based on Kerlinger's (1984) Criterial Referents Theory, I posit that not all of these repositories are given equal weight when individuals assess their ideological self-identification. This, ultimately, will affect how people conceptualize themselves ideologically.

By definition, "A *criterial referent* of an attitude is a construct that is the 'object', the focus of an attitude, that is significant, salient, and relevant for an individual or for groups or individuals" (Kerlinger 1984, 30, emphasis in original). In this case, the criterial referents for ideological self-identification would be those dimensions that individuals' deem relevant to their placement on the liberal–conservative continuum. Kerlinger (1967) argues that not all dimensions of ideology are universally relevant across individuals. Rather, what defines one person's ideology is not necessarily what defines another. For instance, in a review of the research on the contours of ideological self-identification, Robinson and Fleishman (1988) concluded that some respondents defined their ideology "in terms of their attitudes toward government intervention in the economy, while others may answer in terms of attitudes toward social or moral issues (e.g., racial equality, abortion)" (137).

There is also evidence that demonstrates how criterial referents vary by group, as well as by individual. Conover and Feldman (1981) demonstrated that liberals and conservatives defined their ideological labels differently, rather than the opposite of one another. That is, liberals conceptualized being liberal in terms of resistance/support for change, recent social issues and New Deal issues while conservatives defined conservatism as support/opposition to change, socialism/capitalism, and fiscal policies (Conover and Feldman 1981). Stimson (1975) noted that the structure of belief system varied across cognitive ability. Of the nine issues examined, more issues correlated with the liberal–conservative continuum among those high in cognitive ability than those low in cognitive ability. Thus, Stimson concluded that "Because many issue positions are related to these respondents' location on the liberal-conservative scale, their conception of the meaning of the dimension may be said to be broad and abstract-at least relative to lower ability

---

[2] Issue positions and political symbols can be classified in more than one category simultaneously.

respondents" (Stimson 1975, 402). Scholars (e.g. Kerr 1952) have also demonstrated that the information people use to define *liberal* and *conservative* varies systematically by geography and party identification, as well.

Therefore, I argue that these definitions also vary systematically by race. That is, the criterial referents that Blacks use to define their ideological self-identification are different from other racial groups. Ideological self-identification can be thought of as the weighted sum of each of the policy domains. In some cases, the weights on the referents may be zero, indicating that a particular ideological domain has no bearing on ideological self-identification at all. As Markus (1983) explains "Self-schemas are knowledge structures about the self that derive from past experience and that organize and guide the processing of the self-relevant information contained in the individual's social experiences" (547). Further, self-schemas are a manifestation of enduring personal concerns (Markus 1983). Prior research (e.g. Dawson 1994) has demonstrated that group interests often serve as a proxy for self-interest. In the case of African Americans, then, personal concerns reflect not just those of the individual but also the race as a whole. If we think of ideology as how much control people believe government should assume over the social, political, and economic world (see Campbell et al., 1960), then Blacks will use the criterial referents in those domains in which African Americans have had the most consistent contact with government or engagement with politics when defining their ideological self-identification.

IDEOLOGICAL CONSTRAINT

In understanding Blacks' conceptualization of the liberal–conservative continuum, it is not only important to discern which policy domains Blacks use to determine their ideological self-identification, but also how each of the domains interacts with the others. Just as historical experiences have determined which issue areas are important to Blacks' ideological self-identification, history has altered the packaging of these domains. Thus, Blacks not only have a unique set of criteria they use to identify themselves as *liberal* or *conservative,* they also have a distinct bundling of these domains, which has led to an alternative source of ideological constraint.

Like ideological thinking in general, those with high levels of political sophistication have been shown to exhibit more stability in their attitudes

(Stimson 1975).[3] For instance, Jacoby (1991) found that on issues where the policy alternatives were not straightforward, there were large differences between those with high levels of education and those with low levels of education in their ideological identification and issue positions.[4] In a study that compared political elites with the mass public, Jennings (1992) found that party delegates showed more ideological constraint than the average American citizen. Also, this relationship held even when the mass public was stratified by their political activism; party elites demonstrated more consistency and stability than the most activist members of the mass public.

Additionally, attitude stability has been linked to aspects of the political environment. Nie and Andersen (1974) note an increase in issue stability from 1952 to 1972. They argue that the structure of mass attitudes is sensitive to the nature of American politics and that heightened salience to politics (in this case, that brought on by the politics of the 1960s) leads to greater attitude constraint.

More recently, Ellis and Stimson (2012) argue that the root of ideological inconsistency lies in the difference between individuals' operational versus symbolic ideologies. Symbolic ideology represents the labels people assign to themselves, given the psychological attachment they have developed to ideological symbols. Operational ideology, on the other hand, is citizens' ideas about the proper role of government. Further, they demonstrate that Americans often have a discrepancy between their operational and symbolic ideologies, due to a symbolic attachment to the term *conservative* and an affinity for liberal public policies.

The trouble with these studies is that they assume that there is a capital "T" truth with respect to how issues should fit together and that inconsistency is equated with instability. They have not allowed for the possibility that citizens come to politics from various angles and that the path that leads them to the political world affects how they interconnect different ideas. Thus, there are some cases where life's circumstances leads to a divergent imaging of politics that is logically coherent given the situation.

---

[3] More recently, however, Ansolabehere, Rodden, & Snyder (2008) found high levels of policy constraint, even among the less sophisticated. Furthermore, both high and low political sophisticates exhibited considerable policy content in their political evaluations.

[4] This study also found that on "easy" issues, such as race, gender roles, guaranteed jobs, and negotiations with Russia, there were no statistical differences between those with high levels of education and those with low levels of education in their ideological identification and issue positions (Jacoby 1991).

For no other group is this truer than for African Americans. Blacks have developed a worldview that is rooted in the tumultuous race relations experienced over the course of U.S. history (Philpot 2007; Dawson 1994). The preeminent scholar in Black Politics, the late Hanes Walton, Jr., was innovative in stating that any study that failed to acknowledge the systemic, structural, and contextual factors influencing African-American political thought and behavior did not accurately capture the Black experience in America (see Walton 1985). Further, Knoke (1979) demonstrated that Blacks have distinct distributions of the economic, social, and racial dimensions of political beliefs, which he attributes to Blacks' occupation of the lowest level on America's racial stratification. Therefore, in order to understand why Blacks possess the ideological consistency that they do, we must look at how the historic relationship between Blacks and the U.S. government have shaped their beliefs about the proper size and scope of government.

Converse (1964) provides the framework for understanding how Blacks' conceptualization of the liberal–conservative continuum has come to differ from that of Whites with his discussion of the sources of ideological constraint. Constraint "may be taken to mean the success we would have in predicting, given initial knowledge that an individual holds a specified attitude, that he holds certain further ideas and attitudes" (Converse 1964, 207). Converse identifies three sources of ideological constraint – logical, social, and psychological. Although very rare, logical sources of constraint of a belief system that are based purely on objective, logically consistent idea elements. For example, "One cannot believe that government expenditures should be increased, that government revenues should be decreased, and that a more favorable balance of the budget should be achieved all at the same time" (Converse 1964, 209). Social sources, the most common sources of constraint, are those "package" idea elements together for mass consumption. From this standpoint, a small group of trusted opinion leaders have determined "what goes with what" and diffused this information as a bundled belief system to the whole of society (Converse 1964, 212).

Alternatively, psychological sources of constraints allow individuals and groups to reimagine idea elements into belief systems that differ from the masses. Whereas these idea elements may not appear to be bound by any strict logical constraints to the outside observer, citizens may "have *experienced* them as logically constrained clusters of ideas, within which one part necessarily follows from another" (Converse 1964, 211, emphasis in original).

Often such constraint is quasi-logically argued on the basis of an appeal to some superordinate value or posture toward man and society, involving premises about the nature of social justice, social change, "natural law," and the like. Thus a few crowning postures – like premises about survival of the fittest in the spirit of social Darwinism – serve as sort of glue to bind together many more specific attitudes and beliefs, and these postures are of prime centrality in the belief system as a whole (Converse 1964, 211).

Hence, the life experiences of individuals empower them with the autonomy to repackage political ideas into customized belief systems (see Lane 1962). In what follows, I trace the historical process that has led Blacks to package the ideological dimensions the way they do and why certain constructs are more important than others.

LAISSEZ-FAIRE DIMENSION

And one day we must ask the question, "Why are there forty million poor people in America?" And when you begin to ask that question, you are raising questions about the economic system, about a broader distribution of wealth. When you ask that question, you begin to question the capitalistic economy."

> – Martin Luther King, Jr.

Elements of classic liberalism can be found in the Declaration of Independence as our nation's founders, particularly Thomas Jefferson, were strong supporters of individualism, private property, minimal government, and free enterprise (McClain and Tauber 2010). For the better part of U.S. history, the county's economy has followed a "laissez-faire" approach, with minimal regulation from the federal government. From its inception, however, the U.S. capitalist system has been unjust for African Americans.

The foundation of the American economy was built by exploiting Black labor. Ideas of White supremacy, coupled with economic interests and the need to maximize profits was the basis of slavery (Fredrickson 1981). In the industrialized North, racial subjugation was used to suppress labor costs in manufacturing jobs. Around the turn of the twentieth century, for instance, factory owners would recruit cheap Black labor from the South to work in northern factories. Employers would also use African-American workers as strike breakers during labor conflicts (Valocchi 1994).

It was not until the Great Depression that the government took a more active approach in addressing some of the market forces and racial policies that disadvantaged Blacks economically (Walton and Smith 2010). Arguably, the greatest expansion of the federal government occurred during Franklin Roosevelt's Administration under the New Deal policies. Aimed at temporarily meeting the needs of the staggering number of unemployed Americans,

> the federal government took on a wide array of responsibilities previously left to the states or market forces, including universal access of the elderly to retirement income, welfare for fatherless children, and government-supported public works jobs for the unemployed. In addition to the beginnings of the modern welfare state, the New Deal also expanded the power of the regulatory state with respect to banking, agriculture, the stock market, and the relationship between workers and their employers (Walton and Smith 2010, 33).

On their face, the New Deal policies were universal. But the discriminatory nature of the Works Progress Administration, the National Industrial Recovery Act, and the Agricultural Adjustment Act, in particular, had deleterious effects on African-Americans' ability to secure work (Valocchi 1994). Thus Blacks, whose unemployment at that time was roughly 20 percent, twice that of Whites (Sundstrom 1992), were limited in their ability to benefit from New Deal legislation.

A second great expansion of the federal government occurred with President Lyndon Johnson's Great Society, which not only included the War on Poverty but also consumer and environmental protection, education and job training, urban development, and civil rights (Brown-Collier 1998). The Great Society also established a number of government entities charged with addressing discrimination in the workforce. The Equal Employment Opportunity Office was created in 1964 to track workplace diversity and investigative instances of discrimination. Established in 1965, the Office of Federal Contract Compliance forced private firms relying on federal contracts to adopt racial quotas with respect to their hiring (Collins 1983).

As a result of these government interventions, there was an increased demand for African-American labor (Collins 1993). With many racial barriers in the labor market dismantled, Blacks were allowed to enter higher prestige jobs from which they had previously been barred. Subsequently, Black earnings increased and "the purchasing power of the average black family rose by half" (Levitan and Taggart 1976, 610).

This changed during the mid to late 1970s, as a result of the increased suburbanization of employment. Improvements in transportation and lower costs of production led many industries to relocate outside of central cities, leaving high density, predominantly Black urban areas without a source of low-skilled jobs. At the same time, an ever-increasing globalized economy and a move away from manufacturing, has yielded a net loss in high-wage, low-skilled jobs in the United States in general (Wilson 1996).

By this time, the demand for jobs became the principal item on the African-American agenda. To this aim, a broad coalition of Blacks, liberal Whites, labor groups, and religious groups pursued legislation that would guarantee "a job to all willing and able to work" (Walton and Smith 2010, 219). Originally, the Full Employment and Balanced Growth Act (also known as the Humphrey–Hawkins Act), would have done just that. Because of political pressure and the fear of inflation, the clause in the bill that would require Congress to create public-sector jobs if individuals were unable to find employment in the private sector was eventually removed. When the Humphrey–Hawkins Act was passed in 1978, it was largely symbolic (Walton and Smith 2010; Stricker 2007).

Making matters worse was a subsequent conservative backlash to Johnson's Great Society. President Ronald Reagan, supported by a majority Republican Senate, reduced funding to cities. Among the programs cut were grants that would have funded "urban mass transit, economic development assistance, urban development action grants, social service block grants, local public works, compensatory education, public service jobs, and job training" (Wilson 2008, 562). President Reagan also called for an "across-the-board" reduction in the personal income tax rate. The federal tax rate among the nation's poorest during this time, however, actually increased. Consequently, income inequality grew between the very top of the income distribution and disadvantaged groups like Blacks and Hispanics, the less educated and younger Americans during the 1980s and 1990s (Danziger and Gottschalk 1995).

Currently, Black unemployment fluctuates between 12 and 13 percent ("Table A-2. Employment status of the civilian population by race, sex, and age" 2014). While this is certainly lower than Blacks' peak unemployment rate of 19.5 percent in 1983, the Black unemployment rate remains twice that of Whites. In fact, at any given time period, Black–unemployment ranges from 1.67 to 2.77 times that of White unemployment (Desilver 2013).[5]

Because of changes in the American economy and the spatial mismatch between Black workers and growth industries, it is unlikely that Black

[5] These figures are based on data collected by the Bureau of Labor Statistics, which started collecting unemployment data by race in 1954.

unemployment will improve without an aggressive course of action. Even when Whites had reached full employment during the Clinton Administration, Black unemployment was just under 10 percent, effectively leaving them in a state of recession. Thus, scholars argue that Blacks will not reach full employment unless the government uses "a combination of sound fiscal and monetary policies and targeted job creation, public works, and service programs" (Walton and Smith 2010, 295). Because of this, much of Blacks' understanding of the general laissez-faire dimension is entangled with the social welfare dimension. In other words, the laissez-faire dimension by itself will be less important to Blacks' ideological self-identification than how government intervenes on behalf of Blacks to overcome economic downturns vis-à-vis social programs, public sector jobs, etc.

RACIAL DIMENSION

States' rights, as our forefathers conceived it, was a protection of the right of the individual citizen. Those who preach most frequently about states' rights today are not seeking the protection of the individual citizen, but his exploitation...The time is long past—if indeed it ever existed—when we should permit the noble concept of States' rights to be betrayed and corrupted into a slogan to hide the bald denial of American rights, of civil rights, and of human rights.
– Robert F. Kennedy

In the quest for equal protection under the law, Blacks have had to appeal to the federal government to help shield them from the States' attempts at circumventing the Constitution and other civil rights statutes. To be sure, the exercising of States' rights has been a euphemism for constricting the civil rights of Blacks since the *Plessy* v. *Fergusson* case in 1896 (Lansing 1976). The States, particularly but not exclusively in the South, have not only sought to maintain a segregated society, but have also gone to great lengths to disenfranchise Black voters, limit Blacks educational opportunities, and restrict Blacks residential mobility (Walton and Smith 2010).

Although the federal government has not always been an ally, there have been at least two eras in which it was necessary for federal government to step in to enforce Blacks' civil rights. Perhaps the greatest federal intervention on behalf of Black rights occurred during Reconstruction. By the end of the Civil War, most White southerners were willing to accept that slavery was over. Fearing freedmen would seek vengeance on

them, however, southern states adopted Black Codes to restrict Blacks'
rights. By forcing Blacks into labor contracts with Whites, Black Codes
effectively ensured that Blacks would remain a cheap source of labor in
the South. Blacks who chose not to work or who quit their jobs could be
arrested and imprisoned. Black Codes also restricted where Blacks could
rent or own property, prohibited Blacks from testifying in court against
Whites, imposed a curfew on them, and prevented their use of firearms
(Franklin and Moss 1988).

Radical Republicans in Congress proposed the Fourteenth Amendment,
which would give Blacks equal protection under the law, to combat the
South's Black Codes (Walton and Smith 2010). Not surprisingly, the South
rejected the Fourteenth Amendment. In response, Congress passed the
Reconstruction Act of 1867, which divided the ex-Confederate states[6] into
five military districts. Each district had to draw up a new constitution,
which included suffrage rights for Black males, and submit it for approval
by Congress. Further, unless the states ratified the Fourteenth Amendment,
they would not be readmitted into the Union (Franklin and Moss 1988).

Although the Fourteenth Amendment was ratified in July 1868, it did
not protect Black suffrage rights. In fact, states in the North and the
South denied the franchise on the basis of race. With the passage of the
Fifteenth Amendment in March 1870, however, Black males would be
granted the constitutional right to vote in local, state, and federal
elections (Walton 2001).

Feeling disenfranchised at all levels of government, Southern Whites
were outraged. Consequently,

Secret societies grew and spread when it became apparent to Southerners that
their control was to be broken by Radical Reconstruction. For ten years after
1867 there flourished the Knights of the White Camelia, the Constitutional
Union Guards, the Pale Faces, the White Brotherhood, the Council of Safety,
the'76 Association, and the Knights of the Ku Klux Klan. Among the numerous
local organizations were the White League of Louisiana, the White Line of
Mississippi, and the Rifle Clubs of South Carolina. White Southerners expected
to do by extralegal or blatantly illegal means what had not been allowed by
the law: to exercise absolute control over Negroes, drive them from and their
fellows from power, and establish "white supremacy." Radical Reconstruction
was to be ended at all costs, and the tactics of terrorist groups were the first
step of Southern white leaders toward achieving this goal (Franklin and Moss
1988, 226).

---

[6] Tennessee was exempt from the Reconstruction Act of 1867 since, by that time, it had
   already ratified the Fourteenth Amendment (Franklin and Moss 1988).

Congress responded by passing the Ku Klux Klan Acts, making it a punishable crime for states' violations of Blacks' Fourteenth and Fifteenth Amendment rights (McClain and Tauber 2010; Walton and Smith 2010). The president was also given authority to prevent these crimes using the U.S. Army and Navy (Franklin and Moss 1988).

A dispute over the 1876 presidential election, however, led to the end of Radical Reconstruction. In exchange for Republican Rutherford B. Hayes assuming the presidency, southern states were given home rule and the use of federal marshals, supervisors, and military to oversee elections in the South was forbidden (Franklin and Moss 1988). Thereafter, Blacks lived in the oppressive system of Jim Crow.

To ensure Blacks were completely disenfranchised, southern states held constitutional conventions to adopt "color blind" measures that did not violate the Fifteenth Amendment. Leading the charge was Mississippi which, in 1890, imposed a poll tax and literacy tests on voters. Mississippi also barred ex-convicts from the franchise. In 1898, Louisiana added the "grandfather clause" to the disenfranchisement tools. Under the grandfather clause, only males whose fathers and grandfathers were eligible to vote on January 1, 1867 were qualified to vote, but no Blacks were in Louisiana at that time. By 1910, North Carolina, Alabama, Virginia, Georgia, and Oklahoma all had constitutional provisions to disenfranchise Blacks (Franklin and Moss 1988). Even when Blacks met the qualifications needed to cast ballots, Whites would use coercion, trickery, and violence to ensure Blacks could not vote (Walton and Smith 2010).

In 1875, Tennessee adopted its first Jim Crow laws, with the rest of the South quickly following suit. A strict color line was established, keeping Blacks and Whites separate in both public and private spaces. Lynching, rape, and other forms of extreme violence were used to enforce the color line, especially in the Midwest and South where lynching was most prevalent. Further, the post-World War I era brought with it a revival of the Ku Klux Klan (Franklin and Moss 1988). And African Americans, who fought for freedom abroad and continued this fight on the home front, witnessed the scope and severity of Jim Crow laws unrelentingly increase (Woodward 1955).

After decades of African-American activism, all three branches of the federal government – the Supreme Court, the President, and Congress – finally responded during the 1950s and 60s with actions aimed at dismantling Jim Crow. For instance, President Harry Truman became the first president to adopt a national civil rights agenda, calling for Congress to pass anti-lynching legislation and a ban on poll taxes and employment discrimination. He also issued executive orders banning discrimination in the military and federal employment (Walton and Smith 2010).

The Supreme Court and the Interstate Commerce Commission dealt a series of striking blows to segregation in the 1950s. Most notably was a series of cases involving school desegregation, which began with institutions of higher education and culminated with the landmark *Brown* v. *Board of Education of Topeka*. Beyond public schools, the Supreme Court and the Interstate Commerce Commission erased racial lines in other public venues.

In 1950 the Supreme Court ruled that the segregation of Negroes on dining cars of interstate railways was an undue burden on interstate commerce. Although an increasing number of Negroes were traveling on commercial airlines that had never been segregated, those who continued to travel by rail experienced little or no difficulty in securing first-class accommodations and in traveling across state lines without being segregated. In 1955 the Interstate Commerce Commission decreed that all racial segregation on interstate trains and buses must end by January 10, 1956. The decree applied also to waiting rooms in railway and bus terminals (Franklin and Moss 1988, 414).

While this decree had no jurisdiction over the segregated conditions of intrastate travel, it did go a long way in reversing the 60-year-old *Plessy* decision.

The South fought vehemently against desegregation. To avoid compliance, southern leaders turned public schools over to private organizations and made it a punishable crime to teach in or attend a mixed race school. Georgia, Mississippi, and Virginia passed resolutions declaring that the federal government had trespassed on the sovereignty of the states. Southern members of Congress issued the "Southern Manifesto," condemning the federal government's usurpation of state power and calling for resistance to desegregation's implementation. And, as was the case in the past, the South also resorted to violence, bombing Black homes and churches, and terrorizing and murdering civil rights activists (Franklin and Moss 1988).

Still, momentum with regards to civil rights legislation continued. In January 1964, the Twenty-fourth Amendment, which outlawed the poll tax, was ratified. Later that year, Congress passed the seminal 1964 Civil Rights Act, "the most far-reaching and comprehensive law in support of racial equality ever enacted in Congress" (Franklin and Moss 1988, 449). The 1964 Civil Rights Act not only banned discrimination in most public facilities, it authorized the federal government and the Attorney General to take action when there was noncompliance (Walton and Smith 2010). One year later, the 1965 Voting Rights Act (VRA) was passed eliminating racial barriers to the franchise. The VRA, recognizing the South's previous attempts to circumvent Blacks' Fifteenth Amendment rights, gave the executive branch the power to enforce voting rights in the States. This included using federal poll watchers to observe elections and requiring federal approval to any changes in the voting laws in seven states: Alabama, Georgia, Louisiana, Mississippi, South Carolina, Virginia, and North Carolina. The South begrudgingly complied with the VRA and the Justice Department estimated that in the five years after its passage, "almost as many blacks registered in Alabama, Mississippi, Georgia, Louisiana, North Carolina, and South Carolina as in the entire century before 1965" (Davidson 1992, 21).

After the VRA's passage, the South had shifted from focusing merely on preventing Blacks from voting to preventing Black political incorporation. In a practice known as "candidate diminution," White southerners would abolish offices, extend the terms of White incumbents, and require insurmountable qualifications for running for office in order to prevent Black candidates from winning elections. Additionally, Southern states would employ tactics that would dilute the Black vote, such as racial gerrymandering, holding at-large elections, and nominating multiple African-American candidates for the same office (Davidson 1992). Therefore, when the Voting Rights Act was extended in 1982, it was amended to include language that prohibited states from impeding the ability of Blacks to elect representatives of their own choosing (Katz, Aisenbrey, Baldwin, Cheuse, and Weisbrodt 2006).

In the post-civil rights era, racism in many places has become so institutionalized that the racist intent of such laws have long since been forgotten. The 1964 Civil Rights Act initially enabled Blacks to sue states, regardless of whether their practices led to disparate impact or disparate treatment. In the 2000 *Alexander* v. *Sandoval* case, the Supreme Court ruled that individuals only had the right to sue the states in cases where there was disparate treatment. Without proof of intent, Blacks found it very difficult to file institutional racism suits. African-American leaders, such as Congressman John Lewis, have attempted to use legislation to override the *Sandoval* decision, but with limited success (Walton and Smith 2010).

Part of the problem is that the majority of White America does not believe that racial discrimination is an obstacle obstructing Black success. As Table 2.1 indicates, Blacks are more likely than Whites to

TABLE 2.1 *Perceptions of most important national problem (in percent), by race and decade*

	1960s		1970s		1980s		1990s		2000s	
	Blacks	Whites	Blacks	Whites	Blacks	Whites	Blacks	Whites	Blacks	Whites
Agricultural	0.4	2.8	0.8	0.9	0.3	1.5	0.1	0.2	0.0	0.0
Economics	8.6	9.3	37.8	50.3	18.3	36.2	14.3	27.9	11.0	15.7
Foreign Affairs	29.4	54.5	10.9	14.1	19.7	25.6	11.1	12.9	8.8	11.9
Government Functioning	1.9	2.0	4.3	5.0	2.1	2.6	2.7	4.6	2.2	6.1
Labor Issues	1.3	0.9	0.4	0.5	0.1	0.2	0.0	0.0	0.0	0.0
Natural Resources	0.2	0.3	0.5	2.1	0.5	2.2	1.2	2.9	0.0	0.0
Public Order	5.7	6.5	11.9	9.9	15.4	7.7	27.6	20.3	30.8	21.2
Racial Problems	25.9	8.8	3.1	1.8	1.6	0.2	4.4	1.0	8.8	0.2
Social Welfare	23.8	14.5	29.5	14.6	41.2	23.4	38.3	30.0	38.5	41.7

Note: Percentages are weighted values.
Source: American National Election Study Cumulative Data File, 1948–2008.

indicate that racial problems are the most important problems facing the nation. Thus, one of the largest gaps in Black/White opinion is in beliefs about the appropriateness of government intervention in guaranteeing racial equality. While the majority of Whites oppose these programs, Blacks overwhelmingly support government efforts to ensure equal employment and educational opportunities (Kinder and Winter 2001). Furthermore, this gap remains persistent over time (Schuman, Steeh, Bobo, and Krysan 1997).

In the post-civil rights era, however, the importance of racial issues has been superseded by other issues, like social welfare issues. To be sure, only 8.8 percent of Blacks in the 2000s thought that racial problems were the most important problems facing the nation. When we disentangle the analyses to look at year instead of decade (not shown), we see that even during 1984 and 1988, when Jesse Jackson ran for the Democratic Party's presidential nomination, less than 4 percent of Blacks in both years named race as the most important national problem. In 1992, in the wake of the Rodney King riots, about 5 percent of Blacks indicated that race was the most important national problem. Instead, we see Blacks responding that public order was one of the most important problems that year (16.2 percent of Blacks indicated that this was the most important national problem). So despite the gap between Blacks and Whites in opinions on whether the government should ensure racial equality, the racial policy dimension will not be an important factor in Blacks' placement on the liberal–conservative continuum. Rather, the importance of race to Blacks will be actualized through the salience of other policy dimensions, such as social welfare.

MILITARY DIMENSION

Once let the black man get upon his person the brass letters, U.S., let him get an eagle on his button, and a musket on his shoulder and bullets in his pockets, and there is no power on earth which can deny that he has earned the right to citizenship in the United States.
– Frederick Douglass

As the above quote suggests, African Americans have used the military to gain recognition as citizens. Even if temporarily, Black military service, particularly during wartime, "gave lie to notions of their racial inferiority, providing evidence against leading rationalizations of the nation's racial hierarchies" (Klinkner and Smith 1999, 19). Consequently, Blacks have served in almost every military conflict throughout

U.S. history (Walton and Smith 2010). For instance, approximately 5,000 free and enslaved Blacks served in the Continental Army and Navy during the Revolutionary War. Military service enabled freedmen to raise their status in their communities; for slaves, it provided a pathway to freedom in those states that formally abolished slavery either during or immediately after the Revolutionary War. After the issuance of the Emancipation Proclamation, both freedmen and slaves were heavily recruited into the Union Army. In total, 186,000 Blacks fought as Union troops in the Civil War. These soldiers risked imprisonment and death for acts of mutiny for demanding fair treatment and equal pay for services rendered. W.E.B. DuBois saw military service during World War I as a means of escaping Jim Crow and achieving the rights of full citizenship. He urged college-educated African Americans to enlist in the armed forces to demonstrate the race's worth, particularly that of its leadership. DuBois, Black leaders, and the returning Black soldiers, however, became disillusioned by this strategy due to the institutionalized injustice within the military and the unchanging state of race relations in the U.S. Still, Blacks would continue to trade wartime service in exchange for the promise of equality and full citizenship (Nalty 1986).

Beyond citizenship, Blacks sought material benefits through military service as well. For instance, as a result of their service during World War II, Blacks were able to translate their veteran status into increased income. "Whereas for young white men, net of other matters, a stint in the military during World War II counted in income terms for something like a single year more of formal education, for blacks, military service contributed as much as did two or three more years of formal education" (Modell, Goulden, and Magnusson 1989, 840–1). Using U.S. Census data to calculate the difference in income between veterans who served in World War II and non-veterans, Browning et al. (1973) also found that there was a significant income advantage among Blacks to having veteran status.

For many, if not all ethnic minority men, military service can positively affect their subsequent chances in the opportunity structure of civilian society. Geographic mobility and personal independence, education, occupational training of various kinds, and experience in bureaucratic structures, all make it easier for the veteran to obtain those civilian jobs that provide better pay (Browning, Lopreato, and Poston 1973, 77).

Black veterans serving in World War II were also able to benefit from the G.I. Bill. While segregation, discrimination, and the under-funding of historically Black educational institutions of higher education prevented Blacks from using the G.I. Bill at the same rate as their White counterparts (see Herbold 1994), Black veterans attained a higher level of education in the post-war period than non-veterans (Turner and Bound 2003). The G.I. Bill helped further integrate predominantly White colleges and universities, expanded the breadth of offerings at Historically Black Colleges and Universities which had previously pigeonholed Blacks into a limited set of vocations, "and helped provide a foundation for the gradual growth of a black middle class" (Herbold 1994, 108).

At the same time, working in war-related industries as civilians also offered Blacks the opportunity to increase their social standing. For instance, using retrospective work histories from the Palmer Survey, Collins found that Black men working in war-related industries in the 1950s earned significantly more than those who had not (Collins 2000, 776). During this time, Blacks had been barred from many of the unionized manufacturing jobs in the North (Myrdal 1944) as well as non-farm sector jobs in the South (Margo 1990). War-time industry jobs gave Blacks access to higher paying jobs than they would have normally otherwise had (Collins 2000, 776). Without the war industry jobs, Blacks' employment opportunities would have been further limited.

The history of Blacks in the military is not without the same scars of racism that mark overall U.S. race relations. As Bowers, Hammond, and MacGarrigle (2005) explain:

For once the African-American had been freed of his bondage and had gained some rights of citizenship, it made sense that he should serve in the nation's armed forces. Yet vast hostility to blacks remained in the very fabric of the society, so much so that the integration of whites and blacks within the armed forces seemed out of the question. As a result, although black units were often brigaded with white regiments or incorporated into white divisions, black soldiers were never included in all-white units. They served their time in the Army apart, segregated into battalions, regiments, and divisions reserved exclusively for them (263–264).

The branches of the armed forces put restrictions on the number of Blacks that could enlist, the capacity they were allowed to serve, and their ability to be commissioned as officers. It was not until 1948, when President Truman issued an executive order banning discrimination in the armed services, that these restrictions began to be lifted (Nalty 1986).

Even with a desegregated military, racial disparities persisted. For example, rather than draft White college students, the Department of Defense implemented "Project One Hundred Thousand" during the

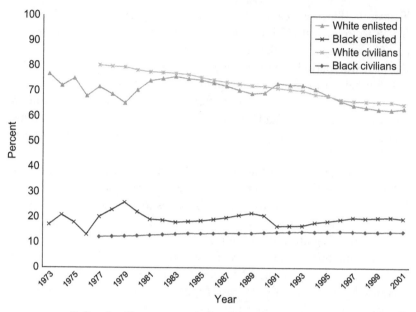

FIGURE 2.1 Enlisted military versus civilian labor force, by race and year
Note: Civilian group is comprised of comparable 18- to 24-year-olds.
Source: Bureau of Labor Statistics and Department of Defense.

Vietnam War. This policy widened the pool of draftees to incorporate men who did not previously meet military qualifications. Approximately 40 percent of the first round of men drafted under this program were nonwhite (Murray 1971). Once drafted, Blacks were disproportionately represented in combat units and less likely to enter officer training programs (Moskos 1973; Murray 1971). Nevertheless, Blacks serving in the military during the Vietnam War still believed that their military service was a means of career advancement (Moskos 1973) and were less likely than Whites to believe that the draft was unfair (Murray 1971).

In the modern-day All Volunteer Force (AVF), Blacks remain enlisted in the armed forces disproportionately relative to their numbers in the general U.S. population (Teachman and Tedrow 2008). Looking at Figure 2.1, we can see that in 2001, African Americans made up 19.5 percent of those enlisted in the military, while they only constituted 14 percent of the civilian workforce. In contrast, Whites are slightly underrepresented in the military relative to their comparable civilian

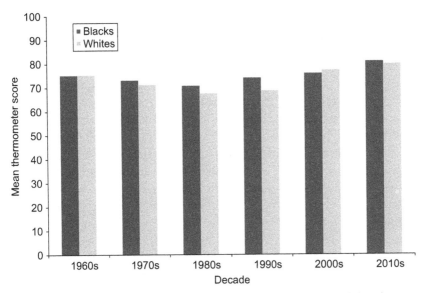

FIGURE 2.2 Mean military feeling thermometer scores, by race and decade
Note: Values are weighted means.
Source: American National Election Study Cumulative Data File, 1948–2012.

group. Furthermore, Blacks in the military report higher levels of job satisfaction, and receive better pay and promotion opportunities than their civilian counterparts (Phillips, Andrisani, Daymont, and Gilroy 1992). Blacks during the AVF era are also more likely to reenlist in the military than Whites, especially if they are married (Burk and Espinoza).

Furthermore, public opinion data demonstrates that Blacks continue to evaluate the military extremely highly. On a standard feeling thermometer, which ranges from 0 to 100, African Americans consistently score the military between 71 and 81 (American National Election Studies and Stanford University 2015). These evaluations are on par with those of Whites, who rate the military between 68 and 80 on the same scale (see Figure 2.2).

To summarize, the military issue dimension does not simply denote ideas about patriotism for Blacks. Among African Americans, the military has been a way to demonstrate racial equality. The military and related wartime industries have also served as important sources of employment for Blacks, particularly during times when other areas of employment were not open to them. Therefore, I expect the military policy dimension to be an important predictor of Black ideological self-identification.

Likewise, because Blacks have viewed the military as means through which to utilize the federal government to attain social and economic equality, being conservative on the military dimension should lead Blacks to be liberal on the social welfare dimension. As evidence, Parker (2009) examined the policy attitudes of Black veterans and non-veterans in the South during the 1960s. Parker found that veterans were less supportive of social welfare policies than non-veterans. Still, 89 percent of veterans (compared to 97 percent of non-veterans) believed that the government should help people get medical care at low cost. Eighty-five percent of veterans and 91 percent of non-veterans also believed that the federal government should help build more local schools, while 81 percent of veterans and 91 percent of non-veterans agreed that the federal government should guarantee employment for anyone seeking a job (Parker 2009, 159). Therefore, inasmuch as the military symbolizes a path towards social mobility for Blacks, military conservatism should be positively correlated with other attitudes capturing support for federal social welfare spending.

SOCIAL WELFARE DIMENSION

To be a poor man is hard, but to be a poor race in a land of dollars is the very bottom of hardships.

– W.E.B. DuBois

As Quadagno (1994) explains, "According to a long-standing tradition in political theory, Americans oppose all forms of government intervention because of an encompassing liberal culture in which individual rights are sacred, private property is honored, and state authority is distrusted" (5). Thus, for the greater part of United States history, there existed no national welfare state. The United States even lagged behind European nations in its development of programs aimed at protecting the social rights of its citizens.

A notable exception came shortly before the end of the Civil War in response to the recognition that the country would need to integrate newly freed slaves into society. In March 1865, Congress passed a bill that established the U.S. Bureau of Refugees, Freedmen, and Abandoned Lands. Also known as the Freedmen's Bureau, this military bureau, set up under the U.S. Department of War, was the nation's first social welfare agency. The Freedmen's Bureau regulated labor contracts between Black agricultural workers and Southern planters, established special courts to try minor civil cases in jurisdictions where Blacks otherwise had no access to courts, registered Black voters, established Black educational institutions, and served as a relief agency for the needy living in the South, which had been devastated by the Civil War (Goldberg 2007).

Almost immediately, the Freedman's Bureau was met with opposition. For instance, President Andrew Johnson vetoed the 1866 Freedmen's Bureau Bill.[7] In his veto message, he wrote: "The idea on which the slaves were assisted freedom was that on becoming free they would be a self-sustaining population. Any legislation that shall imply they are not expected to attain a self-sustaining condition must have a tendency injurious alike to their character and their prospects" (Walton and Smith 2010, 218). Other groups, such as White Southerners and Northern Democrats, questioned whether Blacks were fit for any privileges that came with full and equal citizenship. A third source of opposition was rooted in disagreement in the expansion of the federal government and the use of the military in civic affairs. There were also those opponents who believed that the Freedmen's Bureau provided preferential treatment to Blacks, instead of protecting all of the labor class. Finally, the Democratic Party alleged that the Freedmen's Bureau was merely an electioneering machine, rife with corruption (Goldberg 2007).

On the other hand, Blacks supported the Freedmen's Bureau. As Goldberg (2007) explains, "freedpeople sought recognition as honorable, rights-bearing citizens whose wartime services entitled them to state assistance. They demanded that the government furnish them with land or, failing that, safeguard their autonomy as laborers and protect them from coercive and abusive employers" (50). Nevertheless, the Freedmen's Bureau's opponents eventually won and the agency was dissolved in 1872, existing only 7 years (Walton and Smith 2010).

Besides the Freedmen's Bureau, the responsibility for the social welfare of the poor had primarily been in the hands of private charities. While there had been a few inadequately funded workers' compensation, old-age pension, and mothers' pension programs at the state-level, the United States had no national social programs until 1935. The Great Depression, however, forced the nation to adjust its hands off approach to the economy and providing for the social welfare of Americans.

---

[7] Congress was able to override President Johnson's veto, resulting in a 2-year extension in the Bureau's length of operations and a broadening of its powers. Under the 1866 Freedmen's Bureau Bill, Black rights were expanded to include, among other things, the right to take up arms against the violent attacks of the Ku Klux Klan (Goldberg 2007).

To address Americans' financial hardship and restore faith in the U.S. economy, President Franklin Roosevelt ushered in a "new era of government intervention" with the New Deal (Quadagno 1994, 19). The cornerstone of the New Deal was the Social Security Act of 1935, which provided old age insurance, unemployment compensation, Aid to Dependent Children, and Old Age Assistance. Access to these programs was not universal. Agricultural workers and domestic servants, who were predominantly Black, were not eligible to receive old-age insurance or unemployment compensation. The Civilian Conservation Corp (CCC), a nature conservation program that enabled young men to build their skill set while earning money, systematically failed to enroll Blacks into the program at a rate comparable to their population.[8] The National Recovery Administration, which set the standards for fair competition, wages, and hours, routinely undervalued the work in areas where Blacks were heavily concentrated. Lastly, the Federal Emergency Relief Administration, which provided grants to states for unemployment relief, paid Blacks lower wages than Whites and only hired Blacks as unskilled laborers after all Whites needing jobs had been employed (Weiss 1983). This left Blacks, who were in disproportionate need of relief[9], without adequate welfare assistance.

African Americans were further discriminated against during the implementation of the New Deal's housing policies. In addition to reducing the required down payment needed to purchase a home, regulating interest rates, and extending the length of mortgages, the National Housing Act of 1934 established the Federal Housing Administration (FHA). Because the FHA insured loans from default for lenders, it took a conservative approach by only insuring mortgages in low risk neighborhoods. In a process known as *redlining,* the FHA refused to insure loans in high-risk neighborhoods, which incidentally were those with large Black populations. Furthermore, the FHA encouraged homeowners to use restrictive

---

[8] Nationwide, only 5 percent of the CCC enrollees were African American. In Mississippi, where the Black population was over 50 percent, Blacks constituted only 1.7 percent of the CCC enrollment (Weiss 1983, 54).

[9] Because of the 70 percent decrease in the price of cotton, two-thirds of Black farmers in the early 1930s yielded no profit. In cities like Harlem, median Black wages decreased by 40 to 50 percent between 1929 and 1932. In Cleveland, 53.8 percent of Black families had incomes less than $500, compared to 26.1 percent of White families. At the same time, 18.3 percent of White families, but only 1.1 percent of Black families, had incomes of $2,000 or more. Finally, Black unemployment exceeded 50 percent in some large cities, compared to the nationwide unemployment rate of 25 percent (Weiss 1983, 46–7).

covenants, which prohibited the sale of homes to African Americans to prevent neighborhoods from integrating. As a result of redlining and restricted covenants, very few Blacks were able to benefit from this New Deal policy that enabled so many working class Americans to fulfill the dream of home ownership (Quadagno 1994).

In 1944, Congress established the Veterans Administration (VA), to help administer the G.I. Bill of Rights. In exchange for at least 90 days of active duty without a dishonorable discharge, World War II veterans were guaranteed insured, low-interest, long-term mortgages for purchasing a home, farm, or business. Even with veteran status, however, Blacks were unable to secure loans from lending institutions (Onkst 1998). "By 1962 the VA and FHA had financed more than $120 billion in new housing. Less than 2 percent was available to nonwhite families and most of that on a segregated basis" (Quadagno 1994, 91). Instead, Blacks were filtered into racially segregated, substandard housing located in central cities that isolated Blacks from industrial jobs, which were all moving out to the suburbs (Quadagno 1994). Thus, while the New Deal lifted the United States out of the Great Depression, its policies also created large concentrations of poverty-stricken Black neighborhoods in some of America's largest cities (Stricker 2007).

Although the Roosevelt Administration formally forbade discrimination in the implementation of New Deal policies, the governing of these programs was left to the states. This meant that the federal government had no control over the day-to-day operation of these relief programs. It is important to note that the racial consequences of the New Deal were not random. "Rather, they reflected a compromise reached with southern Democrats over the structure of the welfare state" (Quadagno 1994, 20).

Because of the ongoing racial ramifications of the nation's economic policies, the fight for full citizenship encompassed both the struggle for fundamental legal and constitutional rights and access to material benefits, such as land, education, and employment (Walton and Smith 2010). To be sure, class and race issues in the U.S. overlapped considerably. By the Civil Rights Era, Black agenda included dismantling the "tripartite system of racial domination" – Whites' political, economic, and personal control over Blacks (Morris 1984, 1).

Shortly after the 1963 March on Washington for Jobs and Freedom, President Johnson declared an "unconditional war on poverty" and began preparing his plan to combat poverty in the U.S. On August 20th, 1964, Congress passed the Economic Opportunity Act as part of the War on Poverty. This comprehensive set of antipoverty programs addressed job training, community action, health care, housing, and education. If the New Deal had purposefully sought to exclude African Americans, Johnson's War on Poverty specifically targeted Blacks as beneficiaries. With community action as the centerpiece, the War on Poverty sought to integrate Blacks into "local politics, local job markets, and local housing markets" (Quadagno 1994, 31). The goal of the War on Poverty was to not only provide the poor with income support, but to provide them with the education and training necessary to sustain long-term gainful employment (Brown-Collier 1998).

The War on Poverty had a significant economic impact on African Americans in a variety of ways. The most obvious benefit would be the cash and in-kind transfers Blacks received, which lifted many Black families above the poverty line. There was also the considerable improvement in education:

Black pre-schoolers were more likely to enroll than whites, largely because of federally financed early education programs. High school completion increased significantly and compensatory programs provided vital resources to the schools where black youths were concentrated. At the college level, absolute and relative enrollment gains were dramatic, the direct result of government aid programs" (Levitan and Taggart 1976, 611).

As a consequence, African Americans were able to move into more prestigious, professional, higher paying occupations (Levitan and Taggart 1976).

The War on Poverty also expanded Blacks' opportunity for federal employment. Between 1960 and 1970, the percentage of Black government employees doubled, going from 13 percent to 27 percent. Compare this to White public sector employment, which only increased from 12 percent to 15.6 percent over the same decade (Collins 1983, 373). Additionally, the community action piece of the War on Poverty served as a launching pad for future Black politicians.

When Johnson declared the War on Poverty, there were no black mayors and only seventy elected black officials at any level of government. Five years later there were 1,500; by 1981 5,014 including 170 mayors. Many of the new leaders gained experience and visibility in community action programs where they campaigned for the poverty boards, chaired meetings, lobbied, litigated, and delivered speeches (Quadagno 1994, 57–8).

The War on Poverty and its programs, however, became the scapegoat for adverse economic conditions experienced throughout the late 1970s and early 1980s. Furthermore, President Ronald Reagan blamed the War on Poverty for the social ills produced by welfare dependency, such as crime, drug use, and the breakdown of the American family (Stricker 2007). This conservative backlash to the War on Poverty led to a drastic cut in social welfare spending, especially on programs for children. Changes in benefit calculations and eligibility criteria for Aid to Families with Dependent Children (AFDC) led to a $1,300 to $2,500 decrease in annual income. In addition, Congress eliminated about 750,000 full-time public sector jobs and decreased spending on job training programs by $14 billion (Danziger and Gottschalk 1995, 26–7). By 1991, the child poverty rate among Blacks was 46 percent, compared to 17 percent among Whites (Stricker 2007).

Also by this time, conservatives had succeeded in coupling Blacks with welfare dependency (Stricker 2007; Gilens 1999). Relative to other industrialized nations, Americans are, by far, the least likely to believe that it is the government's responsibility to take care of the poor (Walton and Smith 2010).[10] Tied to this is the belief that welfare recipients are undeserving and most of the people on welfare are Black (Gilens 1999). These attitudes set the stage for the dismantling of the American welfare system.

In 1996, Congress signed into law the Personal Responsibility and Work Opportunity Reconciliation Act (PRWORA), which ended AFDC. Under PRWORA, poor women with children were no longer entitled to welfare benefits. Instead, PRWORA provided Temporary Assistance for Needy Families (TANF), placing a 60-month lifetime maximum on aid and requiring adult recipients to work within 2 years of receiving aid (Walton and Smith 2010). Under this new law, the states are able to design and administer their own programs, including reducing or extending the maximum time limit for cash assistance. In an examination of state TANF time-limit policy, Brock (2009) found that the majority of states with the strictest time limit policies (less than 5 years and/or not extending to children beyond 5-year maximum) had larger African-American populations.

Because of the economic boom experienced during the 1990s, those transitioning off of TANF were able to find and keep jobs (Walton and Smith 2010). If the past is any indicator, however, the Black community

---

[10] In a 1991 Times Mirror Center for the People and the Press study, 23 percent of U.S. citizens believed it was the government's responsibility to take care of the poor, compared to 70 percent of Spaniards, 62 percent of the French, and 61 percent of the British (Walton and Smith 2010).

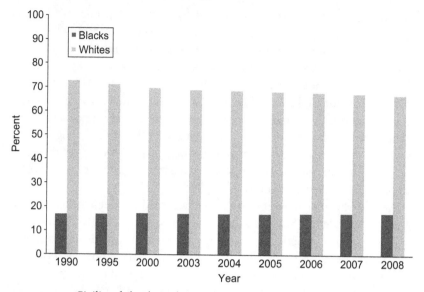

FIGURE 2.3   Civilian federal employees, by year and race
Note: Percentages do not include U.S. Postal Service employees.
Source: U.S. Census Bureau, Statistical Abstract of the United States: 2012.

disproportionately bears the brunt of an economic downturn that is not countered by governmental antipoverty programs. Historically, this has included not only cash and in-kind transfers, but also increased access to higher education and affordable housing (Stricker 2007).

Furthermore, the government is the single most important source of employment for Blacks (Pitts 2011). To be sure, employment in the public sector has traditionally served as a pathway to middle-class status for African Americans (Rubio 2010). The difficulty of attaining private sector jobs plus higher wages in the public sector originally drew Blacks toward government employment (Blank 1985). An examination of migratory patterns of Blacks during the 1970s, indicated that, as they became more upwardly mobile, the Black middle-class relocated out of segregated urban centers to neighborhoods near large public universities, hospitals, or other public services, which were their principal employers (Morton 1985). Even today, Blacks continue to be overrepresented in the federal civilian workforce. As Figure 2.3 indicates, roughly 17 percent of full-time non-military federal employees are African American, even though they constitute about only 13 percent of the workforce. Blacks are 30 percent more likely than non-Blacks to be employed in the public sector. Also, the median wage for Blacks in the public sector is higher than that of Blacks in other industries (Pitts 2011). Therefore, retrenchment in antipoverty programs not only deprives African Americans of their livelihood, it retracts their safety net.

Given the racialized politics surrounding the American welfare state, it is not surprising that an examination of attitudes towards social welfare policies demonstrates large differences in Black and White opinion. Specifically, Blacks are much more likely to support government spending on policies aimed at addressing income disparities. In 1992, the gap between Black and White opinion ranged from an 11.7 percentage point difference on attitudes towards government-provided health insurance to 33.8 percentage points on federal spending for the unemployed (Kinder and Winter 2001). African Americans consistently list social welfare issues – including child care aid to education, unemployment, and health care – as the most important national problems. Up until the 1990s, Blacks were even twice as likely as Whites to believe so (see Table 2.1). Nevertheless, 38.5 percent of African Americans continue believe that social welfare issues are the most important national problems. Hence, the social welfare dimension should be an important predictor of Blacks' ideological self-identification.

RELIGIOUS DIMENSION

> I hope you cannot but acknowledge, that it is the indispensable duty of those, who maintain for themselves the rights of human nature, and who possess the obligations of Christianity, to extend their power and influence to the relief of every part of the human race, from whatever burden or oppression they may unjustly labor under; and this, I apprehend, a full conviction of the truth and obligation of these principles should lead all to.
>
> – Benjamin Banneker

The importance of religion to Black life is well documented (Harris 1999; McDaniel 2008; Calhoun-Brown 1996). To be sure, Blacks are the most religious group in American society ("U.S. Religious Landscape Survey" 2008). Not only does the Black church serve as a source of salvation, it provides Blacks with a social and political hub in many African-American communities (McDaniel 2008).

Blacks' conversion to Christianity, however, was a slow process. A few Blacks had been introduced to Christianity by European missionaries travelling to Africa, while others converted during the trip through the Middle Passage or upon entering the Colonies (McDaniel 2008). Nevertheless, slavery had been in existence for almost two centuries before Christianity had been introduced to Blacks en masse (Raboteau 2004).

The delay was partially driven by the belief that, under the laws of the Church of England, baptized African slaves would have to be freed. In response, several colonies enacted legislation denying baptism as a condition of freedom. Slave owners were also reluctant to allow slaves the time necessary for adequate religious instruction. Again, state legislatures responded by passing laws preventing slaves from working on Sundays and having their Sabbath worship obstructed. Most importantly, many slave owners feared that Christianity would make their slaves rebellious:

> The danger beneath the arguments for slave conversion which many masters feared was the egalitarianism implicit in Christianity. The most serious obstacle to the missionary's access to the slaves was the slaveholder's vague awareness that a Christian slave would have some claim to fellowship, a claim that threatened the master-slave hierarchy (Raboteau 2004, 102).

But by the mid-eighteenth century, a Christian revival movement swept over Europe, which heavily influenced evangelists in North America (Akinyela 2003). Consequently, many more Blacks were being converted to Christianity and Blacks were joining the growing Baptist and Methodist movements in the South (Raboteau 2004).

Missionaries placated southern planters with the promise that Christian slaves would make better slaves. Blacks, who would often outnumber Whites, attended integrated Sunday church services, receiving messages about the virtues of obeying their masters and not stealing or lying. Resenting being preached to about docility and obedience, Blacks held their own prayer services, many in secret at the risk of flogging or other severe punishment. Out of these separate religious gatherings emerged Blacks' unique brand of Christianity, which allowed them to develop customs and rituals to cope with their oppression (Raboteau 2004).

Christianity, as practiced by African Americans, also served as a source of political empowerment and a catalyst to activism. Evidence of the marriage between the Black religion and politics can be found as early as the Revolutionary Era. For instance, slaves in New England petitioned the Governor of Massachusetts for their freedom using a combination of "political rhetoric of the Revolution with appeals to the claims of Christian fellowship" (Raboteau 2004, 291). During the Antebellum Era, early Black Baptist conventions as well as the African Methodist Episcopal Church worked with the abolitionist movement, petitioning government for the end of slavery (McDaniel 2008).

Perhaps the most notable period of African-American religious based political activism occurred during the Civil Rights Movement (Morris 1984; McAdam 1982).

Churches provided the movement with an organized mass base; a leadership of clergymen largely economically independent of the larger white society and skilled in the art of managing people and resources; an institutionalized financial base through which protest was financed; and meeting places where the masses planned tactics and strategies and collectively committed themselves to struggle (Morris 1984, 4).

As the movement gained momentum, particularly in the South, "organizations created to protect Black rights ... were structured through local churches and led by clergy, enabling such groups to obtain funding without fear of outside influence (McDaniel 2008, 73).

The most prominent of these organizations was the Southern Christian Leadership Conference (SCLC), led by Martin Luther King, Jr. The SCLC mobilized a network of Black religious and civic organizations throughout the South to combat Jim Crow. With a strategy of nonviolent direct action, their activities included bus boycotts, voting drives, and fighting for school integration (Morris 1984).

The Black Church continues to be important to contemporary Black politics. First, because of their grassroots network of congregants, Black churches dwarf secular Black civil rights and political organizations in their ability to disseminate political information directly to the Black community. Second, their autonomy from mainstream institutions, regular meeting times, and centrality to African-American life, also enable Black churches to better equip Blacks with the skills needed to participate in politics than secular organizations (Harris 1999). For these same reasons, candidates seeking the Black vote have routinely attended Sunday services or church forums to garner support. Candidates have also appealed to Black clergy to help mobilize voters, as was the case with Jesse Jackson's 1984 run for the Democratic Presidential nomination (Harris 1999; Tate 1993; Calhoun-Brown 1996).

Recognizing variation in political activity among Black churches, however, researchers have made the distinction between political and apolitical churches. (See McDaniel 2008 for an in-depth discussion on this topic.) Calhoun-Brown (1996) describes political churches as follows:

Political churches are usually led by politically active ministers. The political minister may issue pastoral endorsements, help to organize church members as volunteer workers in political campaigns, organize voter registration drives, or serve on ministerial committees for campaign organizations. In political churches parishioners hear announcements about elections, campaigns, candidates, and issues often from the pulpit. Candidates attending service may be given a platform from which to speak – during service itself. Suggested voting slates of candidates perceived to be sympathetic to African American concerns may be available at or distributed by the church. The church may even make financial contributions or give opportunities for congregants to give to campaigns. The political church may not engage in all of these activities, but the environment is such that electoral participation is the communicated norm and political activity is facilitated by the institution itself (942).

As Table 2.2 indicates, Blacks were more likely to hear political messages in their places of worship than Whites. For instance, in 2000 not only were Black clergy 5 percentage points more likely than White clergy to disseminate campaign information from the pulpit, they were three times more likely to encourage their parishioners to vote (Burns, Kinder, Rosenstone, Sapiro, and National Election 2008; Sapiro, Rosenstone, and National Election 2000; Rosenstone, Kinder, Miller, and National Election 1999; Rosenstone, Kinder, Miller, and National Election Studies. University of Michigan. Center for Political 2005).

There is empirical evidence to demonstrate receiving political messages has a direct impact on the political activism of African Americans. In an analysis of the 1984 presidential primary, Calhoun-Brown (1996) found that Blacks who attended a political church were "one and one-half times more likely to recall the primary, one and one-half times more likely to vote in the primary, and one and one-half times more likely to vote in the general election"(946). Likewise, Philpot et al. (2009) found that the single largest predictor of voter turnout for Blacks in the 2008 presidential election was church attendance. This effect was even larger than that of group identification or party mobilization. Thus, the relationship between Black politics and Black religion remains intimately intertwined. Consequently, the religious dimension will be an important determinant of Blacks' placement of the liberal–conservative continuum.

There is also evidence to suggest, however, that being conservative on the religious dimension does not necessarily translate into conservatism on the social welfare dimension. As McDaniel and Ellison (2008) explain:

the black church tradition closely couples the concern for personal spiritual salvation with a focus on community building, liberation, equity, and social justice. This leads to particular focus on antipoverty efforts and support for other programs aimed at creating opportunities for less fortunate persons (190).

TABLE 2.2 *Prevalence of political messages in place of worship, by race and year*

	1994		1996		1998		2000	
	Blacks	Whites	Blacks	Whites	Blacks	Whites	Blacks	Whites
Clergy provided election information	24.0 N=150	17.4 N=880	17.8 N=152	13.9 N=1,119	20.0 N=140	11.4 N=893	18.0 N=167	13.1 N=997
Clergy encouraged R to vote for a particular candidate or party	10.5 N=152	4.3 N=910	8.6 N=152	4.4 N=1,121	9.3 N=140	3.2 N=904	18.1 N=166	4.7 N=993

Note: Values are weighted percentages. Total sample size of racial group appears under percentage.
Source: American National Election Studies, 1994, 1996, 1998, 2000.

In an examination of Houston-area residents, McDaniel and Ellison found that while Black biblical literalists were more likely than Black non-literalists to support increased barriers to receiving abortions; religious Blacks were also more likely to support increased spending on the poor. Based on this, the religious dimension should be positively correlated with the moral dimension but negatively correlated with the social welfare dimension. In other words, religiously conservative Blacks should also be liberal on social welfare.

MORAL DIMENSION

> Foul aspersions upon the character of colored women are assiduously circulated by the press of certain sections and especially by the direct descendants of those who in years past were responsible for the moral degradations of their female slaves. And yet, in spite of the fateful heritage of slavery, even though the safeguards usually thrown around maidenly youth and innocence are in some sections entirely withheld from colored girls, statistics compiled by men not inclined to falsify in favor of my race show that immorality among the colored women of the United States is not so great as among women with similar environment and temptations in Italy, Germany, Sweden and France.
>
> – Mary Church Terrell

At the heart of Black's ideas about moral conservatism is what historian Evelyn Brooks Higginbotham calls the "politics of respectability." Those adhering to the tenets of the politics of respectability engage in politics with dignity and decency in such a way as to counter mainstream society's negative stereotypical images of African Americans. This political mindset requires Blacks to combat racial injustice without public displays of sexuality, violence, or impropriety. "Respectable" Blacks embody middle-class values by maintaining an image of godliness, modesty, and chastity in the eyes of Whites in order to validate their demands for equality and citizenship. It is the reason why club woman and political activist Mary Church Terrell, in a 1898 speech before the National American Woman Suffrage Association convention, felt compelled to speak at length about the morality of Black women, in addition to discussing all of their charitable work, political activism, and acts of racial uplift as justification for attaining voting rights.

The politics of respectability developed out of the need to overcome the well-entrenched beliefs formed about the innate nature of Blacks as intellectually and morally inferior that emerged during slavery. To be sure, in a nation based on the notion that "All men are created equal," the U.S. had to reconcile its beloved sense of liberty with the legalized bondage of African slaves. Consequently, supporters of slavery adopted legitimizing myths about Blacks – "attitudes, values, beliefs, stereotypes, and ideologies that provide moral and intellectual justification" for the creation of a racial hierarchy that so starkly contrasted the ideals of freedom and equality which served as the impetus of the U.S.'s founding (Sidanius and Pratto 1999, 45).

Essentially, "Dehumanizing Black people by defining them as nonhuman and as animals was a critical feature of racial oppression" (Collins 2004, 55). Under this system of racial and economic subjugation, Black male bodies were exploited for their labor. As justification, White society created the myth that Black men were not only mentally deficient, but that they were hypersexualized, bestial, and violent. This stereotype suggested that Black men were wild animals that needed to be domesticated through slavery to save White society, and White women in particular, from their predatory nature (Collins 2004).

Like Black men, Black women were also forced into hard manual labor. Additionally, Black women were routinely raped, in part to exercise political and/or economic power over them and partly to control their fertility and reproduction. Whether it was for labor or for the birthing of more slaves, control over Black women's bodies was not their own. To justify the sexual and physical exploitation of Black women, supporters of slavery created myths about Black female sexuality, painting them as insatiable, animalistic, jezebels (Collins 2004).

As observers of the American slave system correctly predicted (see Tocqueville 1835 for instance), these prejudices outlived the institution of slavery. Therefore, Blacks adopted Victorian patriarchal conventions about family, household, and sexuality (Gaines 1996). By exercising the politics of respectability through their morals and behaviors, Blacks were able to defend against White supremacist attitudes that categorized them as innately inferior. "Respectability was a perceived as a weapon against such assumptions, since it was used to expose race relations as socially constructed rather than derived by evolutionary law or divine judgment" (Higginbotham 1993, 192).

A classic example of the politics of the respectability was the Black Women's Club Movement. The Black Women's Club Movement began in the post-Reconstruction era to address the unmet educational and social welfare needs of African Americans. Initially, clubs were formed at the state and local level and operated independently of one another to serve their respective communities. The Black Women's Club Movement centralized in 1895, when Josephine St. Pierre Ruffin organized the First National Conference of Colored Women in Boston. This conference brought together various clubs from around the country and eventually led to the formation of the National Association of Colored Women (NACW) (Lerner 1974).[11] Founded in 1896, the NACW is the largest and most enduring African-American protest organization in history.

While the NACW's mission was racial uplift and self-help, "At the core of essentially every activity of NACW's individual members was a concern with creating positive images of Black women's sexuality" (Hine 1989, 918). Members of NACW were discouraged from sexual expression. NACW members also built boarding houses, domestic service training centers, hospitals, and nursing training centers with the goal of providing "Black women with protection from sexual exploitation and with dignified work" (Hine 1989, 918).

The 1955 Montgomery Bus Boycott provides another historical example of how Blacks have exercised the politics of respectability as a strategic means of attaining their goals. For several years, Montgomery's Women's Political Council (WPC), a civic group consisting of Black professional women, had targeted Montgomery's segregated bus laws. Led by Jo Ann Robinson, the WPC petitioned several of Montgomery's elected officials to hire more Black bus drivers, increase the frequency of bus stops in Black neighborhoods, and create a more equitable way of seating passengers. Dissatisfied with the unresponsiveness of Montgomery's city government, the WPC decided to force the officials' hands by staging a bus boycott. With little support in the Black community for a boycott, however, what the WPC needed was an incident to spark interest in their plan (Garrow 1985).

On March 2, 1955, fifteen-year-old Claudette Colvin was arrested for assault, violating the segregation law, and disorderly conduct for refusing to relinquish her seat on a segregated Montgomery bus. She was later found guilty of assault in a brief trial, but only sentenced to pay a small fine. Ultimately, it was decided that Colvin's case would not serve as the catalyst for the attack on segregation. First, her case had lost momentum and many of the likely witnesses were starting to waver in support. Second, the small penalty Colvin received resulted in her losing her martyr

---

[11] The formation of the NACW represented the unification of the Colored Women's League, a coalition of 113 organizations, and the National Federation of Afro-American Women, a coalition of 85 organizations (Shaw 1991).

status. Finally, many described Colvin as "immature – prone to break-downs and outbursts of profanity. Worse, she was pregnant" (Branch 1988, 123). As Branch explains, "Even if Montgomery Negroes were willing to rally behind an unwed pregnant teenager – which they were not – her circumstances would make her an extremely vulnerable stand-ard bearer" (Branch 1988, 123).

Eight months later, on December 1, 1955, Rosa Parks was arrested for refusing to move to the back of a segregated bus. Unlike Claudette Colvin, Rosa Parks was believed to be "without peer as a potential symbol for Montgomery's Negroes – humble enough to be claimed by the common folk, and yet dignified enough in manner, speech, and dress to command the respect of the leading classes" (Branch 1988, 130). And so it was that Montgomery's Black community and its supporters used Parks' arrest to spearhead the year-long bus boycott.

Even today, Black politics is marred by a bifurcation between the respectable and unrespectable. For instance, Political Scientist Cathy Cohen develops a theory of secondary marginalization, which she uses to explain Black elites' slow response to the HIV/AIDS crisis in the African-American community. She argues that Black leaders, who have taken it upon themselves the responsibility of preserving the image of the Black community and policing the Black agenda, distinguish between "worthy" and "unworthy" group members when distributing scarce resources that have been secured from mainstream society. Cohen finds that Black political, media, and medical organizations, in their response, differentiated between "the 'innocent victims' of AIDS and those whose 'bad' behavior led to their infection" (Cohen 1999).

Similarly, White (2007) finds a Black ambivalence when it comes to support for food stamps that is rooted in Black identity and beliefs about who is deemed worthy of being incorporated into the group. White ran an experiment where subjects read a story about potential cuts to the federal food stamp program, varying whether the story focused on the impact on inner-city, African-American, poor, or American families. He found that highly identified African Americans concerned about crime were the least supportive of food stamps when they read that said cuts would impact inner-city families. White concludes that this decreased support is the effort of Blacks to distance themselves from marginalized subsets of the African-American community (White 2007).

Still, moral ideology will not be a significant factor underlying Black ideological self-identification. As practiced in the Black community, moral ideology is derived from a self-policing of the meaning of Blackness and who belongs in the group (White 2001). Moral ideology for African Americans is more often applied to intragroup politics than notions of the proper role of government in regulating moral issues.

Previous research has used Blacks' positions on racial issues as the delineating marker between Black conservatives and Black liberals. Reducing the distinguishing factor between these two groups to one element, however, fails to capture the complexity in the ideological thinking of African Americans. First, only focusing on race omits the contribution other policy domains make in shaping Blacks' ideological self-identification. To be sure, when Blacks call themselves *liberal* or *conservative,* they draw upon a range of issue considerations, including military, social welfare, and religious.

Second, through the examination of other policy domains, we are able to get a more robust picture of how race works in the political calculus of Black decision making. As the findings in Chapters 1 and 2 suggest, the racial dimension by itself has declined in significance as the other dimensions have encompassed racial aspects within them. Thus, race remains salient inasmuch as it is intimately intertwined with the other policy dimensions. Furthermore, as race has been incorporated into the other dimensions, the meaning of what it means to be liberal and conservative along those dimensions has been fundamentally altered. For instance, racial justice is currently linked to Black religion so that identifying as conservative not only denotes one's beliefs about the righteous path towards salvation, but also one's commitment to racial uplift as a means to achieving one's place in the hereafter (see also Lincoln and Mamiya 1990; Cone 1969). This understanding of the religious dimension is different than that of Whites and presumably will affect Blacks' ideological self-identification. This we will explore in the next chapter.

Third, through the examination of the various policy areas, we begin to get a picture of ideological self-identification that is both multidimensional *and* hierarchical. As we saw in Chapter 1, Blacks were able to define liberalism and conservatism within six different issue areas. The historical analyses presented in Chapter 2 suggest, however, that not all of these dimensions will be applicable to Blacks' ideological self-identification. The theoretical framework presented in this chapter posited that, when determining their ideological self-identification, Blacks will use those dimensions where they have had the most experience with government and politics. This is another area in which race has an indirect effect on the formation of Blacks' ideological self-identification. Chapter 2 has delineated the historical roots of Blacks' ideological understandings and proposed why it is that Blacks might utilize certain ideological dimensions over others. Based on these findings, it is expected that the most salient dimensions in determining Blacks' placement on the liberal–conservative continuum will be the social welfare, military, and religious domains. With these expectations, Chapter 3 sets out to empirically examine the underpinnings of Black ideological self-identification.

3

Multiple Paths to the Same Place

The Underpinnings of Ideological Self-Identification

One of the main arguments for why the observed relationship between ideological self-identification and party identification is different for Blacks than it is for other racial groups is that Blacks have a unique conceptualization of the liberal–conservative continuum that is rooted in the Black experience. In general, ideological self-identification is structured *multi-dimensionally*. That is, people have a diverse set of policy preferences that enable them to categorize themselves as liberal or conservative across several domains. Based on some subset of these preferences, citizens then make a global assessment of their ideological self-identification. Ideological self-identification is also structured *hierarchically* – not all of these dimensions are universally relevant. In addition to varying by individual, the weight of the dimensions in determining one's placement on the liberal–conservative continuum varies systematically by race. For Blacks, those dimensions for which there is a shared Black experience within the realm of government and politics will be the most salient to African-American ideological self-identification.

The focus of Chapter 3 is demonstrating whether these assumptions about Black ideology are correct. Chapter 1 identified the six distinct policy dimensions in which citizens and elites applied ideological labels. With these policy dimensions in place, Chapter 2 established a set of theoretical expectations regarding which criteria Blacks were most likely to use when determining their ideological self-identification and how these criteria would form a constrained ideology. It was hypothesized that, based on their historical experienced, African Americans' ideological self-identification is largely based on the social welfare, religious, and military issue areas, but that being conservative in one domain did not necessarily translate into being conservative in the other domains. The present chapter sets out to empirically test these claims. Specifically, Chapter 3 examines which issue areas African Americans use when determining whether to label themselves *liberal* or *conservative* and how these domains are bundled together to form a constrained ideology.

While it has been argued that the opposite of conservative is not necessarily liberal (e.g. Conover and Feldman 1981; Kerlinger 1967; Huntington 1957), this dichotomy "has been the single most useful and parsimonious way to classify political attitudes for more than 200 years" (Jost 2006, 654). Furthermore, regardless of whether the liberal-conservative continuum is bipolar or these concepts are orthogonal, the purpose of this project is to discern the meaning behind individuals' *self-identification* as either liberal or conservative.

OPERATIONALIZING IDEOLOGICAL DIMENSIONS

Previously, scholars have used respondents' issue positions as a measure of ideology. (See Layman and Carsey 2002, for example.) If ideology is the superordinate belief system that predicts issues positions (see Lyons and Scheb 1992), then this practice is less than ideal since "ideological sentiments do not translate directly into policy preference" (Levitin and Miller 1979). Alternatively, studies (e.g. Ellis and Stimson 2012) have made use of respondents' attitudes about the proper level of government spending in different areas as measures of ideology. While these measures get closer to the definition of ideology, not all government intervention is spending-related. To overcome the limitations that plague previous studies, I use a set of measures specifically designed to tap into the various dimensions of ideology. These measures were administered as part of the 2010 Post-Midterm Election Study (PMES).[1] Data for the PMES were obtained from a national probability sample of 325 Blacks and a national probability sample of 398 Whites (non-Hispanics). To be eligible for the survey, respondents had to be at least 18 years old. The survey was administered by Knowledge Networks via the internet. The median length of time to complete the questionnaire was 10 minutes and the completion

---

[1] Tasha Philpot of the University of Texas at Austin, was the principal investigator of the 2010 Post-Midterm Election Study. The study was made possible through the generous support of the National Science Foundation.

rate was 63 percent.[2] The survey was conducted between November 23, 2010 and December 7, 2010. Included on the survey instrument was a battery of 18 items that tapped into each of the six dimensions of ideology explored in this books. (See the appendix for exact question wording and coding). The advantage of using the PMES is the ability to use the battery of ideology-related questions not featured on other surveys, e.g. the American National Election Studies. The PMES also has a large enough Black sample to conduct meaningful analyses. For consistency's sake, all ideology measures are coded from zero (most liberal) to one (most conservative).

This first set of analyses examines the distribution of the six dimensions. To assist us in understanding the complexities of Blacks' placement on these dimensions, I augment these analyses with data from the qualitative interviews that were described in the previous chapter. The qualitative data provide an in-depth assessment of what it means to be liberal or conservative in a given policy domain. I also include Whites as a comparison group in these analyses to provide a baseline for understanding how Black ideological self-identification may be conceptualized differently than the general electorate.

We begin with the laissez-faire dimension, which taps into general ideas about the size and scope of government. Here, conservatives believe that the government is wasteful and inefficient and that it undermines capitalism; liberals believe that government should have some control over business. The survey measures used were taken from Comrey and Newmeyer's (1965) Weak Federal Government Scale. This policy domain proved an area where the gap between Blacks and Whites was quite large. The mean difference between Blacks and Whites on this dimension was 0.15, which was statistically significant at the $p < 0.05$ level. Blacks' mean placement was 0.52, right at the center of the measure. There were a few outliers at both ends of the spectrum; however, Blacks were mostly moderate with respect to laissez-faire. The qualitative evidence suggested the Blacks thought that government was needed to provide rules and regulations for society. At the same time, Blacks thought that government needed to respect the privacy of its citizens, especially if no one was getting hurt. There was quite a bit of support among Blacks for public-private partnerships, as well as for the ideal of popular sovereignty.

---

[2] The completion rate was calculated using AAPOR RR6, which takes into account the multiple phases of recruitment and selection into the survey. (See Callegaro and DiSogra 2008b for a detailed explanation.)

On the other hand, Whites' mean placement was 0.67, indicating that Whites were fairly conservative on this dimension. Like Blacks, Whites also believed that government needed to respect the privacy of its citizens as long as no one was getting hurt. Among Whites, however, there was a stronger opposition to government regulating corporations and businesses. White conservatives on the laissez-faire dimension also believed that the government needed to play less of a role in the everyday lives of American citizens:

My personal opinion is it has gotten out of control. How they somehow control our rights by, already from venues they have out here whether it's state or local, federal issues with regards to controlling a little bit more. I mean we're much more of a socialist economy than we want to admit. They say it's enterprise capitalist system, but you know, we're about that close from socialism (Respondent 2, 41-year-old White male).

White conservatives on the laissez-faire dimension believed that government should be limited to providing basic infrastructure, public health, and national security.

The racial dimension represents the extent to which people believe that government intervention is needed to achieve racial equality. It was measured using Dawson's Radical Egalitarianism/Black Conservatism Scale. Racial conservatives believe that there are no systemic barriers prohibiting Blacks from achieving equality. Racial liberals, on the other hand, believe that racism prohibits Blacks from achieving equality and government intervention is needed to level the playing field (see Dawson 2001). With a difference of 0.22, this was the largest difference between Blacks and Whites on any of the ideological dimensions. Whites were fairly moderate, with a mean placement of 0.57. In contrast, Blacks were very liberal. Their mean racial score was 0.35. Furthermore, only 11 percent of Blacks placed above the midpoint on this dimension. The basis of Blacks' placement on the racial policy dimension was the belief that racism still existed and a strong support for racial equality. Almost all of the respondents in the qualitative sample believed it was the government's responsibility to ensure racial equality to at least some degree. Consider the point made by Respondent 69, a Black 33-year-old female from the East Coast:

They [the government] have a responsibility because for one the government was created on inequality of the races and they already owe African-Americans everything they have. They wouldn't have the wealth that they have, and it is because of our race that they have become the dominant race. And they also owe the Native Americans, they owe the Mexicans whose backs they're now standing upon. So yeah, absolutely.

Blacks who did not support government intervention in the area of race, articulated a nationalist rather than a conservative reasoning. Here is one explanation provided by Respondent 70, a 33-year-old Black male from the East Coast:

that's like a slave who's been beaten by his master go onto his master and asking him for help. Again, the government is a huge reason why we're actually in the situation we're in now. And I think it's a slap in the face for us to go to the person who actually wrote the rules for us to be in the situation that we're in now to come help us. So again, we need to come together as a group. Obviously at this point in time in this age everything revolves around money. And I think once we start putting our money literally where our mouth is we can turn the whole thing over by ourselves. We don't even need the government. The Black Panthers proved that.

Most White respondents believed that race should not be an issue, regardless of whether they identified as liberal or conservative. For White racial liberals, this meant that everyone should be treated equally and not judged by their race. One respondent recognized the privilege that came with her Whiteness:

I don't think people think clearly enough about it. I don't think it occurs to people that to be someone who is White in this society means to be someone who has grown up with privileges that people who are not White have not grown up with. Even if we grew up poor we still grew up with things like dolls that look like us on the store shelves. I don't get followed around when I go to a store. My son doesn't get stopped by the police if he's driving through the wrong neighborhood. And I think that there are too few of us who have taken advantage of those and enjoyed that privilege who haven't taken the time to stop and think about that and what that means for the people who haven't enjoyed those privileges and how that has an effect on people's daily lives. It isn't just about the big issues of, you know, getting jobs and the criminal justice system and all of that sort of thing. It's a pervasive thing day by day by day. It seeps into children's souls. And it's important for all of us to be vocal and to acknowledge it when we see it. Say something. Don't just let it pass (Respondent 15, 56-year-old White female).

Most White racial liberals believed that it was the government's responsibility to ensure racial equality, although a few believed that racial equality needed to come from society and that government could not change the hearts and minds of individuals. White racial conservatives indicated that our nation's laws should be colorblind in their enforcement. Respondent 17, a 33-year-old White male from the East Coast, expressed his opinion this way: "I consider myself conservative and specific groups should not be given specific rights separate from other groups. In other words, government provides people and groups and I think that's very wrong and very disgusting." From their point of view, White racial conservatives believed that there were no systemic impediments to racial minorities achieving equality and therefore they did not support affirmative action programs and other government interventions.

The military dimension was captured using items from Comrey and Newmeyer's (1965) Service to Country Scale. On one end of the scale, conservatives believe military service deserves the highest honor; those at the polar end oppose citizens having to serve in the military. Figure 3.2 illustrates the distribution of the military dimension. The mean placement of Blacks on this dimension was 0.55, with a standard deviation of 0.19. This indicates that Blacks were just right of center on this dimension, with most Blacks taking a moderate to slightly conservative position. To give these results substantive meaning, I examined Blacks' self-description of their placement on the military dimension. Most commonly, Blacks responded that they were against the United States going to war. Nevertheless, Blacks also believed that a strong military was necessary in the event that the United States was under attack. Respondent 61, a self-described military moderate, explained the need for a strong military as follows, "Well if somebody were to walk up to you and punch you in your face what are you going to do? And that is the basis of what your natural nature is. So again, as far as the military, there is a time and a place for everything."

On this same dimension, Whites were considerably more conservative, with a mean placement on the military policy scale of 0.63 and median placement of 0.67. Furthermore, Whites experienced significantly more variance in their opinions.[3] The qualitative interviews can be used to help us understand the meaning behind Whites' placement on the military policy scale; the interviews indicate that those at the center of the scale viewed the military as almost a necessary evil. For example, in explaining why she was moderate when it came to the military dimension, Respondent 36 discussed the tradeoff between technological innovations that are derived from military research versus the loss of privacy that comes from these innovations:

I wish we didn't have a need for the military. Unfortunately, we do. Back in the 80s, I was against all wars. Thanks to Star Wars, we now have GPS. Thanks to Star Wars, we now have cell phones. Thanks to Star Wars, we have Google Earth.

---

[3] The statistical significance in the difference of variances was determined using the Levene's Test for Equality of Variances. All reported differences are significant at the $p < 0.05$ level.

Unfortunately, though, we also lost our privacy, thanks to it. Due to the evolution of computers and other sort of things, right now somebody in Washington can aim that missile at the two of us, hi guys [respondent waves out the window]. By the same token, they can also aim it at that little missile silo somewhere else on the earth, hi guys [respondent waves out the window], same people who are looking at us also. So that's why we have a window seat?

On the conservative end, Whites believed that a strong military was needed for national security and self-defense, especially in the War against Terror. White military liberals, in contrast, were anti-war and did not believe the United States should use military force unless absolutely necessary. Most White military liberals specifically named the war in Iraq as an example of why they did not support U.S. military intervention. Finally, White military liberals believed that the United States should be focusing more on domestic problems rather than engaging in international disputes.

The social welfare dimension uses items from Comrey and Newmeyer's (1965) Welfarism Scale. Respondents at the liberal end of this scale believe that government has a social obligation to take care of its citizens, while conservatives believe that it is up to each individual to ensure her own wellbeing without government assistance. The mean Black response on the social welfare dimension was 0.36. There were only a few Blacks who took the extremely conservative position on the social welfare dimension, while the majority of Blacks were liberal to moderate (see Figure 3.1). The qualitative data indicate that most Blacks who were liberal on social welfare indicated it was because they supported helping those in need and supported equality. The Blacks who were conservative on this dimension were against government handouts and were particularly skeptical about the U.S.'s welfare state. Blacks who were conservative on the social welfare dimension believed it was the individual's responsibility to earn a living. Take, for instance, Respondent 63's explanation of why he is conservative:

I think I'm kind of conservative. I think I'm on the fence on this one because I think everybody can work. That's how I feel. Something that you could do to earn an income instead of sitting at home and doing nothing. However sometimes, you know, nobody told you to get pregnant or nobody told you how many children to have or not, what not to do. But some situations you can't help it. But I think that I'm conservative when it comes to that because I think everybody can work.

But again, very few Blacks considered themselves conservative when it came to social welfare.

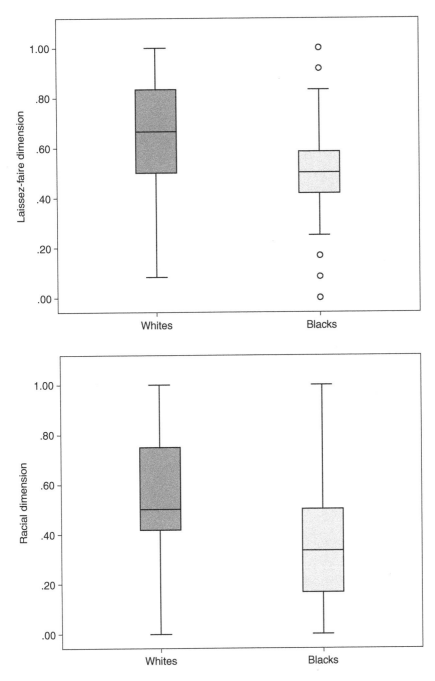

FIGURE 3.1 Distribution of ideological dimensions, by race
Note: Values were calculated using independent sample weights. Ideological dimensions are coded from zero (most liberal) to one (most conservative). Figures represent the medians and IQRs for each ideological dimension.
Source: 2010 Post-Midterm Election Study.

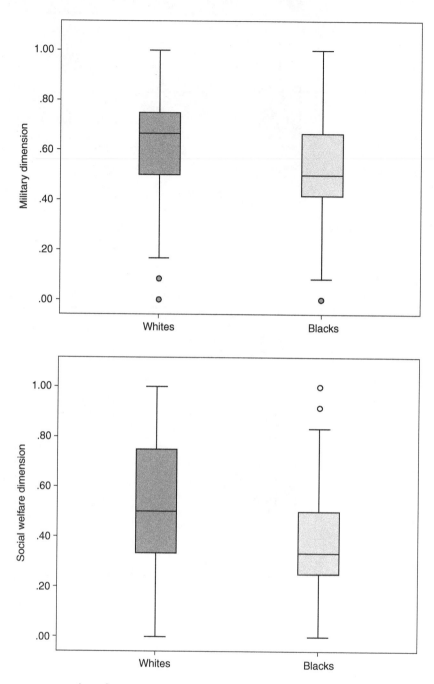

FIGURE 3.1 (*cont.*)

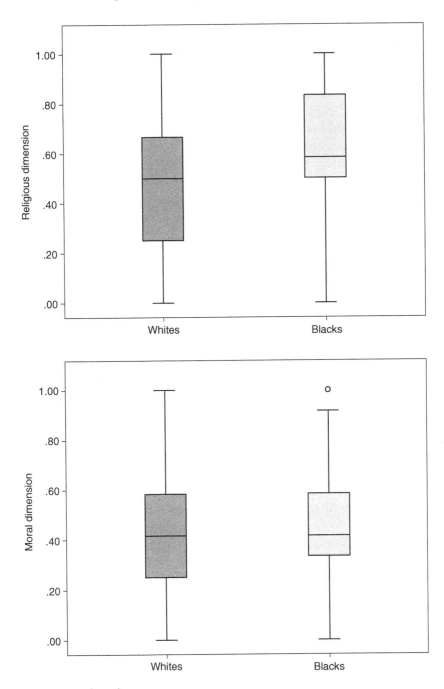

FIGURE 3.1 (*cont.*)

In contrast, Whites were significantly (both substantively and statistically) more conservative on the social welfare dimension. Their median
placement on social welfare was 0.50, with a mean of 0.52 and standard
deviation of 0.25. Put another way, 57 percent of Whites placed at the
midpoint or higher (more conservative) on this dimension, compared to
35.5 percent of Blacks. Whites in the qualitative sample indicated that they
were liberal on the social welfare dimension because they supported social
programs such as housing subsides, universal health care, welfare, and
funding for education. Interestingly, a few White social welfare liberals
believed that government owed it to taxpayers to provide these programs:

> I think we have people come here, they pay taxes, I think the government has
> some responsibility towards us or for that and so if there is social security, health
> care, your total social issues like that, then I think that if we do our part as a
> citizen, then the government has a responsibility to us as well (Respondent 30,
> White female).

In explaining why they were social welfare conservatives, Whites indicated that they supported helping people help themselves, rather than
using government programs like welfare. They also believed that government was inefficient and that welfare abuse was rampant.

The religious dimension captures respondents' beliefs about the extent
to which there should be separation of church and state. These items are
taken from Comrey and Newmeyer's (1965) Religiosity Scale. Religious
conservatives advocate for laws that would incorporate religion into
public lives, while liberals believe that religion is a private matter. The
religious domain is the only dimension in which Blacks were significantly
more conservative than Whites. The median position on the religious
dimension for Blacks was 0.63 and 82.5 percent of Blacks placed at the
moderate to most conservative position on this dimension. For Whites,
the median placement was 0.58. and 62.2 percent had responses that
positioned them at the midpoint of the dimension or higher.

In explaining their religious conservatism, both Blacks and Whites in
the qualitative sample based it on their belonging to a particular church or
the Christian faith. A few articulated it in terms of their adherence to the
Bible or their opposition to issues like abortion and gay marriage. With
respect to politics, religious conservatives believed that politicians should
pray and use their faith to guide their decision-making in order to make
morally sound legislation. Religiously conservative respondents, regardless of race, also believed that religion and religious choices should not be
legislated.

Respondents on the liberal side of the religious dimension usually did not belong to a church or have strict religious beliefs. Others were critical of religious teachings. Most prevalently, religious liberals considered themselves open-minded, respectful of other religions, and thought that everyone was entitled to their own religious beliefs. White religious liberals also used a scientific argument as the basis of their placement on the religious dimension. As Respondent 7, a White 41-year-old male from the Midwest, explains:

My feelings with religion and the Bible is that the Bible is a history book of the Jewish people foremost. . . . I believe that religion years ago or centuries ago was a form to explain things that were unexplainable. And today with technology we can explain earthquakes, we can explain mountains of fire that they're volcanoes, so I think a lot of that, plus a lot of it was handed down by word of mouth so some of it's not to be took in literally I would say.

Religious liberals also believed that religion and politics should not mix. For instance, Respondent 53, a Black female from the East Coast, had the following to say on the matter:

[Religion and politics] are diametrically opposed to one another. Politics I think is driven by personal gain, personal agendas, money, corruption. Religion is supposed to be, I think, your relationship that you have with God and how you live your life spiritually. And I just don't think they're a good mix.

One religious liberal thought religion and politics would necessarily intertwine. Respondent 76, a 63-year-old woman from the Midwest, wondered "how can someone rule and be a good leader unless he knows the Lord." Nevertheless, the majority of religious liberals from both races thought that religion and politics would corrupt one another.

One of the smallest gaps between Blacks and Whites was on the moral dimension. The moral dimension, which was measured using Wald, Owen, and Hill's Moral Conservatism Scale, is "a composite scale of preferences on public issues with a moral dimension" (Wald, Owen, and Hill 1988, 536). Moral conservatives advocate for "traditional" family values, while moral liberals are accepting of different lifestyles. The mean placement of Blacks and Whites on this dimension was 0.45 and 0.43, respectively. Figure 3.1 indicates that while the mean difference between Blacks and Whites was small, Blacks were much more consistent in their placement on this dimension. That is, the variance for Whites was larger than that of Blacks.

Although Blacks in the qualitative sample believed that morality provided a way of knowing the difference between right and wrong, they also believed that few things in life were so cut and dried. Blacks thought that while there should be standards that society should live by, people were only human and bound to make mistakes. Because of this, several Blacks indicated that people should not be judged or condemned for their behavior. When it came to politics, however, most Blacks believed that politicians had an obligation to perform their duties with a high moral standard.

For Whites, morality was also the difference between right and wrong. The definition of right and wrong differed, however, depending on whether a respondent was liberal or conservative. Moral liberals believed morality was personal. They did not oppose premarital sex, stem cell research, and gay marriage, were pro-choice and opposed the death penalty. As Respondent 24 articulated, White moral liberals thought that people should be free to make their own moral choices: "I believe that people should have free agency as long as they don't harm someone else or prohibit someone else, that their moral choices should be theirs alone to make, and I don't think that would be a conservative position." Whites who were moral conservatives considered themselves to hold traditional values, opposed having children out of wedlock and living together before getting married, and were pro-life. With respect to politics, there was a strong consensus among all of the White respondents that government should not dictate morality to its people but should set the example of how to act towards one another. As one respondent stated, "It's impossible to separate [morality from politics]. Morality is how you should run your society and politics is how you do run your society" (Respondent 47, 66-year-old White male).

In order to provide a sense of how people package these policy dimensions together, Table 3.1 presents the intercorrelations of the six dimensions. The top half of the table shows the results for Blacks. The racial policy dimension had a moderate and positive correlation with the social welfare and laissez-faire dimensions. This is consistent with the *New York Amsterdam News* results that demonstrated a racialization of the social welfare dimension and our expectations discussed in Chapter 2 that race would be incorporated into the laissez-faire and social welfare dimensions. The racial dimension was also modestly ($r = 0.11$, $p = 0.06$) correlated with the moral dimension; as racial conservatism increased, so did moral conservatism. Given the role of respectability politics in the Black community, this correlation is wholly understandable as well. As predicted in Chapter 2, the military dimension had a small ($r = -0.07$), yet statistically insignificant ($p = 0.20$) correlation with the social welfare

TABLE 3.1 *Correlation matrix for ideological dimensions, by race*

	Blacks					
	Laissez-faire	Racial	Military	Social Welfare	Religious	Moral
Laissez-faire	1					
Racial	0.29*	1				
Military	0.22*	0.04	1			
Social Welfare	−0.05	0.27*	−0.07	1		
Religious	0.31*	0.01	0.24*	−0.29*	1	
Moral	0.08	0.11*	0.11*	0.13*	0.38*	1
	Whites					
	Laissez-faire	Racial	Military	Social Welfare	Religious	Moral
Laissez-faire	1					
Racial	0.49*	1				
Military	0.32*	0.26*	1			
Social Welfare	0.38*	0.35*	0.14*	1		
Religious	0.27*	0.25*	0.38*	0.05	1	
Moral	0.28*	0.17*	0.32*	0.24*	0.66*	1

Note: Values are Pearson product-moment correlations. Independent sample weights were used to calculate values. All measures are coded from zero (most liberal) to one (most conservative). Starred correlations are statistically significant at the $p < 0.10$ level (two-tailed test).
Source: 2010 Post-Midterm Election Study.

dimension. The more conservative Blacks were on the military dimension, the more liberal they were on social welfare. Also predicted in Chapter 2 was the negative correlation between the social welfare and religious dimensions ($r = -0.29$, $p = 0.00$). As Black respondents became more religiously conservative, they were more likely to believe that it was the government's responsibility to provide a social safety net. As expected, the religious dimension was positively correlated with the moral dimension ($r = 0.38$, $p = 0.00$). The religious dimension was also positively correlated with the laissez-faire domain ($r = 0.31$, $p = 0.00$). Strangely, the social welfare dimension and the laissez-faire dimension were not correlated ($r = -0.05$, $p = 0.36$). This is counterintuitive and contrary to any expectations presented in earlier chapters. If we examine the distribution of these two scales, however, we can see why this is the case (see Carroll 1961). The laissez-faire dimension is distributed normally around its mean while the social welfare dimension is heavily skewed towards the liberal side of the scale (see Figure 3.1). Finally, the moral dimension was positively correlated with the laissez-faire dimension ($r = 0.08$, $p = 0.15$) and the social welfare dimension ($r = 0.13$, $p = 0.02$).

That these results were not just an artifact of how the policy domains were measured is demonstrated in the bottom half of Table 3.1 presents the results for Whites. The most noticeable difference between Blacks and Whites was that, for Whites, all of the ideological dimensions were positively correlated with one another and these correlations were statistically significant, with the exception of the correlation between the social welfare and religious dimensions. The largest correlation was between moral and religious dimensions ($r = 0.66$, $p = 00$). This was almost twice the size of the correlation between these two dimensions among Blacks. An examination of the qualitative data helps to explain this difference. When asked to describe what it meant to be either morally liberal or conservative, Whites were nearly three times as likely as Blacks to describe the moral dimension in terms of religious leaders, organizations, or denominations.[4] Blacks, on the other hand, were more likely to describe this dimension in terms of knowing the difference between right and wrong, traditional values, and the expected behaviors that accompany each side of the moral divide – all in secular terms. There was also a relatively strong correlation between the racial and laissez-faire dimensions ($r = 0.49$, $p = 0.00$) and the laissez-faire and social welfare dimensions ($r = 0.38$, $p = 0.00$). The weakest correlations were between the religious and social welfare dimensions ($r = 0.05$, $p = 0.33$) and between the social welfare and military dimensions ($r = 0.14$, $p = 0.01$). Overall, however, being conservative in one policy domain translated into being conservative in the others among Whites.

---

[4] The list of responses included: The 700 Club, Baptists, belief in the Bible, Bob Jones University, the Catholic Pope, Catholics, Christians, the Christian Coalition, Christian Fundamentalists, churches, dogmatic, Episcopal, Evangelical Christians, Hassidic Jews, Independent Bible Churches, Jehovah's Witnesses, Jerry Falwell, Jesse Jackson, Jesus Christ, Jews, Methodist Presbyterians, Mike Huckabee, the Moral Majority, Mormons, Muslims, New Age religions, not religious, Pat Robertson, being religious, religious leaders, the Religious Right, Southern Baptists, supporting female clergy, supporting a relationship with God, supporting school prayer, televangelists, United Methodist Church, and Word of God Catholics. White respondents gave 41 religious responses; Black respondents gave 14 religious responses.

PREDICTING IDEOLOGICAL SELF-IDENTIFICATION

With the measures of the policy dimensions established, I now turn to the central focus of this chapter, which is examining the predictors of ideological self-identification (ISID). Using the PMES, a model of ISID was estimated to determine the relative effects of the policy dimensions, controlling for political sophistication and standard demographic variables. (See the Appendix for exact question wording and coding.) Model 1 in Table 3.2 examines whether the racial policy dimension, by itself, predicts ideological self-identification for Blacks. Since Blacks do not currently identify race as an important national problem, it was hypothesized that the racial dimension would not be a significant predictor of Black ISID. As hypothesized, this dimension fails to reach a conventional level of statistical significance ($p = 0.50$). Substantively, the effect of the racial dimension on Blacks' ideological self-identification is modest, at best.[5] For instance, when Blacks are liberal on the racial dimension, the probability of them self-identifying as conservative is 0.21. The probability of Blacks self-identifying as conservative when they are conservative on the racial dimension is 0.29.

Model 2 in Table 3.2 then looks at the relative effect of each of the policy dimensions in relation to the racial dimension. In Model 2, the racial dimension also fails to reach statistical significance ($p < 0.10$) and is even smaller. To substantively understand its effect, see the top panel in Figure 3.2 which presents the predicted probability of self-identifying as conservative as racial conservatism moves from its minimum to its maximum (zero to one). Moving from the most liberal end of the racial policy dimension to the most conservative end decreased the probability of self-identifying as conservative by 0.005. Furthermore, this difference was not statistically significant.

In contrast, the religious dimension had a statistically significant effect on Blacks' ideological self-identification. As discussed in Chapter 2, Black religion and Black politics have a long, intimate relationship. Therefore, it was hypothesized that the religious dimension would be a significant predictor of Black ISID. The results support this hypothesis. Among religious liberals, the probability of identifying as conservative was 0.11. The probability of self-identifying as conservative increased to

---

[5] The predicted probabilities for this section were calculated using the prvalue command in Stata 13 (see Long and Freese 2014). Values were calculated by holding the variable for female constant at its mode and all other variables constant at their means.

TABLE 3.2 *Predictors of ideological self-identification, by race*

	Model 1	Model 2	Model 3	Model 4
	Blacks	Blacks	Blacks	Whites
Racial Dimension	0.0263	−0.017	0.086	−0.021
	(0.39)	(0.43)	(0.46)	(0.42)
Laissez-faire Dimension		0.075	0.234	1.691*
		(0.55)	(0.58)	(0.47)
Military Dimension		−0.668	−0.971*	0.039
		(0.43)	(0.46)	(0.36)
Social Dimension		0.699*	0.739*	2.068*
		(0.40)	(0.41)	(0.41)
Religious Dimension		0.767*	1.048*	1.638*
		(0.40)	(0.39)	(0.43)
Moral Dimension		0.323	−0.047	1.536*
		(0.45)	(0.46)	(0.49)
Campaign Interest	−0.513*	−0.444*		−0.190
	(0.22)	(0.22)		(0.23)
Education	−0.719	−0.832		1.069*
	(0.64)	(0.65)		(0.50)
Political Sophistication			−1.695*	
			(0.95)	
Racial * Political Sophistication			−0.946	
			(0.91)	
Laissez-faire * Political Sophistication			−0.567	
			(1.63)	
Military * Political Sophistication			0.248	
			(0.98)	
Social Welfare * Political Sophistication			0.876	
			(1.30)	
Religious * Political Sophistication			−1.127	
			(1.01)	
Moral * Political Sophistication			5.397*	
			(1.78)	
Female	0.039	0.008	−0.012	−0.058
	(0.15)	(0.16)	(0.16)	(0.15)
Age	0.007	0.010*	0.010*	0.012*
	(0.00)	(0.01)	(0.01)	(0.01)
Income	0.339	0.247	0.217	−0.220
	(0.34)	(0.36)	(0.35)	(0.35)
Cut 1	−0.794	−0.345	0.342	3.803
	(0.48)	(0.62)	(0.46)	(0.63)
Cut 2	0.513	1.038	1.738	5.212
	(0.48)	(0.62)	(0.47)	(0.68)
N	312	299	299	369
Log likelihood	−320.87	−298.47	−294.94	−271.65
Pseudo R-square	0.03	0.05	0.06	0.31

Note: Values are ordered probit regression coefficients with applied independent sample weights. Standard errors appear in parentheses. Ideological self-identification is coded 1 (liberal), 2 (moderate), 3 (conservative). Ideological dimensions are coded from zero (most liberal) to one (most conservative). Starred coefficients are statistically significant at the $p < 0.10$ level (two-tailed test).
Source: 2010 Post Midterm-Election Study.

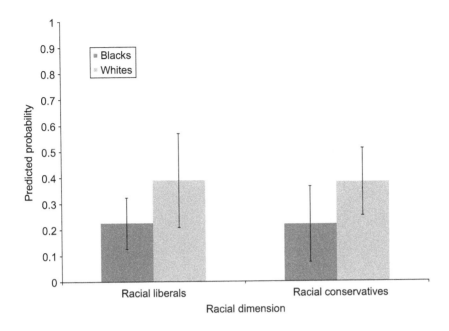

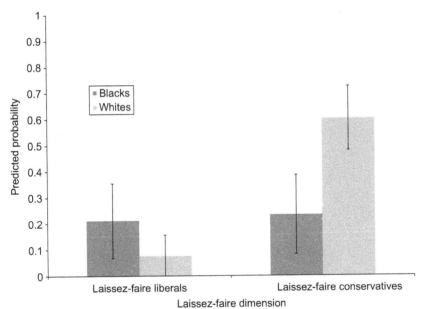

FIGURE 3.2 Probability of self-identifying as conservative, by race and
ideological dimension
Note: Bars represent the predicted probability of self-identifying as conservative, with 90%
confidence intervals. Values are based on ordered probit regression coefficients with applied
independent sample weights. Ideological dimensions are coded from zero (most liberal) to
one (most conservative). Values were calculated by holding continuous variables constant at
their means and dichotomous variable constant at their modes.
Source: 2010 Post-Midterm Election Study.

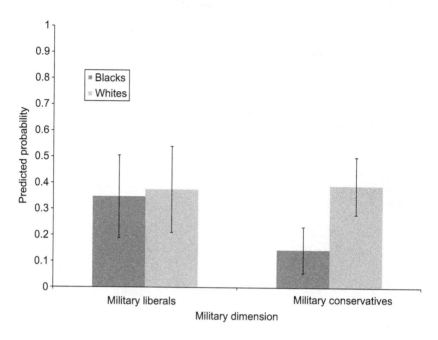

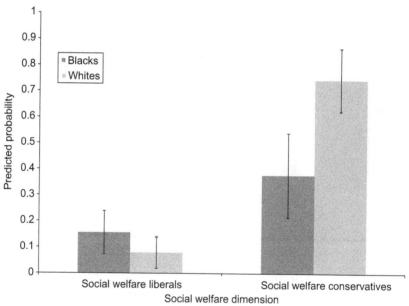

FIGURE 3.2 *(cont.)*

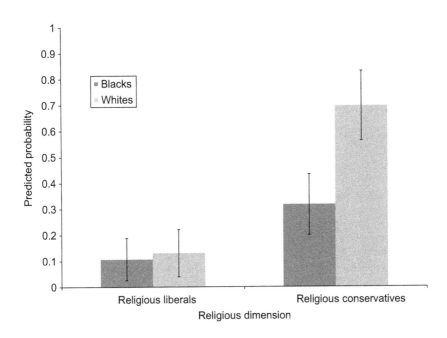

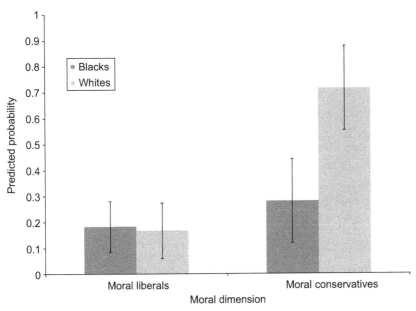

FIGURE 3.2 (*cont.*)

0.32 among religious conservatives (see Figure 3.2). At the $p < 0.10$ level, this 21 percentage point difference is statistically significant.

Qualitatively, Respondent 49, a 51-year-old Black female from the South, provides an example of someone who used the religious dimension to determine her ideological self-identification. When asked why she considered herself conservative, she responded as follows:

> I feel I am Christian based, I do believe that there are certain things that we should be about. . . . I'm not for gay rights as far as marriage is concerned . . . and not just because of the spiritual reason but also because of the economical reason. Being a social worker I believe in two parents. I believe in the male and female parent but also because you can't multiply the Earth if you are of the same sex, so if you want to be same sex it's really okay with me, I don't have a problem with that other than, you know, biblically that's not right. But I'm saying me personally, but when you start looking at them getting married and not necessarily even raising a child but not being able to multiply the Earth. I know that there are a lot of children out there that need homes, don't get me wrong, I know that but on the other hand when we start talking about multiplying the Earth and making sure that generations go on and on then that can't happen with same sex marriages. So for that reason I have an issue with that. So that is one of the things that I believe in, and generally speaking I believe that there should be prayer in schools. I believe . . . that parents should be able to discipline their children. Those are the kinds of things that liberals do not agree with and I whole heartedly agree with those.

Thus, for Respondent 49, the religious dimension served as a lens through which she interpreted the world – including political issues, political candidates, and her own behavior.

The social welfare dimension was another issue area that Blacks utilized when determining their ideological self-identification. In the earlier chapters, the social welfare dimension was the one domain that was consistently salient across years and data sources. A substantial number of Blacks listed social welfare issues as the most important national problem. Thus, it should be no surprise that the social welfare dimension worked as hypothesized and was salient to Blacks' ISID. Figure 3.2 illustrates the predicted probability of self-identifying as conservative for all values of the social welfare dimension. When Blacks were extremely liberal on the social welfare dimension, the probability of identifying as conservative was 0.16. Blacks who were extremely conservative on the social welfare dimension had a probability of 0.38 of self-identifying as conservative on the liberal–conservative continuum. Further, this 22 percentage point difference was statistically significant at the $p < 0.10$ level.

In the qualitative sample, Blacks most often used the social welfare dimension to explain why they self-identified as liberal. For example,

Respondent 22, a 38-year-old Black male from the East Coast, relayed his experience growing up. His explanation for identifying as liberal was:

Because I'm a supporter of tax and spending. Global housing, child subsidies. I was raised like that. My parents were both retired when I was coming up, already. If there wasn't social security, Medicare. Food stamps is an example. We wouldn't have anything.

He also added that his liberal identity was shaped by his employment as a financial aid officer on a college campus. So for Respondent 22, self-identifying as a liberal meant an affinity for programs that helped those in need.

Substantively, the ideological dimensions worked in an intuitive direction. As respondents became more conservative on any of the ideologies, they were more likely to self-identify as conservative. The notable exception was the military dimension. As Figure 3.2 illustrates, when Black respondents went from being extremely liberal to extremely conservative on this dimension, the probability of them self-identifying as conservative *decreased* by 0.20. This difference, however, was not statistically significant at the $p < 0.010$ level. Still, the nature of the connection between the military dimension and Blacks' ideological self-identification was foreshadowed earlier. Undoubtedly, this result is a function of the complex relationship between Blacks and the military, which was discussed in Chapter 2. Empirically, we saw this in the negative correlation between the social welfare and military dimensions for Blacks in Table 3.1. Qualitatively, Respondent 50, a 42-year-old Black woman from the South, explains why military service was attractive to her:

I personally joined the military at the age of 19 because I got tired of paying for my own college and taking care of a child and I could have did what all the other girls did, go to Fort Knox and marry somebody and become a dependent. I couldn't stand that word. I said why do I gotta be his dependent? So instead of going and marry somebody in the military I said, well I'll just join the military then that will keep me independent. So that's what I did. I joined to be independent and not have to depend on someone to take care of me and go wherever they go. I wanted to decide where I went so that was why and to be independent.

Respondent 52, an 80-year-old Black male from the East Coast who also served in the military, believed that the military allowed Blacks to "defend ... the Constitution, defend the person next to you. Defend the ground you're on." He believed that honor was very important in the military and that the military was not as prone to the same racial patronage that he witnessed in American politics.

The remaining two policy domains failed to have a significant effect on the ideological self-identification of African Americans. The probability of identifying as conservative when Blacks were at the most liberal position on the laissez-faire scale was 0.21. When Blacks were at the most conservative position of this scale, the probability of self-identifying as conservative was 0.23, a very small and statistically insignificant ($p < 0.10$) increase of 0.02. Likewise, when Blacks moved from the most liberal to the most conservative position on the moral dimension, the probability of them self-identifying as conservative increased by 0.10. This modest change was not statistically significant ($p < 0.10$).

One of the arguments made in Chapter 1 was that the idiosyncratic relationship between Blacks' party identification and ideological self-identification could not be entirely explained by political sophistication, or a lack thereof. Rather, Blacks' have a conceptualization of their ideological self-identification that is based on their historical interaction with the political world and this unique conceptualization has implications for the correlation between Blacks' party identification and ideological self-identification. The evidence, so far, has supported this argument. Even when controlling for political sophistication[6], Blacks' bundling of the policy domains continues to reflect the historical relationship between African Americans and government and politics discussed in Chapter 2. To further demonstrate that Blacks' ideological self-identification was not a function of political sophistication, Model 3 in Table 3.2 re-estimates the model with the inclusion of interaction terms between the policy dimensions and political sophistication to see whether the effects of any of the issue areas were contingent on political sophistication.[7] If my argument is correct, we would expect to see no difference between high and low political sophisticates in the significance and magnitude in the effect of the policy dimensions on the ideological self-identification. With the exception of the moral dimension, these expectations were largely confirmed.

To get a better sense of what these results mean substantively, Figure 3.3 presents the predicted probability of self-identifying as conservative as Black respondents of varying levels of political sophistication move from

---

[6] Political sophistication in Models 1, 2, and 4 is measured by respondents' level of campaign interest and education. (See the Appendix for coding of each of these variables.)

[7] For these analyses, political sophistication is a dichotomous variable where one represents those Blacks who have at least a college degree and report being very interested in following campaigns and zero represents Blacks who have not received a college degree and do not follow campaigns closely. (See the Appendix for details on variable construction.)

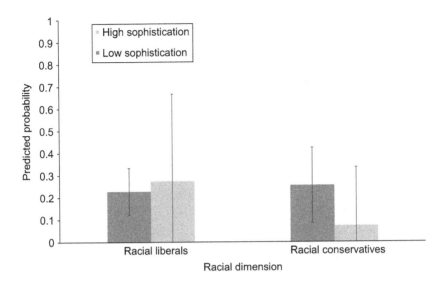

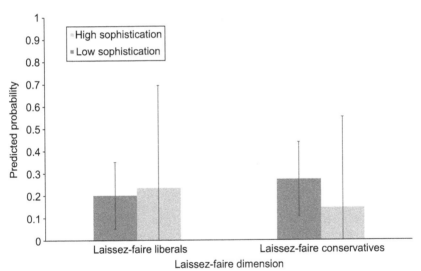

FIGURE 3.3 Probability of self-identifying as conservative, by political sophistication and ideological dimension

Note: Bars represent the predicted probability of self-identifying as conservative, with 90 percent confidence intervals. Values are based on ordered probit regression coefficients with applied independent sample weights. Ideological dimensions are coded from zero (most liberal) to one (most conservative). Values were calculated by holding continuous variables constant at their means and dichotomous variable constant at their modes.

Source: 2010 Post-Midterm Election Study.

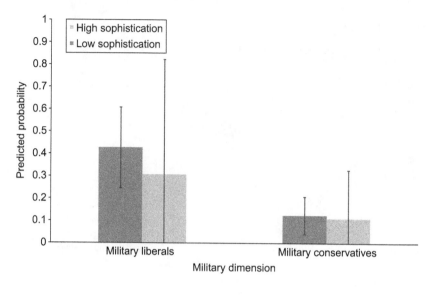

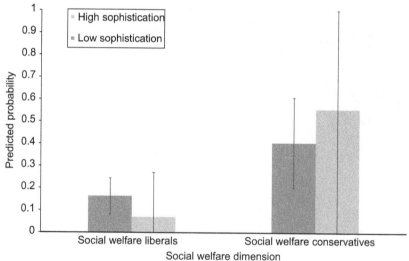

FIGURE 3.3 *(cont.)*

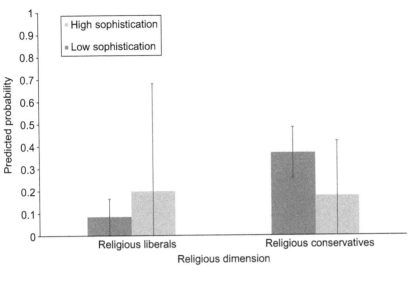

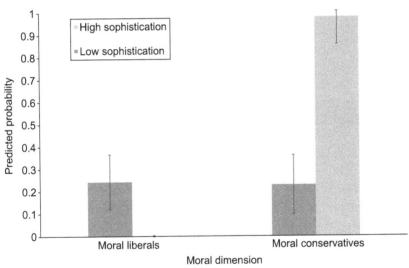

FIGURE 3.3 (*cont.*)

one end of each policy domain to the other.[8] Consistent with Model 2, the racial and laissez-faire dimensions did not significantly increase the probability of Blacks self-identifying as conservative. When Blacks with low political sophistication moved from the most liberal position to the most conservative position on the racial dimension, their probability of self-identifying as conservative increased by 0.02. Among Blacks with high political sophistication, there was a 0.20 increase. Based on the 90 percent confidence intervals, however, these differences were not statistically significant. Further, the differences between low and high political sophisticates were not statistically significant. This was also true for the 0.07 difference between laissez-faire liberals and conservatives with low political sophistication and the 0.08 difference between laissez-faire liberals and conservatives with high political sophistication. With respect to the social welfare dimension, the probability of self-identifying as conservative increased from 0.16 to 0.40 as Blacks with low political sophistication moved from the liberal end of this dimension to the conservative end. Further, this difference was statistically significant. Among Blacks with high political sophistication, this difference was 0.48. The difference between liberals and conservatives on the social welfare dimension was not statistically significant (p < 0.10) among political sophisticates, even though the difference was substantively large. The difference between Black conservatives and liberals on the religious dimension among those with low political sophistication was 0.29; this difference was both substantively large and statistically significant. Among high political sophisticates, this difference was 0.02. This much smaller difference was statistically insignificant. There were also statistically insignificant differences between military liberals and military conservatives among both low and high Black political sophisticates. For Blacks with low political sophistication, the difference in the probability of self-identifying as conservative when moving from the most liberal to the most conservative position on the military scale was 0.31. That difference among Blacks with high political sophistication was 0.20. To sum, there were no statistically significant differences between Blacks with low political sophistication and those with high political sophistication in the use of the racial, laissez-faire, social welfare, military, and religious dimensions, even though some of the observed differences appeared substantively large.

---

[8] Predicted probabilities were calculated using the margins command in Stata 13 (see Williams 2012). Dummy variables were held at their modes while all other variables were held at their means. Respective 90 percent confidence intervals are presented with each value.

The only dimension where there was a significant difference between Blacks with low political sophistication and those with high political sophistication was on the moral dimension. Among Blacks with low political sophistication, moving from the most liberal position to the most conservative position on the moral dimension decreased the probability of self-identifying as conservative by 0.01, a very small and statistically insignificant difference ($p < 0.10$). For political sophisticates, moving from the most liberal to the most conservative position on the moral dimension increased the probability of self-identifying as conservative by 0.98. Moreover, this difference was significantly different from low political sophisticates ($p < 0.10$). As discussed in Chapter 2, the moral dimension is an encapsulation of respectability politics for Blacks. While respectability politics serves as an internal policing mechanism within the Black community, it also has provided the public face of Black politics. Nevertheless, there exists within respectability politics an intraracial class struggle to control the Black agenda. By definition, respectability politics is a reflection of middle-class values and preferences, while the poor and working classes are treated as deviant. As sociologist Mary Pattillo explains:

The black middle class was the race's best foot forward, and could serve as a positive image of blacks who were not far removed from the ugliness of slavery. Embodying respectability meant modeling sexual conservatism, patriarchal family relations, financial sobriety, reserved comportment, and intellectual achievement. Not only did the poor fall outside the bounds of righteousness, but so too did loose women, practitioners of ecstatic religious, gays and lesbians, figures from the criminal underworld, and any manner of blacks who did not adhere to the most puritanical of strictures. The upright character of some middle-class blacks was a sign to whites of blacks' readiness for full citizenship and all of the benefits that entailed. Respectability proved that racism and racial discrimination were unfounded. Therefore, the best of the race, the talented tenth, the black middle class, the black elite, the black bourgeoisie must stand in front as the example of and beacon toward racial progress (Pattillo 2007, 104–5).

In other words, inasmuch as the poor and working classes did not conform to middle class ethos, they undermined Black's quest for racial uplift (Du Bois 2007 [1899]). Even in contemporary politics, Blacks continue to "pathologize" the behaviors of poor and working class African Americans (Cohen 2004; White 2007; Wilson 1996) and the plight of these groups struggle to make it on to the Black agenda (Cohen and Dawson 1993). A closer examination of the PMES indicated that class divisions helped explain why there was such a significant difference between Blacks with low and high levels of political sophistication on the moral dimension. The mean income among Blacks with low levels of political sophistication was $25,000 to $29,999. Blacks with high levels of political sophistication had a mean income of $40,000 to $49,999. A reasonable conclusion one can draw from these data is that Black political sophisticates, as a result of their higher level of political engagement and higher income bracket, are more likely to abide by the politics of respectability than their low political sophistication counterparts.

Finally, as further evidence that Blacks' conceptualization of their ideological self-identification contributes to the idiosyncratic correlation between ideological self-identification and party identification, I provide parallel analyses for Whites. If Blacks have a different conceptualization of the liberal–conservative continuum than Whites, we would expect to see a different set of dimensions predict Whites' ISID. Additionally, we also expect to see differences in the relative weights that Blacks and Whites assign to these dimensions. The results confirm these expectations. Model 4 in Table 3.2 indicates that the strongest predictors of ideological self-identification for Whites were the social welfare, religious, laissez-faire, and moral dimensions.

To illustrate this substantively, Figure 3.2 presents the predicted probability of Whites self-identifying as conservative by ideological dimension.[9] Consistent with earlier findings demonstrating the saliency of this domain for Whites, the general laissez-faire dimension had a relatively large effect on Whites' placement on the liberal–conservative continuum. Among White laissez-faire liberals, the probability of self-identifying as conservative was 0.08. This probability increased by 0.54 among those Whites who were extremely conservative on the laissez-faire dimension. Moreover, this difference was statistically significant at the $p < 0.10$ level. To further demonstrate the impact of the laissez-faire dimension on Whites' ISID, I incorporate data from the qualitative interviews. Consider Respondent 7, a White male from the Midwest who was raised conservative but now considered himself liberal. His decision to reclassify himself was partially driven by his position on laissez-faire issues:

Reaganomics worked very good [sic] for me. All I knew, I was young at the time and I was working all the time. But I didn't realize the spending that the government did and the deficit and things like that.

---

[9] The predicted probabilities for this section were calculated using the prvalue command in Stata 13. Values were calculated by holding the variable for female constant at its mode and all other variables constant at their means.

In theory, Respondent 7 liked the idea of fiscal conservatism but voiced skepticism over conservatives' use of the term "fiscal conservatism" to cut domestic spending, only to spend millions of dollars on defense. For him, identifying as liberal was not only a rejection of Reaganomics as he had experienced it, but also disillusionment with spending on the wars in Iraq and Afghanistan under a Republican president.

The social welfare dimension was also a strong predictor of Whites' ideological self-identification. Looking at the center right panel of Figure 3.2, we see that the probability of White social welfare liberals self-identifying as conservative was 0.08. Among social welfare conservatives, the probability of identifying as conservative on the liberal-conservative continuum increased to 0.74, a statistically significant difference ($p < 0.10$) of 0.66. Qualitatively, an example of someone using the social welfare dimension as a determinant her ideological self-identification would be Respondent 36, a 50-year-old White woman from the South. When asked why she considered herself liberal, Respondent 50 had this to say:

I'm an Eleanor Roosevelt, Michael Moore liberal. I believe that it is the job of everyone to help their neighbor to the best of their ability. And that we evolve as time evolves. The notions of conservatism of yesteryear, okay, some of them have limited grounds, but I believe that we're a culture that evolves and you need to be liberal in your beliefs and open to the fact that as time changes, you must evolve with the times.

Respondent 50 believed that it was important to help those in need at any costs, even if it meant "giving up a little of yourself."

Finally, the religious and moral policy dimensions were also significant in predicting Whites' ideological self-identification. Figure 3.2 presents the probability of identifying as conservative as the religious dimension increases from its minimum to its maximum. Among White religious liberals, the probability of identifying as conservative was 0.13. The probability of self-identifying as conservative increased to 0.70 among religious conservatives. Further, this difference was statistically significant at the $p < 0.10$ level. To illustrate, Respondent 23 used the religious dimension to describe why he was liberal, "A lot of the issues that I hear talked about these days in terms of religion and the state, I think it's uniformly a bad idea for the state to get involved in any sort of religious consideration. In point of fact, I'm probably best described as an atheist in that regard." Respondent 23, a 54-year-old White male from the East Coast, was raised a Quaker but no longer practiced any religion. He firmly believed in separation of church and state and believed that religion should not be expressed in the public sphere.

Likewise, Figure 3.2 indicates that the probability of White moral liberals identifying as conservative was 0.17. For moral conservatives, the probability of identifying as conservative was 0.72, a statistically significant ($p < 0.10$) difference of 0.55. An example of using the moral dimension as an underlying determinant of one's ideological self-identification would be Respondent 4's description of why she considered herself liberal. Respondent 4, a White 50-year-old woman from the Midwest, described her beliefs as follows:

I just think I have a lot of liberal views on different things. I don't know, I consider conservative people to be more uptight or more ... Oh I don't know. I mean for instance it's like my kids or whatever. I let their girlfriends or whatever come stay with them at the house. So I don't know, I just think I am.

For her, being liberal was associated with being "progressive" and "open-minded" when it came to sexual relationships.

Neither the racial nor the military dimensions were important predictors of White ideological self-identification. The difference in probability between White racial liberals and White racial conservatives in self-identifying as conservative was 0.008, a substantively small and statistically insignificant difference. With respect to the military dimension, the difference between White military conservatives and White military liberals was 0.01. Again, not only was this difference substantively small, it failed to reach conventional levels of statistical significance.

Taken together, these findings suggest that the criterial referents Blacks use to determine their ideological self-identification are different than those used by Whites. First, Blacks used fewer ideological dimensions to predict their ideological self-identification. Second, when Blacks and Whites used the same criterion to determine their ideological self-identification, e.g. religious and social welfare, the weight of that criterion differed by race. Further, these differences were statistically significant.[10] Lastly, Blacks' conceptualization of their ISID was not a function of their levels of political sophistication. On only one dimension did Blacks' levels of political sophistication predict differences in placement on the liberal-

---

[10] To test the statistical significance in the difference in coefficients across racial groups, a version of the model was estimated that included multiplicative terms representing the interaction between each ideological dimension and race. The race variable was a dummy variable coded 0 (Whites) and 1 (Blacks), so that a statistically significant multiplicative term indicated a significant difference among Blacks on that dimension.

conservative continuum. And even then, these differences could be traced back to the historical relationship between Blacks and the political environment discussed in Chapter 2. Given the differences between Blacks' and Whites' conceptualization of ideological self-identification, it should be no surprise then that their respective relationships between party identification and ideological self-identification differ as well.

CONCLUSION

With combination of data sources, Chapter 3 has helped us ascertain the basis of Blacks' ideological self-identifications. As Sanders (1986) explains,

[P]eople's ideological self-placement is related to their views on political issues, particularly within the issue area they most strongly associate with liberalism and/ or conservatism. Their self-placement is not haphazard or random, nor is it simply a matter of amorphous but potent political symbolism. Rather, there is a strong issue content to such identification. Liberalism and/or conservatism may rarely function as tightly constrained ideologies, but when people say they are liberals or conservatives, it is likely to reflect their feelings on, at least, some issues. And if we ask them, broadly, what area they think these terms refer to, we can easily ascertain which issues their ideological self-placement is likely to reflect (Sanders 1986, 133).

In other words, ideological self-identification is not simply a symbolic attachment to ideological labels. Instead, people base their ideological self-identification on their political experiences and preferences. Blacks are certainly no exception.

Moreover, these results suggest that ideological self-identification varies systematically by race. The underlying determinants of Blacks' placement on the liberal–conservative continuum are significantly different from that of Whites. When thinking about whether they are liberal or conservative, African Americans use their beliefs about the religion and social welfare, whereas Whites use their beliefs about social welfare, morality, religion, and the proper role of government. Furthermore, the strength and direction of these relationships differ by race. Take for instance the military dimension, which just barely failed to meet conventional levels of statistical significance ($p = 0.12$) as a predictor of Blacks' ideological self-identification. Being conservative on the military dimension increased the likelihood that Blacks would identify as liberal whereas it increased the probability Whites would identify as conservative, although not significantly so.

As argued earlier, the basis of these differences are rooted in the Black experience. Whites have not been privy to this experience and, therefore, have a fundamentally different understanding of the liberal-conservative continuum. As Walton (1985) explains:

Similar demographics do not make groups equal – politically or socially. The politics of race, which expresses itself in poll taxes, white primaries, racial gerrymandering, racial poverty, and numerous discriminatory institutional political arrangements does not permit both groups to have equal access, resources participation, representation, and finally rewards (Walton 1985, 12).

As a consequence, the packaging of ideological constructs is different for Blacks than they are for Whites.

Finally, the results demonstrate that the racial policy domain is not the most salient dimension that separates Black liberals from Black conservatives, as suggested by prior work on this subject. Racial considerations are important, however, inasmuch as race has shaped Blacks' policy orientations in the other issue domains. Furthermore, racial considerations determine how ideological self-identification gets translated in partisan attachments and political behavior. This latter point will be the focus of Part II of this book.

PART II

4

The Tie That Binds

The History and Nature of Black
Group Consciousness

We've got to face the fact that some people say you fight fire best with fire,
but we say you put fire out best with water. We say you don't fight racism
with racism. We're gonna fight racism with solidarity.
– Fred Hampton

Part I of this book was devoted to explaining the idiosyncratic relationship
between Blacks' party identification and ideological self-identification as a
function of Blacks' unique conceptualization of the liberal–conservative
continuum. The central argument of Part I was that citizens organize
ideological information multi-dimensionally along a number of distinct
policy domains, including laissez-faire, racial, military, social welfare, religious, and moral. Further, when individuals are asked to place themselves
on the liberal–conservative continuum, these dimensions are weighted
hierarchically by some pre-assigned saliency determined by the individual.
Not only can the saliency of the dimensions vary by individual, they
vary by groups. In the previous chapter, the evidence demonstrated that
the use of the dimensions in determining individuals' ideological self-
identification varied systematically by the race of the individual. That is,
Blacks used a different set of criteria when placing themselves on the
liberal–conservative continuum than did Whites. Interestingly, the results
suggested that the racial dimension was not the dividing line between
Black liberals and Black conservatives. Instead, race had an indirect effect
inasmuch as it was incorporated into the other policy domains.

I argue that race plays an additional role in explaining the nonconventional relationship between Blacks' party identification and ideological
self-identification. Although Blacks' attitudes about racial policies do not

predict their ideological self-identification, race still factors heavily when it comes to whether Blacks' ideological self-identification will correlate with their party identification. Specifically, I contend that the relationship between party identification and ideological self-identification for Blacks is contingent on racial group consciousness. Therefore, Part II of this book is devoted to examining the moderating role of group consciousness in the relationship between Black's party identification and ideological self-identification. Whether or not Black conservatives ultimately deviate from the Democratic Party depends on their level of racial group consciousness. Chapter 4 begins this line of inquiry by taking a step back to look at the roots of Black group consciousness and how prevalent it currently is in the Black community.

Group-based political thinking is not unique to African Americans. Social groupings abound in American society and their importance to politics has been duly noted (see Mendelberg 2005 for a review). To be sure, we are constitutionally mandated to classify ourselves into various ascribed categories every ten years. In addition to the groups into which we are born, there exists no shortage of professional organizations, religious and educational institutions, advocacy groups, sports teams, celebrity fan clubs, fraternal associations, etc. we can join with minimal cost or effort. According to the 2008 American National Election Study, 44.8 percent of respondents belonged to at least one voluntary association (ANES 2009). Yet, not all of our group memberships carry the same meaning and importance.

For Blacks, racial group membership supersedes other group memberships, at least with respect to politics (Dawson 1994). African Americans exhibit unmatched levels of group consciousness, which is evidenced by their support for political parties and candidates (Gurin et al., 1989; Philpot and Walton 2007). While, it was once anticipated that group consciousness would dissipate as more Blacks attained higher levels of income and education (Dahl 1961), this has not happened (McClerking 2001; Harris-Lacewell 2004). How do Blacks maintain their connectedness with the race in the face of growing heterogeneity?

Answering this question is the goal of this chapter. I begin by reviewing the process by which objective group membership gets transformed into group consciousness. Second, I provide a brief history of the prevalence of Black group consciousness. I follow this with a discussion of the determinants of Black group consciousness and the psychological process that leads to Black racial consciousness formation. Finally, I conclude this chapter with a look at the nature and predictors of contemporary Black group consciousness. Chapter 4's objective is to provide the foundation for understanding why racial group consciousness would be a mitigating factor between Blacks' ideological self-identification and party identification.

THE PROCESS OF FORMING GROUP CONSCIOUSNESS

Our individual orientations towards groups to which we belong can be thought of as a continuum. On one end is objective group membership; on the other is group consciousness (McClain, Johnson Carew, Walton, and Watts 2009). Somewhere between group membership and group consciousness lies group identity. Whereas objective group membership is simply belonging to a group without assigning affect or meaning to that membership, group or social identity is "that *part* of an individual's self-concept which derives from his knowledge of his membership of a social group (or groups) together with the value and emotional significance attached to that membership" (Tajfel 1981, 255). In general, people readily generate feelings of attachment to social groups, even when group distinctions are arbitrary (Billig and Tajfel 1973; Rabbie and Horowitz 1969; Doise, Csepeli, Dann, Gouge, Larsen, and Ostell 1972; Tajfel 1970). The basis of these group attachments rests on recognition of shared social characteristics and values with other group members, along with a fondness for this similarity (Huddy 2003). Factors that highlight and make salient group distinctiveness also foster the development of group identity (see McGuire and Padawer-Singer 1976, for example). A strong and enduring group identification (particularly the kind that will ultimately translate into group-based political outlooks and activism) is most prevalent, however, when one's in-group is in competition for valuable and finite resources with one or more out-groups (Sherif and Sherif 1966). Moreover, group identity intensifies when an individual perceives his or her in-group as having an illegitimate disadvantage when it comes to the distribution of and access to these resources (Coser 1957).

Individuals may hold multiple, overlapping, and sometimes competing group identities simultaneously. Note that not every identity is equally salient. Furthermore, the salience of identities may vary over time and context (Tajfel 1981). Still, there is nothing inherently political about group identities.

In contrast, group consciousness is intrinsically political. Although it is a precursor to group consciousness, group identity and group consciousness are not the same (Chong and Rogers 2005; McClain et al. 2009). By definition, group consciousness not only connotes a sense of identification with a group but the awareness that group membership has political implications. While group identity encompasses a person's recognition of shared characteristics with others perceived to be similar, group consciousness "refers to a set of political beliefs and action orientations arising out of this awareness of similarity" (Gurin, Miller, and Gurin 1980, 30).

Nevertheless, group identity stimulates group consciousness formation. Group identity links the individual to the group and is the foundation for forming a preference for one's in-group (Conover 1988). Having a strong, intense identification with the group fosters a sense of political cohesion with other group members (Huddy 2003). Group identity leads group members to attribute the failures of the group to situational and external factors; successes are credited to internal characteristics of the group (see Hewstone 1990).

This latter point, the propensity to view group failures as structurally determined, is perhaps most important in understanding the link between group identity and group consciousness, particularly among minority groups. A social hierarchy of groups, by itself, does not cultivate group consciousness. Rather, group consciousness arises from group members' perceptions that the stratification system which deems them inferior to another group does so arbitrarily instead of based on merit (Tajfel and Turner 1979; Gurin et al. 1989). Consequently, members of subordinate groups that develop a sense of group consciousness view their placement in the lower strata as illegitimate, "resulting in a sense of relative deprivation and discontent with one's position in society" (Miller, Gurin, Gurin, and Malanchuk 1981, 495).

In addition to dissatisfaction with structural inequality, Gurin et al. (1980) identify two additional conditions that lead to the transformation of group identity into group consciousness. First, group consciousness develops out of an individual's close, intimate, and abundant contact with her in-group and is further intensified by having only superficial, nominal contact with the superordinate out-group. Second, the evolution of identity into consciousness is facilitated by channels and institutions controlled by the in-group that transmit information aimed at heightening group members' awareness of their relative deprivation and that question the legitimacy of the existing social order.[1]

---

[1] Though significantly weaker, group consciousness can develop in dominant groups (Gurin et al. 1980). Group consciousness among superordinate groups entails justifying relative

Group consciousness is multidimensional and encompasses both cognitive and affective orientations towards an in-group. As discussed above, *group identification* is a component of group consciousness and represents one's psychological sense of interconnectedness with the group. The second component, *polar affect*, represents a preference for an individual's in-group over her out-group. A third aspect of group consciousness is *polar power*, which is the perceived level of resources and status of an in-group relative to an out-group. Finally, *individual vs. system blame* represents ideas about whether a group's position in society is derived from systemic forces or individual attributes. Miller et al. argue that these four elements "presumably form a political ideology that for subordinate groups represents a shift from a situation in which group members simply accept their status to one in which they express a sense of grievance as victims of injustice, perceive a lack of legitimacy in the social hierarchy, and eventually set about collectively to correct the injustices" (Miller et al. 1981, 497).

Racial consciousness is a form of group consciousness. For those with racial consciousness, "the race becomes an object of loyalty, devotion, and pride. By virtue of this fact it becomes an entity, a collective representation" (Brown 1931, 90). Individuals who develop racial group consciousness not only exhibit an identification and affinity with their racial group but also an ideology about the legitimacy of the groups' relative position in society. With respect to racial minorities in the United States, racial consciousness "would entail the development of a schema containing information about the group's relatively deprived status, a causal attribution for that status that places the blame outside of the group, and a sense of sympathy for the in-group and anger towards those outsiders seen as responsible for the group's status" (Conover 1988, 62). Note, however, that the motivation driving racial consciousness is one's need to identify with and progress one's in-group, rather than discriminate against the out-group (Brewer 2001).

THE HISTORY OF BLACK GROUP CONSCIOUSNESS

Although Black political consciousness is regarded as a fairly new phenomenon (Cross 1991; Smith 1981), aspects of Black consciousness have

---

advantage and seeking to protect the status quo. The expression of group consciousness among members of a dominant group increases when subordinate strata challenge the dominant group's position in society (Gurin 1985).

existed since slavery (Singer 1962; Cone 1970). As evidence, Singer (1962) points to the development of African-American institutions that emerged as a result of forced segregation and discrimination. During Reconstruction, Blacks opened businesses that catered to other Blacks. There was also a growth in independent Black churches led by Black preachers. By the early twentieth century, groups such as the Niagara Movement, the National Association for the Advancement of Colored People, and the National Urban League were founded for the purposes of addressing the political and economic fate of Blacks (Singer 1962).

Evidence of racial consciousness among Blacks can also be found during the 1920s. In an effort to escape the oppression of Jim Crow, many Blacks moved from the South to northern cities like Chicago and New York during the period following both World Wars known as the Great Migration. Faced with substandard living and working conditions, however, Blacks became increasingly cynical of the North's promise of the "good life." In New York, this discontent fueled an artistic and literary movement which focused on America's race problem, referred to as the Harlem Renaissance. Many of the works produced during this time confronted racism and celebrated the Black experience. With respect to group consciousness:

Those who contributed to the literature of the Harlem Renaissance were deeply aware of their belonging to a group that not only was a minority but also was set a apart in numerous ways, many of which were degrading. If black writers accepted this separateness, it was not so much because they wanted to be what others wanted them to be; that is, a distinct and even exotic group in the eyes of the more patronizing whites. Rather, it was because their experiences had given them some appreciation of their own distinct and unique cultural heritage and traditions (Franklin and Moss 1988, 326).

As a result of the Harlem Renaissance, Black consciousness and racial pride flourished (Warren 1990).

Also in New York City at this time, Marcus Garvey started the United Negro Improvement Association (UNIA). Garvey advocated Black self-reliance, entrepreneurship, education, and self-defense. Most notably, the UNIA planned to facilitate the emigration of some Blacks back to Africa (Hanks 2003). Unlike the Niagara Movement and the Harlem Renaissance, which largely focused on the Black elite, the movement led by Garvey had a larger mass appeal because it "addressed [Blacks] concrete needs, offering a way out of poverty and showing them how to leave the land of racism, violence and deceit" (Warren 1990, 18). Garvey is credited for providing the foundation for contemporary Black

Nationalism and promoting a lasting sense of racial solidarity and Black group consciousness (Blake 1969).

Class divisions, however, stifled group cohesiveness, particularly in the North. Prior to the 1960s, research in the area of urban politics demonstrated that Blacks' level of racial solidarity lagged behind that of other ethnic groups (Singer 1962). This research attributed lower levels of group consciousness to conflicting political goals between the small Black middle class and the larger lower class (Banfield and Wilson 1963). Nevertheless, the pending Black Power Movement would change this.

Scholars (Jackson 1987; Cross 1991) regard the highpoint of racial consciousness to be the Black Power Movement of the mid-1960s to early-1970s. The introduction of the phrase "Black Power" into the African-American lexicon is most commonly attributed to Stokely Carmichael, one of the leaders of the Student Nonviolent Coordinating Committee (SNCC), who first publicly used the term during a speech delivered as part of the Meredith March in Greenwood, Mississippi in 1966 (Condie and Christiansen 1977). Accompanied by visual symbols such as raised fists, dashikis, and Afros, Black Power called for Black political, economic, and social unity. Rather than advocating integration and assimilation as had been done in earlier phases of the Black Freedom Struggle, the Black Power worldview emphasized Black beauty, cultural distinctiveness, and racial independence (Killian 1981; Carmichael and Hamilton 1967).

Black Power, as a worldview, proliferated throughout the African-American community. Not only did SNCC adopt it as its guiding philosophy, so too did the Congress of Racial Equality (Condie and Christiansen 1977). While the concept originated among college student groups, the Black Power Movement sought to actively incorporate the Black working-class (Levenstein 2006).

The civil-rights revolution, by facilitating the growth, development, and diversification of the black middle class and by removing the legal basis of status inferiority, contributed to the development of a black ethnic tradition in politics; the movement also encouraged the emergence of new leadership and muted the status-welfare dichotomy in urban black politics. The central contribution of black power was to make race-specific this emergent communal solidarity and thereby to contribute directly to the incipient representation of blacks in the polity (Smith 1981, 434–5).

By bridging the gap between the Black working- and middle-class, the movement achieved unprecedented breadth and impact, both domestically and abroad (Joseph 2009). Thus, the Black Power Movement fundamentally altered Blacks' "notions of identity, citizenship, and democracy" (Joseph 2009, 1003).

The legacy of the Black Power Movement endures. The emergence of Black studies departments throughout institutions of higher learning in the United States is a direct result of the Black Power Movement (Joseph 2003). Although many have since suffered a decline in strength and size (Jackson 1987), this period is also marked by the emergence of independent Black organizations with missions aimed at furthering the political interests of African Americans (Gurin et al. 1989). Organizations such as the Congressional Black Caucus continue to operate in the American political arena today.

THE DETERMINANTS OF BLACK GROUP CONSCIOUSNESS

Currently, Blacks exhibit higher levels of racial group consciousness than other racial groups in American society (Sears and Savalei 2006). Given the determinants of group consciousness, this should come as no surprise. A sense of connectedness with other Blacks comes from the recognition that Blacks occupy a subordinate social, political, and economic position in the United States. Black racial consciousness is born out of the U.S.'s system of racial stratification that dates back to the arrival of the first Africans in the United States. For early generations of African Americans, racial consciousness developed as a result of discrimination and forced segregation (Ferguson 1938). While formal legal barriers to racial equality have been dismantled, Blacks continue to lag behind Whites in terms of income, wealth, housing, education, and access to health care (see Greenblatt 2003 for instance). Blacks also recognize such inequalities and attribute them to systemic discrimination (Dovidio, Gaertner, Kawakami, and Hodson 2002; Schuman et al. 1997). As a result, contemporary Black group consciousness is a function of perceived illegitimacy of racial inequality. For example, Dawson (1994) demonstrates that Blacks who believe African Americans are economically subordinate to Whites are more likely to exhibit a sense of interconnectedness with other Blacks. Likewise, Gurin et al. (1989) find that Blacks' sense of common fate was highest among African Americans who were "discontent with the economic and political powerlessness of blacks as compared to whites and with the belief that racial disparities are largely illegitimate [and] the result of structural barriers (232–233).

Furthermore, despite gains in Blacks' socioeconomic status and the passing of fair housing legislation, U.S. cities have only experienced modest declines in Black-White racial residential segregation (Krysan,

Couper, Farley, and Forman 2009; Massey and Denton 1993). Many Whites still view Blacks as undesirable neighbors and associate high-density Black neighborhoods with suppressed property values, failing schools, and high crime rates (Logan, Stults, and Farley 2004). At the same time, Blacks in cities like Atlanta, Detroit, and Boston often forgo moving to more affluent, White neighborhoods out of fear of racial hostility (Krysan and Farley 2002). Thus, the majority of Blacks are still residentially clustered in high-density Black areas.

Blacks who live in predominantly Black neighborhoods have less frequent and intimate contact with Whites (Sigelman, Bledsoe, Welch, and Combs 1996). Moreover, this type of residential homogeneity has consequences for Black group consciousness. For instance, Demo and Hughes (1990) found that Blacks who experienced greater interracial contact during childhood felt less close to other Blacks. Similarly, in a study of Detroit-area residents, Bledsoe et al. (1995) found that Blacks living in racially mixed neighborhoods expressed moderately lower levels of racial solidarity.

Finally, American race relations provided the impetus for the development of a multitude of Black indigenous institutions that advocate racial solidarity and oppose the status quo (Gosnell 1935; Harris-Lacewell 2003; Myrdal 1944). Such institutions include Black media, Black fraternal and civic organizations, historically Black colleges and universities (HBCUs), and Black churches. As Dawson (2001) explains, "these networks and institutions have been largely responsible for crystallizing the shared historical experiences of African Americans into a sense of collective identity" (11). Although the post-Civil Rights era has witnessed a decline in their membership, a high percentage of Blacks remain connected to these institutions.

The Black church, for instance, is one of those entities that have maintained their significance to the Black community. African Americans are more religious than any other group in the United States. Blacks are more likely than the general population to report that religion is very important and are more likely to pray and attend religious services (Sahgal and Smith 2009). Fifty-nine percent of Blacks belong to a historically Black Protestant denomination (Sahgal and Smith 2009) and a significant number of Blacks attend predominantly African-American churches in non-Black denominations (Dawson, Brown, and Jackson 1998). These Black churches have not only served as a means to achieving salvation, but have been a source of education, civic training, and political mobilization (Harris 1999; McAdam 1982). In addition, many

African-American churches socialize their congregants into engaging in activities aimed at addressing racial inequality and social injustice (McDaniel 2008; Cone 1970). Thus, religiosity among Blacks has been found to be a determinant of feelings of closeness to Blacks (Allen, Dawson, and Brown 1989). Reese and Brown (1995) and Calhoun-Brown (1996) find that religiosity, along with attending a church that promoted political awareness and activism, were positively correlated to various elements of group consciousness.

Black media are another important source of group-centered messages that promote racial unity. While there is no hard and fast definition of what constitutes Black media, we can think of them as those media outlets that are primarily owned and/or operated by African Americans and target Blacks as their central audience (Wolseley 1990; Harris-Lacewell 2004). Black media, particularly the Black press, provide African Americans with alternative, Afro-centric viewpoints aimed at countering the often negative portrayals of Blacks in mainstream media (Wolseley 1990; Allen et al. 1989; Vercellotti and Brewer 2006). Over 90 percent of Blacks report consuming some form of Black media (e.g. Black newspapers, Black music, Black movies) (Dawson et al., 1998). Allen, Dawson, and Brown (1989) find that consumers of Black media tend to exhibit feelings of closeness toward Blacks, express support for Black autonomy, and possess positive stereotypes about Blacks. Additionally, Harris-Lacewell (2004) finds that Black media consumption is positively correlated with Black linked fate and the belief that Blacks should rely on themselves rather than others.

THE PSYCHOLOGY OF BLACK GROUP CONSCIOUSNESS FORMATION

At the individual level, Psychologist William Cross provides the theoretical framework for understanding how the determinants of Black group consciousness manifest themselves psychologically (see Cross 1991). Cross's theory of Nigrescence – or the "process of becoming Black" – has five phases: pre-encounter; encounter; immersion-emersion; internalization; and internalization-commitment. Pre-encounter Blacks lack an Afro-centric identity. On one end of the pre-encounter spectrum, Blacks may recognize their race but not consider it an important facet of their lives. At the other end, pre-encounter Blacks may hold anti-Black attitudes and view their race as a negative attribute.

The encounter phase exposes Blacks to "those circumstances and events that are likely to induce identity metamorphosis in an individual" (Cross 1991, 199). The encounter may be weekly trips to the family's church, daily exposure to some form of Black media, or witnessing the election of the nation's first Black president. Encounters can even be as subtle as conversations with one's family members. For instance, Demo and Hughes found that feelings of closeness towards Blacks were heightened by receiving pre-adult messages about "what it is to be black" and "how to get along with black people" (Demo and Hughes 1990, 368). Whether it is one large-scale dramatic event or several small occurrences over time, these episodes serve to chisel away at the existing pre-encounter identity and push Blacks towards a more Afro-centric worldview.

During the immersion-emersion phase, one's existing identity is dismantled while a new Black identity is simultaneously created. All things associated with Blackness are embraced and an affective attachment to the race is formed. At the same time, the individual will reject Euro-centric entities and develop anti-White sentiment (Worrell, Cross, and Vandiver 2001). For example, adolescent Blacks in the immersion-emersion phase will seek out Black peer groups and social networks while abandoning existing relationships with Whites. They may also choose to consume predominantly Black media sources and avoid information channels that do not have an Afro-centric point of view. Immersion-emersion, however, is a period of transition that is marked by cognitive dissonance regarding one's identity and intense feelings of rage, anxiety, and guilt (Vandiver, Fhagen-Smith, Cokley, and Cross 2001).

This psychological unsteadiness is resolved during the internalization stage where the individual is left with a new salient Black identity that can be used: "(1) to defend and protect the person from psychological insults that stem from having to live in a racist society; (2) to provide a sense of belonging and social anchorage and; (3) to provide a foundation or point of departure for carrying out transactions with people, cultures, and situations beyond the world of Blackness" (Cross 1991, 210). Blacks in this stage have now accepted their Blackness without the glorification of all things African and African-American and the condemnation of all things associated with Whiteness (Vandiver et al. 2001).

The final stage of Nigrescence is internalization-commitment. Although Cross does not use this terminology, this fifth phase is where group consciousness is formed. Here is where Blacks translate their personal racial identities into a means of actively addressing racial issues and disparities.

The political goals of the race are particularly salient to Blacks in the internalization-commitment phase and they believe racial group-based collective action is the appropriate means of achieving these goals.

CONTEMPORARY GROUP CONSCIOUSNESS

If group consciousness moderates the relationship between ideological self-identification and party identification such that it adheres Black conservatives to the Democratic Party despite their policy preferences, then it is important to know (1) what the current distribution of Black group consciousness is; and (2) what differentiates those Blacks with high group consciousness from those with low group coconsciousness. Unfortunately, existing survey data do not contain consistent measures that would allow us to assess Blacks' group consciousness over time. There are, however, two data sources – the 2010 Post-Midterm Election Study (PMES) and the 2012 Religious Worldviews Study (RWS) – that enable us to look at the nature of present-day Black group consciousness at two time points. Using the items featured on the 1972 and 1976 National Election Studies used by Miller et al. (1981) as a template, both the PMES and the RWS contain questions designed to gauge the four dimensions of group consciousness – group identity, polar affect, polar power, and individual vs. system blame. The methodology of the PMES has previously been described in Chapter 3. Data for the RWS[2] were obtained from a national probability sample of 547 Blacks and a national probability sample of 599 Whites. To be eligible for the survey, respondents had to be at least 18 years old and Christian.[3] The survey was administered by Knowledge Networks via the internet. The survey was conducted between October 5, 2012 and October 17, 2012, the median length of time to complete the questionnaire was 24 minutes and the completion rate was 60 percent.[4]

---

[2] The principal investigator of the Religious Worldview Study was Professor Eric L. McDaniel of the University of Texas at Austin. The study was made possible through the generous support of the National Science Foundation.

[3] Although the 2012 RWS only features Christian respondents, the sample is fairly comparable to the 2010 PMES. One study estimates that roughly 85 percent of African Americans identify as Christian (see "U.S. Religious Landscape Survey" 2008).

[4] The completion rate was calculated using AAPOR RR6, which takes into account the multiple phases of recruitment and selection into the survey. (See Callegaro and DiSogra 2008a for a detailed explanation.)

Group identity is measured using responses to the question, "Do you think that what happens generally to Blacks in this country will have something to do with what happens in your life?" Responses to this question were coded on a 0 (low group identity) to 1 (high group identity) scale. Figure 4.1 presents the distribution of responses. The mean level of group identity for the 2010 sample of Blacks was 0.63, with a standard deviation of 0.31. Seventy-three percent of the sample reported having either some or a lot of group identity. In 2012, the mean level of group identity for Blacks was 0.64, with a standard deviation of 0.32. As indicated in Figure 4.1, fewer Blacks had either some or a lot of group identity in 2012 than they did in 2010 (69 compared to 73 percent).

Measuring polar affect requires assessing Blacks' preferences for their in-group relative to their out-group. To do so, the differences between Blacks' placement of *Blacks* and *Whites* on a feeling thermometer were used. The feeling thermometer scale (see Appendix for exact question wording) runs from 0 (cool feelings towards a group) to 100 (warm feelings towards a group). Polar affect was calculated by subtracting the feeling thermometer scores for *Whites* from the *Blacks* feeling thermometer. This variable was then scaled from 0 (Blacks prefer Whites) to 1 (Blacks prefer Blacks). On average, Blacks feel warmer towards other Blacks (mean = 0.58, standard deviation = 0.13 in 2010; mean = 0.57, standard deviation = 0.14 in 2012). As Figure 4.1 illustrates, 35 percent of Blacks in 2010 had a preference for other Blacks, compared to 13 percent who preferred Whites, and 52 percent who preferred the two groups equally. In 2012, 49 percent of Blacks preferred Blacks, while 8 percent preferred Whites and 43 percent did not prefer one group over the other.

To measure polar power, respondents first read the following statement: "Some people think that certain groups have too much influence in American life and politics, while other people feel that certain groups don't have as much influence as they deserve." They were then asked whether or not they thought Blacks and Whites had too much influence, the right amount of influence, or too little influence. Responses to the Black power question were then subtracted from the White power question to determine the perceived relative position of each group. Polar power was scaled from zero to one, where zero indicated Blacks were believed to have greater influence than Whites and one indicated that respondents believed that Whites have more influence than Blacks. With a mean of 0.83, Blacks in both sample years believed that Whites had significantly more influence in American life and politics than Blacks. Specifically, 78 percent of Blacks in 2010 indicated that Whites had more

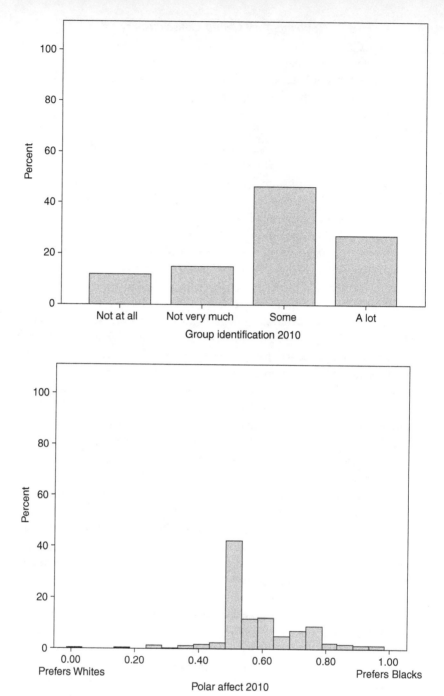

FIGURE 4.1 Distribution of Black group consciousness dimensions, 2010 and 2012
Note: Figures are weighted values.
Source: 2010 Post-Midterm Election Study and 2012 Religious Worldviews Study.

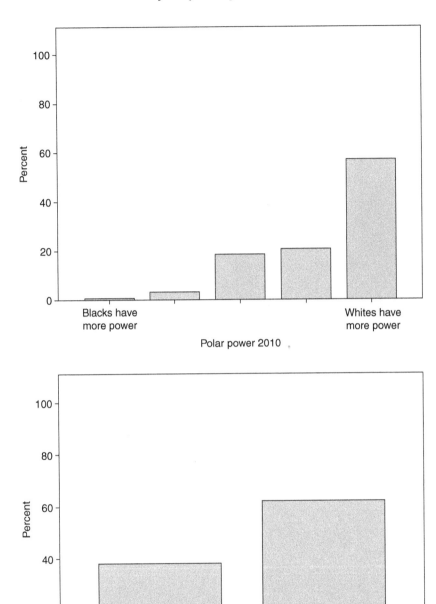

FIGURE 4.1 (*cont.*)

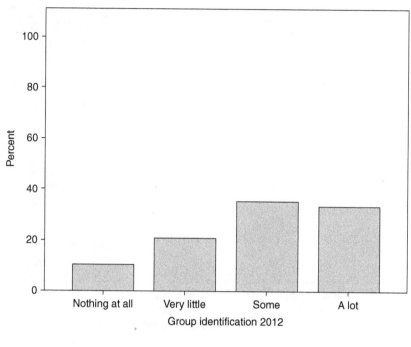

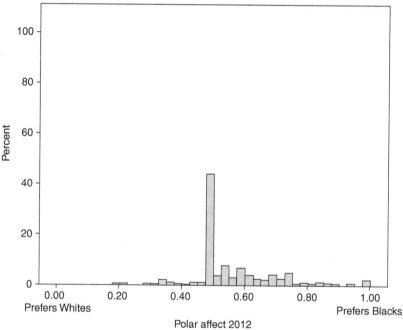

FIGURE 4.1 (*cont.*)

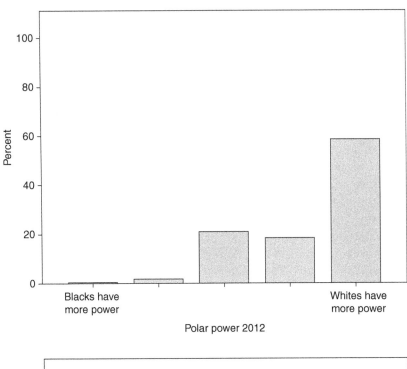

Polar power 2012

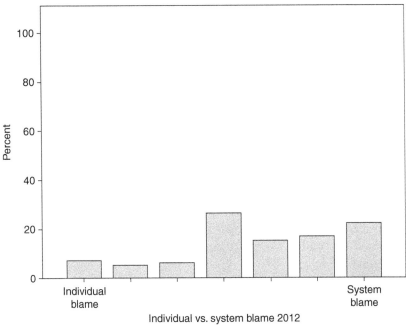

Individual vs. system blame 2012

FIGURE 4.1 (*cont.*)

power, 4 percent thought Blacks had more power, and 18 percent saw no difference (see Figure 4.1). In 2012, 77 percent of Blacks in the sample believed Whites had more power, 2.2 percent believed Blacks had more power, and 21 percent thought there was no difference between Blacks and Whites.

The fourth dimension of group consciousness, individual vs. system blame, was measured using responses to the question. "Which of these two statements do you agree with: (a) It's lack of skill and abilities that keep many Black people from getting a job. It's not just because they're Black. When a Black person is trained to do something, he is able to get a job; or (b) Many qualified Black people can't get a good job. White people with the same skills wouldn't have any trouble." In 2010, this question was asked as a forced choice. Agreement with statement (a) was coded zero; agreement with (b) was coded one. In 2012, respondents were asked to place themselves on a seven-point scale, where statements (a) and (b) were at each end of the scale. Responses were coded from zero, indicating strongest agreement with statement (a) to one, indicating strongest agreement with statement (b). As illustrated in Figure 4.1, about two-thirds of Blacks in 2010 agreed that systemic forces were responsible for racial inequality. About 55 percent of Blacks in 2012 attributed systemic barriers to inequality, while 27 percent took a neutral position, and 19 percent believed individual attributes were responsible for racial disparities.

Finally, group identity, polar affect, polar power, and individual vs. system blame were added together to create an additive index of group consciousness.[5] For ease of interpretation, the group consciousness index was rescaled from zero (low group consciousness) to one (high group consciousness). The mean level of group consciousness in the 2010 sample is 0.66 (standard deviation = 0.21). The mean level of group consciousness in 2012 was 0.67, with a standard deviation of 0.15. Figure 4.2 presents the distribution of group consciousness. About 53 percent of the sample in 2010 exhibited levels of group consciousness higher than the mean, while 45 percent had levels that were below the mean. Similarly, 51 percent of the 2012 sample had group consciousness levels that exceeded the mean, while 43 percent had group consciousness levels below the mean.

[5] All four measures were positively correlated with one another. The inter-item correlations in 2010 ranged from 0.22 to 0.34 and the Chronbach's alpha was 0.54. The inter-item correlations in 2012 ranged from 0.04 to 0.22 and the Chronbach's alpha was 0.33.

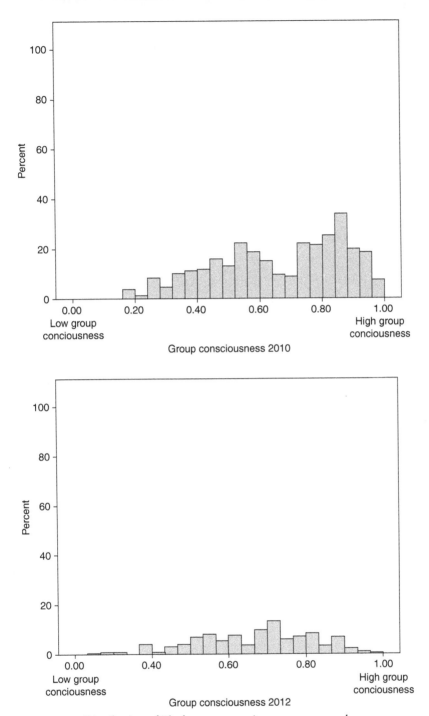

FIGURE 4.2 Distribution of Black group consciousness, 2010 and 2012
Note: Figures are weighted values.
Source: 2010 Post-Midterm Election Study and 2012 Religious Worldviews Study.

TABLE 4.1 *Demographic profile of low and high group-consciousness Blacks*

	2010		2012	
	Low	High	Low	High
% Married	29	24	36	38
% Female	52	57	58	57
% Living in the South	51	51	52	57
% Home Owners	39	51	52	42
% Employed	44	50	53	50
% College Degree	17	21	54	55
Median Church Attendance	Once a week	Once a week	16	24
			Once a week	Once a week
Mean Age	44	44	45	46
Median Income	22,500	27,500	32,500	45,000
% Attended HBCU			11	10
% Belongs to Black Organization			13	15
% Attends a Majority Black Church			67	73
% Living in Large City			24	30

Note: Figures are weighted values. Low group consciousness is at or below the median and high group consciousness is above the median (median = 0.71 in 2010 and 0.69 in 2012).
Source: 2010 Post-Midterm Election Study and 2012 Religious Worldviews Study.

Table 4.1 presents a demographic profile of Blacks with high and low group consciousness.[6] Many of the demographic differences between high and low group consciousness Blacks are modest, at best. For instance, the average age for Blacks in the 2010 sample, irrespective of group consciousness is about 44 years old. Likewise, low consciousness Blacks in the 2012 sample were on average 45 years old, while those with high group consciousness were 46 years old. Blacks with low group consciousness in 2010 were more likely to be married and male than those with high group consciousness. In 2012, high group-consciousness Blacks were more likely to be married and male. None of these differences, however, were statistically significant (p < 0.10). High and low group consciousness Blacks did differ significantly in income and home ownership in

[6] Low group consciousness is defined as those Blacks with levels of group consciousness at or below the median (0.71 in 2010 and 0.69 in 2012) and high group consciousness have levels above the median.

2010; those African Americans with high racial consciousness made more money and were more likely to own their own homes. Blacks with high group consciousness in the 2012 sample also had household incomes that were significantly higher than those with low group consciousness, although the difference in homeownership was not statistically different from zero. In 2012, those Blacks with high group consciousness were also more likely to have a college degree and live outside of the South than those with low group consciousness.

Additional demographic questions were asked in the 2012 Religious Worldviews Study that were not asked of the 2010 respondents. The bottom of Table 4.1 presents those results. Those Blacks with low group consciousness were no more likely than high group-consciousness Blacks to have attended a historically Black college or university (HBCU), belong to an organization working to improve the status of Black Americans, or live in a large city. High group consciousness Blacks were, however, significantly (p < 0.10) more likely to have attended a majority Black church (73, compared to 67 percent).

Beyond demographics, there are other factors that help explain levels of group consciousness. The qualitative interviews became particularly useful in illustrating these differences. Respondents were asked a series of questions related to what it meant to be Black. The purpose of these questions was to allow respondents to describe orientations towards the race in their own words (see Appendix for exact question wording).

A few respondents described their connection to the race in terms of phenotype. When asked about whether race affected her life, one woman responded with the following:

Yes, because I am Black and I am darker than most Blacks. Well not most Blacks, but a certain portion of Blacks. I'm darker, of darker skin. Darker hue, so because of that it affects not just what White folks do to me or any other minority but also what Black folks do to me too. So yes, I do believe that it plays a role (Respondent 50).

This sentiment was echoed among other respondents who also felt that their skin color contributed to their connection to their race. For them, they noted that it was not just about looking different but what type of information their skin color conveyed to the outside world. Black male respondents, in particular, discussed their susceptibility to police brutality regardless of their education and class level. As one respondent explains, "You know ... being a middle class Black male, I mean anytime I go out you know, I know the potential's always there for it [police brutality], for something to happen ... just because of who I am or what I look like" (Respondent 52).

Respondents also discussed other forms of discrimination based on phenotype as a reason for their racial orientations. Many respondents believed that Blacks were perceived by Whites to be "intimidating" and "threatening," which affected how they were treated in American society. In a similar vein, a 30-year-old Black male from Michigan believed that race was an important factor in determining his fate because of media portrayals:

Doesn't matter how much money I have. It doesn't matter how much education I have. It doesn't matter how many different languages I can speak, I'm still a Black man in this country. And as long as I'm involved in issues that concern the poorest, most ignorant, most down-trodden, most hopeless African American person in this country, as long as that person is affected then it will affect me. Because the media still portrays me as him. The media still portrays his struggle as mine. The media still portrays his violence as mine. So no, I'll never be able to get outside of that shadow as long as I can turn on the news and see enough stories of negativity as it pertains to African Americans then it doesn't matter how much education, how much money, what nice neighborhood I move to and what nice car I drive somebody is still going to be looking over their shoulder as being maybe the cousin of that Black guy on the news, so yeah (Respondent 1).

A number of other respondents pointed to the higher standard Blacks are held to in order to appear equally qualified as other candidates for jobs and promotions. Finally, most respondents indicated at some point there had been lost opportunities in general that resulted from their skin color.

For these reasons, several respondents believed that collective action was an appropriate means for Blacks to achieve their goals. One Black male from Maryland indicated that Black progress "makes paths" for him, while another thought that there was strength in numbers. Several respondents pointed to the accomplishments that resulted from Black collective action, including the Civil Rights Movement and the election of President Barack Obama. Finally, three respondents talked about Black collective action in terms of social responsibility. Respondent 60, a 24-year-old Black male from Maryland, even indicated that his group consciousness was the reason why he became an educator. This particular respondent believed that it was his responsibility to "enlighten the next generation" of Blacks.

This process worked in reverse for one respondent, a 39-year-old Black male from New York, who did not have a strong sense of

Black group consciousness. When asked about his feelings towards his race, he responded:

I'm light skinned. Some people think I look Hispanic. I think the way I talk, also. I speak very proper, so I tend to speak also more like a White person and there is some Irish in my blood line, on my father's side ... Black people come in different sizes and shapes and we don't all talk the same, but I kind of feel as a Black person that I'm kind of more on the outside more. I think maybe I personally identify more with White people in some ways. I'm more comfortable being around them than I am with people of my own race, mostly I'm more comfortable around Hispanic people, also (Respondent 26).

In his case, not being perceived as being part of the group led to a breakdown in connectedness with the race.

Most of the respondents with lower levels of group consciousness, however, pointed to their successes as the reason why race was not an important factor in determining their political, economic, or social fate. For instance, Respondent 56, a 32-year-old Black female from New Jersey, talked about group politics in terms of the need for economic policies. She indicated that she had participated in Head Start and received subsidized housing and financial aid when she was younger. Since she was now a college graduate with a well-paying job and it would be unlikely that she would need those programs in the future, those types of policies were no longer important to her. Similarly, a 22-year-old Black male college student from Michigan thought that the success or failure of one African American should not affect the rest of the race. Although he thought that being Black did make achieving success more challenging, race should not deter people from their objectives:

I mean just me being a young, Black male it's always going to be harder for me to get something that someone else is going to do. It's harder for me to get some-where...whereas if I was a White male I could just say hey come in, I'm here. Me being a Black male I say hey, I'm here. And I have to constantly do more of what's expected of me. Just, you know, or for a longer period of time just to get, where a White male just came in and took him a month or two to get there. So it would take me like triple to get there. In a way it's unfair. But at the same time I look at it as making me stronger. You know, then when I get to where I want to be it makes it ten times sweeter (Respondent 9).

None of these respondents saw the need for Black collective action. As one Black male respondent from New York indicated, "I think that we're responsible for our own choices ... But with a lot of the opportunities that are afforded African Americans, I think that we are in a better position to chart our own course" (Respondent 18).

The common thread throughout these interviews is that racial group consciousness is determined by whether individual Blacks find Blackness to be escapable. When Blacks can transcend their race as a result of phenotype or by individual-level achievement, levels of group consciousness are lower. In cases where Blacks find themselves bound by outside perceptions of the race, despite individual-level achievements, racial consciousness is high. This helps explain why Black group consciousness is higher among those with greater wealth and education. Furthermore, the findings regarding respondents' various encounters with Blackness are consistent with Cross's theory of how group consciousness is formed.

CONCLUSION

Delineating the relationship between Blacks' party identification and ideological self-identification requires examining the multifaceted function race plays in this association. While scholars have certainly looked at race as an explanatory variable in models measuring both Black ideology and Black party identification, these studies have failed to capture the complexity of race's role as a moderator of the relationship between these two predispositions. Hence, Part II of this book embarks on this task. Specifically, the second half of this book is devoted to exploring whether varying levels of group consciousness can explain why some Black conservatives will support the Republican Party and others will not.

Chapter 4 began this inquiry by tracing the historical and contemporary roots of group consciousness in the Black community. Using data from the 2010 Post Midterm Election Study and the 2012 Religious Worldviews Study, it was determined that just over half (55 percent) of African Americans exhibited levels of group consciousness above the mean, which was 0.67 on a scale that ran from zero to one. The results also suggested that what separated Blacks with low group consciousness from those with high group consciousness was not a set of demographic characteristics. Rather, Blacks with high group consciousness felt a sense of group oneness with other Blacks as a result of their inability to escape the effects of race in American society. Those with low group consciousness believed that they were able to transcend racial barriers and that race did not impact their lives.

While developed out of a system of discrimination and oppression, Black group consciousness has been used as a source of political empowerment (see Foster 2010 e.g.). As this chapter's opening quotation by slain civil rights activist and Black Panther Fred Hampton suggests, African Americans' sense of group solidarity has been used throughout Blacks' quest for universal freedom and citizenship. This was further detailed in this chapter in order to set the stage for the examination of this construct's role in determining how Blacks apply their ideological self-identification when determining their party identification. To be sure, Chapter 4 has provided context for understanding why and how racial considerations remain important to Black political thinking and decision-making. With this in mind, Chapter 5 demonstrates that Black group consciousness serves as the tie that binds Black conservatives to the Democratic Party, even though their ideological self-identification would predict otherwise.

5

The Invisible Link

Group Consciousness as a Moderator of Ideological Self-Identification

In understanding why there exists a nonconventional relationship between Blacks' party identification and ideological self-identification, the central argument of this book has been two-pronged. First, citizens organize ideological information along a multitude of policy dimensions, including laissez-faire, racial, military, social welfare, religious, and moral. When placing themselves on the liberal–conservative continuum, Blacks not only use a different set of dimensions than do Whites, they also assign different weights to these dimensions. Further, this multidimensional, hierarchical conceptualization of Blacks' ideological self-identification is rooted in their historical interaction with the American political environment. Second, the applicability of Blacks' ideological self-identification to their party identification is moderated by a sense of group consciousness. As levels of Black group consciousness wane, Blacks are more likely to deviate from their identification with the Democratic Party. Providing empirical evidence in support of the second part of this argument is the focus of Chapter 5.

Already, scholars have demonstrated that racial group interests strongly correlate with Blacks' political evaluations. Dawson (1994) found that "perceptions of African-American racial and economic group interests and their consequences...played an important role in both 1984 and 1988 in predicting both African-American party identification and perceptions of which party best advances Black interests" (116). Tate (1993) found that racial considerations, even more than class considerations, predicted Blacks' policy attitudes. Just how racial considerations *moderate* the relationship between Blacks' political evaluations and other political predispositions such as ideology, however, has yet to be explored.

Therefore, I offer an additional layer to our understanding of the relationship between race and party identification by examining the moderating role of racial group consciousness on political ideology. Specifically, I contend that the relationship between party identification and ideological self-identification for Blacks is contingent on racial group consciousness. When group consciousness is high, Blacks regardless of ideology will identify with the Democratic Party. I argue, however, that Democratic Party identification is most likely to decline among Blacks with low levels of group consciousness. In what follows, I provide an overview of the literature on the relative role of social groups and ideology in determining party identification and candidate evaluations. I then make the case for studying the effect of social groups and ideology in conjunction with one another. Third, I specifically focus on African Americans and explore whether group consciousness is a plausible explanation for the differences between Black Republicans and Democrats. Lastly, I provide empirical evidence to support the hypothesized relationship between Black group consciousness, ideological self-identification, and party identification.

IDEOLOGY VS. SOCIAL GROUPS

The basis for positing that group consciousness masks the relationship between ideological self-identification and party identification can be found in the initial conceptualization of party identification described in Campbell et al.'s (1960) seminal work, *The American Voter*. The example of ideology used in the book is the liberal–conservative continuum, whereby individuals organize politics along a left-to-right spectrum. Self-placement on the continuum, for instance, depends on how much citizens believe "government should assume interest, responsibility, and control" over the social, political, and economic world (Campbell et al. 1960, 194). With respect to party identification and subsequent political behavior, Campbell et al. argue that ideology provides a link between issue concerns and party identification. Those who place themselves on the left end of the spectrum are more likely to identify with the party and support candidates that are currently perceived to be more "leftist" or liberal. The same is true for those on the right-hand of the ideological continuum identifying with the party and candidates perceived to be more conservative. And although they find evidence to support this argument, they also find that the ability to organize politics along abstract, ideological lines is not common throughout the American electorate.

To be sure, Campbell et al. find that people organize politics in terms of social groups more often than they do ideologically. When asked to describe political parties, individuals often respond by indicating which groups they associate with which parties. This method of conceptualizing politics enables citizens to evaluate candidates and parties based on how hostile or sympathetic parties and candidates are perceived to be towards groups to which citizens belong or with which they sympathize. From this logic, voting blocs like African Americans occur when citizens form distinct, politically cohesive groups based on their desire to act in the group's best interest.

The discussion of group-relevant considerations in making political evaluations, inferences, and decisions is particularly relevant to our current endeavor. Specifically, the goal of this chapter is to explore when we can expect cohesiveness to breakdown among African-American voters. Chapter 12 of *The American Voter* (1960) is especially instructive for this line of research. In it, Campbell et al. examine the influence of social group membership on voting behavior. In doing so, two questions concern them: (1) how and why do individual members of a group deviate from group political standards; and (2) what accounts for the variance in distinctiveness over time of certain social groups? They argue that answering these questions requires understanding: "(a) the relationship of the individual to the group; (b) the relationship of the group to the political world; and (c) the relationship of the individual to the political world" (299).

Campbell et al. go on to clarify that membership in the group is a necessary but not sufficient condition for such group distinctiveness. Rather, it is psychological identification with the group that helps explain why individuals abide by group standards. Put another way, a lack of identification with the group helps explain deviant behavior. Furthermore, when explaining group-based political action, Campbell et al. argue that proximity matters. That is "as proximity between the group and the world of politics increases, the political distinctiveness of the group will increase" (311). Groups with individual members that view group-based political action as appropriate are more likely to behave distinctively as a group.

When translating group distinctiveness into political behavior, Campbell et al. argue, party identification provides a link between social groupings and the political world, much like ideology. Individuals support parties and their candidates based on which of these is perceived to be best for the group. In looking at various social groups in the United States,

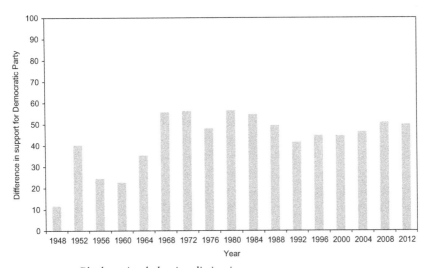

FIGURE 5.1 Black voting behavior distinctiveness, 1952–2012
Note: Values are the weighted mean difference (in percent) in Democratic Party presidential candidate support in two-party vote division between Blacks and non-Blacks. Positive values represent greater support for the Democratic Party; negative values represent greater support for the Republican Party than the residual group.
Source: American National Election Studies Cumulative Date File, 1948–2012.

Campbell et al. found that African Americans were among the most distinct politically. Specifically, they found that Blacks significantly and consistently deviated from the average vote of non-Blacks. Campbell et al. only looked at three elections, but if we update their findings, we can see that this behavior persists over time. Figure 5.1 illustrates the difference between Blacks and non-Blacks when it comes to voting for the Democratic Party's presidential candidates in a given year. At least since 1952, Blacks have been markedly more Democratic than non-Blacks. At its lowest in 1948, the gap between Blacks and non-Blacks was 11.7 percentage points, when 64.7 percent of Blacks voted for the Democratic presidential candidate, compared to 53 percent of non-Blacks. The high point of distinctiveness occurred during the 1980 election. Black support for incumbent Democratic President Jimmy Carter was 93.3 percent, while his support among non-Blacks was just 36.9 percent. In the last four presidential elections, Black support for Democratic presidential candidates has been about 45 percentage points higher than non-Blacks.

Much of the work following *The American Voter* has focused on the relative weight of social groups versus ideology in predicting party identification and vote choice, demonstrating that ideology is more important than originally thought. For instance, Carmines and Stanley (1992) examine whether social group membership or ideology accounted for the movement of northern Whites into the Republican Party during the 1970s and 1980s. They found that ideology was the strongest predictor of this partisan shift, overriding the importance of group ties. Abramowitz and Saunders (2006) similarly found that in 2004, ideology was a stronger predictor of party identification than social group membership. In fact, for many of the groups examined, they find that "the connection between social identity and party identification is much weaker or nonexistent" (184). Still, research in this area has yet to examine how group considerations and ideology might work in tandem with one another.

Nevertheless, there is evidence to suggest that the impact of ideology on political evaluations is contingent on a number of factors. Early studies argued that the ability to evaluate candidates based on a set of abstract ideological ideals was a skill reserved for a few, highly sophisticated voters (Campbell et al. 1960; Converse 1964). Subsequent studies also support the notion that "more sophisticated voters will employ ideology as a rational cognitive structure that determines issue positions as well as the evaluation of political parties and candidates" (Lyons and Scheb 1992, 574). Beyond political sophistication, there is some evidence to suggest that education, gender, and race are associated with the ability to think along ideological lines (Luttbeg and Gant 1985). In addition, research has found that political context plays a significant role in determining whether ideology influences political evaluations. For instance, Field and Anderson (1969) found that the percentage of ideologues was greater in 1964 than 1956 because the 1964 election featured a presidential candidate who made hard ideological distinctions between himself and his opponent. Further, scholars contend that the relationship between ideology and candidate evaluations is stronger when candidates emphasize ideology during the campaign and have more consistent issue positions (Pierce 1970; Lyons and Scheb 1992; Nie, Verba, and Petrocik 1979; Levitin and Miller 1979).

If the use of ideology in political evaluations is sensitive to both the political environment and demographic differences, then Black group consciousness seems like another plausible reason for why the relationship between ideology and party identification is different for Blacks and Whites. According to Miller, Gurin, Gurin, and Malanchuk (1981), group consciousness "involves identification with a group *and* a political awareness or ideology regarding the group's relative position in society along with a commitment to collective action aimed at realizing the group's interest" (495). As an attitude construct, then, group consciousness combines the identification and proximity discussed in *The American Voter* needed to restrict deviant group behavior, particularly as it relates to party identification and candidate evaluations.

As discussed in Chapter 4, Blacks possess unprecedented levels of racial group consciousness (Sears and Savalei 2006). I argue that these high levels of group consciousness are the reason why the correlation between Blacks' ideological self-identification and party identification is not higher. Unlike previous arguments that offer racial considerations as the determinant of Black partisanship (e.g., Gurin et al. 1989; Tate 1993; Dawson 1994), I contend that group consciousness moderates the relationship between ideological self-identification and party identification. African Americans employ what Dawson (1994) dubs the *Black Utility Heuristic*. The assumption behind the Black Utility Heuristic is that "as long as race remains dominant in determining the lives of individual blacks, it is 'rational' for African Americans to follow group cues in interpreting and acting in the political world" (Dawson 1994, 57–58). As a lens through which African Americans interpret the social, economic, and political world, Dawson argues that the Black Utility Heuristic has shaped the formation of Blacks' party identification. Although he does not empirically test this conceptualization, Dawson (1994:64) argues that Black party identification is a function of socioeconomic status and perceptions of racial group interests. This, I believe, is an oversimplification of Black partisanship. To be sure, Black party identification is also a function of Black ideological self-identification. Nevertheless, when determining which party to support, Blacks must weigh their ideological considerations against their racial considerations. Because of the strength of racial group consciousness among Blacks, the effect of ideological considerations will often be muted. This does not mean, however, that ideological self-identification is not part of the decision calculus. The strength of the relationship between ideological self-identification and party identification depends on Blacks' levels of group consciousness. Therefore, if we are to fully understand Black partisanship, we must account for how group consciousness moderates other predispositions as well as its direct effect on Black party identification.

Based on this argument, the relationship between party identification and ideological self-identification will be strongest when group consciousness is at its lowest. Rooted in historical events, public policies, and political symbols, Blacks have developed distinct images of the two major parties, whereby the Democratic Party is currently considered more racially liberal than the Republican Party. Furthermore, Blacks perceive a greater difference between the Democratic Party and Republican Party on race than do Whites (Philpot 2007). African Americans also view the Democratic Party as significantly more "pro-Black" than the Republican Party. Consequently, racial considerations are a strong determinant of Black partisanship (Tate 1993). Therefore, I argue that when group consciousness is high, Blacks will use racial considerations to make assessments of their own partisanship, regardless of their placement on the liberal–conservative continuum. By definition, Blacks with low group consciousness do not view the socio-political world through a racialized lens and will not be considering which party is best for the race when making partisan evaluations. Instead, these Blacks will use alternative considerations, i.e., the liberal–conservative continuum, to make political evaluations. While Black liberals with low group consciousness may not be basing their political preferences on their sense of connectedness with the group, their ideology will still lead them to identify with the Democratic Party. On the other hand, Black conservatives with low levels of group consciousness are most likely to deviate from the race in terms of their party identification. Their policy preferences suggest that there is incongruence between them and the Democratic Party and their lack of group consciousness means that they are not using a racial calculus to make political decisions. Therefore, there should be nothing binding them to the same preferences of other Blacks. Black conservatives with low group consciousness, nevertheless, constitute a very small proportion of the Black electorate, which is why we continue to witness such a strong Democratic Black voting bloc.

GROUP CONSCIOUSNESS AND THE BLACK CONSERVATIVE

But to what extent does Black group consciousness prevail among Black conservatives? Scholars assume that an adherence to Black conservative ideals does not exist simultaneously with a sense of group consciousness (e.g., Harris-Lacewell 2004). While this may be true among Black elites, I argue that this assumption is incorrect when it comes to non-elite Black conservatives. West (1993) posits that African-American conservative elites tend to have little or no connection to the Black community. Clarence Page (1996) argues in his book, *Showing My Color: Impolite*

Essays on Race and Identity, that there is a distinction between "Black conservatives" and "conservative Blacks":

The former is a relatively small, if high-profile, movement of avowed conservatives who happen to be Black. The latter best describes the Black masses who harbor many conservative attitudes, but part company with traditional conservative party lines, especially the line that says Black people make too much of racism (194–5).

Thus, we would expect this second group of Black conservatives to exhibit similar levels of group consciousness to Black liberals. As demonstrated in Chapter 4, the elements that foster Black group consciousness, such as Black identity and a politicized view of group-based inequality (Miller et al., 1981), permeate the lives of the vast majority of African Americans.

Therefore, while levels of racial consciousness may be lower among the Black conservatives at the mass-level, a sense of group oneness with other Blacks is not altogether absent among these individuals. Evidence provided by the 2010 PMES and the 2012 RWS support this claim (see Table 5.1). Looking first at the 2010 sample, of the four dimensions of group consciousness, Black liberals and conservatives only differed significantly in their levels of group identity. This difference was 0.15, indicating that Black liberals on average had some group identity (mean = 0.68, standard deviation = 0.31) while Black conservative group identity ranged from not very much to some (mean = 0.53, standard deviation = 0.32). In terms of polar affect, both groups felt slightly warmer towards Blacks than Whites (liberals: mean = 0.59, standard deviation = 0.14; conservatives: mean = 0.58, standard deviation = 0.13). Both Black liberals and Black conservatives also overwhelmingly believed that Whites had more influence than Blacks in American politics (liberals: mean = 0.83, standard deviation = 0.22; conservatives: mean = 0.83, standard deviation = 0.23). About 58 percent of Black conservatives and 68 percent of Black liberals believed that racial inequality was due to systemic, rather than individual, factors; but this difference was not statistically significant (p = 0.23). Finally, the difference between Black liberals and Black conservatives on the additive group consciousness index was 0.07, with Black liberal group consciousness being slightly higher. This last difference was substantively small but statistically significant (p = 0.05). In the 2012 sample, the only statistically significant difference (p = 0.04) between liberals and conservatives was in their beliefs about individual vs. system blame. Whereas 66 percent of Black liberals indicated that racial

TABLE 5.1 *Mean level of group consciousness, by ideology*

	2010			2012		
	Liberal	Conservative	Difference	Liberal	Conservative	Difference
Group Identity	0.678 (0.31) N=89	0.527 (0.32) N=74	0.151*	0.686 (0.31) N=204	0.646 (0.35) N=97	0.040
Polar Affect	0.587 (0.14) N=87	0.576 (0.12) N=77	0.011	0.581 (0.13) N=206	0.566 (0.14) N=98	0.015
Polar Power	0.832 (0.23) N=89	0.807 (0.25) N=74	0.025	0.842 (0.22) N=203	0.834 (0.24) N=95	0.008
Individual vs. System Blame	0.675 (0.47) N=89	0.582 (0.50) N=67	0.093	0.663 (0.30) N=205	0.584 (0.33) 97	0.079*
Group Consciousness	0.692 (0.20) N=87	0.627 (0.21) N=67	0.065*	0.693 (0.15) N=198	0.663 (0.15) N=94	0.030

Note: Values are weighted means. Standard deviations appear in parentheses. Group identity is coded from 0 (low group identity) to 1 (high group identity). Polar affect represents respondents' preference for Whites subtracted from their preference for Blacks and is coded from 0 (prefers Whites) to 1 (prefers Blacks). Polar power represents respondents' belief that Blacks have more influence in American politics subtracted from their belief that Whites have more influence in American politics and is coded from 0 (Blacks have more power) to 1 (Whites have more power). Individual vs. system blames is coded from 0 (individual attributes are responsible for racial inequalities) to 1 (systemic forces are responsible for racial inequalities). Group consciousness is an additive index composed of group identity, polar affect, polar power, and individual vs. system blame and ranges from 0 (low group consciousness) to 1 (high group consciousness). Liberals include extremely liberal, liberal, and slightly liberal. Conservatives include extremely conservative, conservative, and slightly conservative. Starred values are significant at the p < 0.10 level (two-tailed test).
Source: 2010 Post-Midterm Election Study and 2012 Religious Worldview Study.

equality was due to systemic barriers, 58 percent of Black conservatives believed the same. As was the case in 2010, Blacks in the 2012 sample, regardless of ideology, overwhelmingly believed that Whites held more power than Blacks (liberals: mean = 0.84, standard deviation = 0.22; conservatives: mean = 0.83, standard deviation = 0.24). Black liberals and conservatives in this sample also had, on average, at least some level of group identity and had a slight preference for Blacks over Whites. Overall, the difference between Black liberals and conservatives in group consciousness was 0.03, with Black liberals having a mean placement of 0.69 (standard deviation = 0.15) and Black conservatives placing slightly lower on the group consciousness index at 0.66 (standard deviation = 0.15). Moreover, this difference was not statistically significant (p = 0.11).

More telling were the differences in group consciousness between Black Democrats and Black Republicans. The first three columns of Table 5.2 present the results for the 2010 sample. Although this difference failed to reach statistical significance (p = 0.11) the mean level of group identification among Black Democrats was 0.67, compared to Black Republicans' level of 0.49 (standard deviation = 0.27) on this item. Black Republicans felt slightly warmer towards Blacks than Whites, while Black Republicans felt neutral. The difference between the two was statistically significant (p = 0.05). Although Black Republicans were significantly less likely than Black Democrats to think Whites had more power and influence than Blacks, their placement on this item was still 0.61 (standard deviation = 0.28). This indicated that both groups, regardless of party identification, believed strongly that Whites had the upper hand in American politics. In contrast, only 44 percent of Black Republicans (compared to 65 percent of Black Democrats) indicated that Blacks subordinate position in society was a result of structural forces, but this difference was not statistically significant (p = 0.22). With regards to overall levels of group consciousness, the difference between Black Democrats and Black Republicans was 0.18, a statistically significant difference (p = 0.02). The last three columns of Table 5.2, which present the 2012 results, corroborate the 2010 findings but are not as impressive. Black Republicans and Democrats did not significantly differ in terms of their group identity in the 2012 sample (p = 0.71), nor did they when it came to polar affect. Both groups preferred Blacks over Whites, with no statistically significant difference between Republicans' and Democrats' placement on this dimension (p = 0.70). Black Republicans' placement on the polar power measure was 0.70 (standard deviation = 0.24), indicating that they believed that Whites held significantly more influence in American politics

TABLE 5.2 *Mean level of group consciousness, by party identification*

	2010			2012		
	Democrats	Republicans	Difference	Democrats	Republicans	Difference
Group Identity	0.665	0.487	0.178	0.659	0.612	0.007
	(0.31)	(0.27)		(0.32)	(0.38)	
	N = 208	N = 8		N = 395	N = 8	
Polar Affect	0.589	0.499	0.090*	0.585	0.605	0.062
	(0.14)	(0.21)		(0.14)	(0.15)	
	N = 208	N = 9		N = 395	N = 8	
Polar Power	0.842	0.607	0.235*	0.852	0.700	0.139*
	(0.23)	(0.28)		(0.21)	(0.24)	
	N = 205	N = 8		N = 390	N = 8	
Individual vs. System Blame	0.654	0.440	0.214	0.656	0.642	0.112
	(0.48)	(0.53)		(0.29)	(0.34)	
	N = 205	N = 8		N = 394	N = 8	
Group Consciousness	0.687	0.504	0.183*	0.690	0.641	0.083
	(0.21)	(0.22)		(0.14)	(0.16)	
	N = 201	N = 8		N = 383	N = 8	

Note: Values are weighted means. Standard deviations appear in parentheses. Group identity is coded from 0 (low group identity) to 1 (high group identity). Polar affect represents respondents' preference for Whites subtracted from their preference for Blacks and is coded from 0 (prefers Whites) to 1 (prefers Blacks). Polar power represents respondents' belief that Blacks have more influence in American politics subtracted from their belief that Whites have more influence in American politics and is coded from 0 (Blacks have more power) to 1 (Whites have more power). Individual vs. system blame is coded from 0 (individual attributes are responsible for racial inequalities) to 1 (systemic forces are responsible for racial inequalities). Group consciousness is an additive index composed of group identity, polar affect, polar power, and individual vs. system blame and ranges from 0 (low group consciousness) to 1 (high group consciousness). Democrats include strong Democrats and weak Democrats. Republicans include Strong Republicans and weak Republicans. Starred values are significant at the p < 0.10 level (two-tailed test).
Source: 2010 Post-Midterm Election Study and 2012 Religious Worldview Study.

than Blacks. Black Democrats, however, placed 15 points higher, which yielded a statistically significant difference (p = 0.04). The average placement on the individual vs. system blame measure for Black Republicans was 0.64 (standard deviation = 0.34), compared to 0.66 (standard deviation = 0.29) for Black Democrats, yielding a negligible difference between the two. Overall, the difference between Black Democrats and Black Republicans in their levels of group consciousness was 0.05, with Black Democrats having higher levels of group consciousness in 2012.

Therefore, what differentiates Black conservatives from Black liberals are not the former's orientations towards their race. Racial consciousness appears to be more of a defining characteristic between Black Democrats and Republicans than between Black liberals and conservatives. In fact, Black conservatives are closer to Black Democrats with respect to their levels of group consciousness than they are to Black Republicans, with Black Republicans appearing to be the outliers when it comes to racial solidarity. Given that Black conservatives are not completely void of group consciousness, the proposed hypothesis is plausible; group consciousness may be a moderator of ideological self-identification.

MODERATING IDEOLOGICAL SELF-IDENTIFICATION

In order to test whether racial group consciousness had a moderating effect on the expression of Blacks' ideological self-identification, an ordered probit model was used to estimate the effect of ideological self-identification on party identification, given varying levels of group consciousness. Doing so requires including an interaction term between group consciousness and ideological self-identification (ISID) so that the effect of ideological self-identification is now contingent on group consciousness. With the addition of the interaction term, the effect of ISID on party identification is no longer just the coefficient on that variable, but the first derivative of party identification with respect to ideological self-identification, represented by the following equation: $\frac{\partial PID}{\partial ISID} = \beta_{ISID} + \beta_{ISID*GC} * Group\ Conciousness$; where β_{ISID} is the coefficient on ideological self-identification and $\beta_{ISID*GC}$ is the coefficient on the variable representing the interaction between group consciousness and ISID and Group Consciousness (see Kam and Franzese 2007). Based on the results presented in the first column of Table 5.3, the effect of ISID on party identification in 2010 was $-0.575 + 1.932 * Group\ Conciousness$.

TABLE 5.3 *The effect of ideological self-identification on party identification and party affect, by group consciousness*

	2010		2012	
	Party ID	Party Affect	Party ID	Party Affect
Ideological	−0.575	−0.108	0.558	0.308*
Self-Identification	(0.92)	(0.14)	(0.99)	(0.15)
Group Consciousness	−2.142*	−0.316*	−1.837*	−0.161*
	(0.88)	(0.12)	(0.94)	(0.09)
Ideological	1.932*	0.279	0.054	−0.347*
Self-Identification *	(1.34)	(0.21)	(1.53)	(0.20)
Group Consciousness				
Age	−0.009*	−0.001	−0.003	−0.001
	(0.01)	(0.00)	(0.01)	(0.00)
Female	−0.311*	0.019	−0.645*	−0.041*
	(0.17)	(0.02)	(0.16)	(0.02)
Income	0.018	−0.051	−0.466	0.010
	(0.42)	(0.06)	(0.40)	(0.05)
Education	1.798*	0.236	1.093	0.163
	(0.76)	(0.11)	(0.77)	(0.10)
Campaign Interest	−0.052	−0.003		
	(0.23)	(0.03)		
Political Interest			−0.541*	−0.086*
			(0.28)	(0.04)
Cut1	−0.063		−0.562	
	(0.81)		(0.72)	
Cut2	1.667		1.177	
	(0.88)		(0.70)	
Constant		0.370*		0.306*
		(0.11)		(0.08)
N	300	299	515	514
Pseudo R-square/R-square	0.08	0.10	0.11	0.15
Log likelihood	−196.51		−296.24	

Note: Coefficients for Party identification are weighted ordered probit estimates. Coefficients for Party affect are weighted OLS estimates. Standard errors appear in parentheses. Party identification is coded 0 (Democrat), 0.5 (Independent), and 1 (Republican). Party affect is coded 0 (prefers the Democratic Party) to 1 (prefers the Republican Party). Ideological self-identification is coded 0 (liberal), 0.5 (moderate), and 1 (conservative). Group consciousness is coded from 0 (low group consciousness) to 1 (high group consciousness). Starred values are significant at the $p < 0.10$ level (two-tailed test).
Source: 2010 Post-Midterm Election Study and 2012 Religious Worldview Study.

In 2012, the effect of ISID on party identification was $0.558 + 0.054 *$ *Group Consciousness*. Note also that the significance tests on the interaction terms included in each model only denote whether the effect of ISID on party identification is significant when levels of group consciousness are equal to zero. Because the inclusion of the interaction term makes the standard errors of the estimated effects conditional on different levels of group consciousness, tests of significance have to be calculated for different levels of group consciousness as well (see Friedrich 1982).

Because these are non-linear, interactive models, perhaps the most intuitive way to understand these effects is to calculate differences in the predicted probability of identifying as Republican, Independent, and Democrat for Black conservatives at various levels of group consciousness. These results are presented in Figure 5.2, along with their respective 90 percent confidence intervals.[1] Looking first at the top panel of Figure 5.2, we see that regardless of group consciousness, the probability of identifying as Republican in 2010 was incredibly low. There was evidence to suggest, however, that the relationship between ideology and group consciousness worked in the hypothesized direction. The probability of Black conservatives with no group consciousness identifying as Republican was 0.04. Among Black conservatives with the highest level of group consciousness, the probability of identifying as Republican was 0.03. Still, this was a very small and statistically insignificant (p < 0.10) difference. The 2012 sample yielded more impressive results. Among Black conservatives with no group consciousness, the probability of identifying as Republican was 0.12. When group consciousness was equal to one, Black conservatives had a near zero chance of identifying as Republican. Although the probability of identifying as Republican was larger in 2012 among Black conservatives as levels of group consciousness waned, this effect was not statistically significant. It is likely that these incredibly modest effects were a result of the relatively few Black Republicans in the sample.

Stronger support for the argument that group consciousness moderates the relationship between Blacks' ideological self-identification and party identification comes from the examination of Independents. Among Black conservatives with high group consciousness, the probability of identifying as Independent in 2010 was 0.35. When Black conservatives had no group consciousness, their probability of identifying as Independent was 0.41, although this 6 percentage point difference was not statistically significant. In 2012, however, the probability of identifying as Independent increased from 0.11 to 0.60 as Black conservatives' group consciousness waned; and this difference was statistically significant (p < 0.10).

---

[1] Predicted probabilities were calculated using the margins command in Stata 13 by holding categorical and continuous variables constant at their means and dichotomous variables constant at their modes.

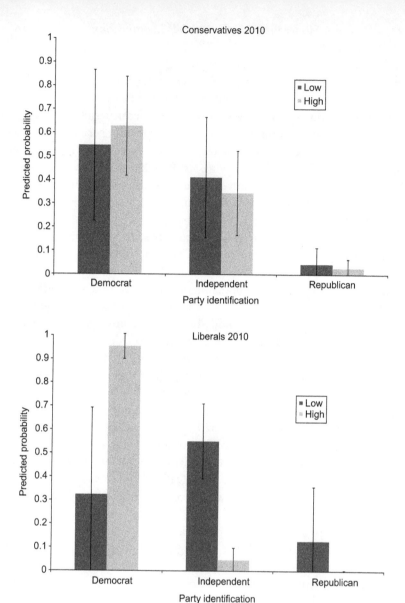

FIGURE 5.2 Party identification, by group consciousness and ideological self-identification, 2010 and 2012

Note: Bars represent the predicted probability of self-identifying as Democrat, Republican, or Independent, with 90 percent confidence intervals. Liberals include extremely liberal, liberal, and slightly liberal. Conservatives include extremely conservative, conservative, and slightly conservative. Democrats include strong Democrats and weak Democrats. Republicans include strong Republicans and weak Republicans. Group consciousness is coded from 0 (low group consciousness) to 1 (high group consciousness). Values are based on weighted ordered probit regression estimates.

Source: 2010 Post-Midterm Election Study and 2012 Religious Worldview Study.

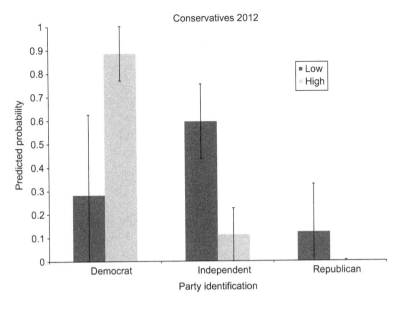

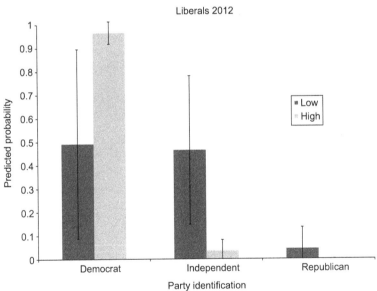

FIGURE 5.2 (*cont.*)

Also interesting was the weakening of Democratic identification that occurred as Black conservatives' group consciousness decreased. Among the Black conservatives in the 2010 sample, those with low group consciousness had a 0.55 probability of identifying as Democrat. This increased by 0.08 to 0.63 among those with high group consciousness, a modest but statistically insignificant ($p < 0.10$) difference. Similarly, Black conservatives with low levels of group consciousness in the 2012 sample had a 0.28 probability of identifying as Democrat, while their high group consciousness counterparts had a 0.89 probability of identifying as Democrat. This difference of 0.61 was statistically significant at that $p < 0.10$ level.

Self-identified liberals were also examined to see to what extent group consciousness affected their propensity to identify with the Democratic Party. Moving to the lower left quadrant of Figure 5.2, we see that the probability of Black liberals with no group consciousness in the 2010 sample identifying as Democrats was 0.32. The predicted probability of Black liberals identifying as Democrats increased to 0.95 when their levels of group consciousness reached the highest point of the index. Moreover, this 0.63 difference was statistically significant. Likewise, in 2012, the probability of Black liberals identifying as Democrat if they had no group consciousness was 0.49. Among Black liberals with high group consciousness, the probability of identifying as Democrat was 0.97. This 48 percentage point difference was also statistically significant. These results suggest that, even among self-identified liberals, the eroding of group consciousness can lead to a breakdown in Democratic Party identification. As was the case with their conservative counterparts, this did not translate into identification with the Republican Party. Although Black liberals with low group consciousness had a greater chance of identifying with the GOP than those with high group consciousness, this difference was not statistically significant ($p < 0.10$). This was true in both survey years. Instead, lowering group consciousness among Black liberals leads to a greater likelihood that they would identify as Independent. In 2010, the difference in probability of identifying as Independent between high and low group-consciousness Black liberals was 0.50 and in 2012 the increased likelihood of low group-consciousness Black liberals identifying as Independent was 0.44. In both sample years, these differences were statistically significant.

As a robustness check, party affect was included as an alternative measure of partisan evaluations. To assess the effect of ISID on party affect given respondents' levels of group consciousness, a comparable model was estimated using OLS. Based on the results in Table 5.3, the effect of ISID on party affect in 2010 was -0.108 + 0.279 * *Group Consciousness*. In 2012, the effect of ISID on party affect was 0.308 - 0.347 * *Group Consciousness*. Substantively, Figure 5.3 helps to make sense of these results by illustrating the predicted party affect as group consciousness increases.[2] Black conservatives in the 2010 sample preferred the Democratic Party over the Republican Party, regardless of group consciousness. Black conservatives with no group consciousness, however, felt 4 degrees warmer towards the GOP than Black conservatives with high group consciousness (0.33 among high group consciousness Blacks, compared to 0.37 among those with low group consciousness Blacks). This difference, however, was not statistically significant. In contrast, Black conservatives with no group consciousness in the 2012 sample preferred the Republican Party over the Democratic Party; their mean placement on the party affect measure was 0.60. Among Black conservatives with high group consciousness, party affect was 0.09, indicating a strong preference for the Democratic Party. The difference between high and low group consciousness Black conservatives in the 2012 was statistically significant. Likewise, Black liberals in the 2010 sample with no group consciousness felt fairly indifferent between the Democratic and Republican Parties (party affect = 0.48). When group consciousness was high, Black liberals' party affect was 0.16. There was a similar distinction between Black liberals with high and low group consciousness in 2012, as well. At the point where group consciousness was zero, party affect among Black liberals was 0.29; it was 0.13 when group consciousness was one. In both sample years, these differences were statistically significant.

Finally, additional analyses were run to examine to what extent President Obama had an anchoring effect on Blacks to the Democratic Party. Both the PMES and RWS were collected during President Obama's tenure in office. It might be the case that, in the age of Obama, the relationship between the Democratic Party and African Americans is completely fixed and this might explain the observed results. During other administrations when a Black man does not occupy the nation's highest office, however, Black conservatives might be more open to the Republican Party's appeals and we would see a greater likelihood of Black conservatives with low

---

[2] Predicted values were calculated using the margins command in Stata by holding categorical and continuous variables constant at their means and dichotomous variables constant at their modes.

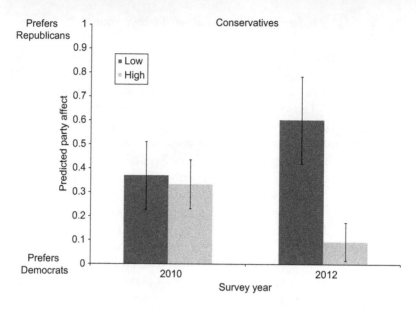

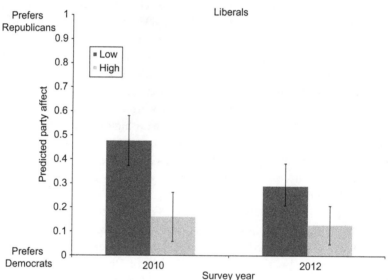

FIGURE 5.3 Party affect, by group consciousness and ideological self-identification, 2010 and 2012

Note: Bars represent the predicted party affect of self-identified conservatives and liberals, with 90% confidence intervals. Liberals include extremely liberal, liberal, and slightly liberal. Conservatives include extremely conservative, conservative, and slightly conservative. Group consciousness is coded from 0 (low group consciousness) to 1 (high group consciousness). Party affect represents respondents' preference for the Democratic Party subtracted from their preference for the Republican Party and is coded 0 (prefers the Democratic Party) to 1 (prefers the Republican Party). Values are based on weighted OLS estimates.

Source: 2010 Post-Midterm Election Study and 2012 Religious Worldview Study.

group consciousness supporting the GOP. To examine this proposition, I used the American National Election Studies (ANES) Cumulative Data File. Data from the ANES Cumulative Data File were obtained by pooling cross-section cases from the biennial ANES time series studies. Although each times series study varies in sample size, they all have the same pre- and post-election design and feature the same subset of core questions (American National Election Studies and Stanford University 2015). Respondents had to be at least 18 years old to be eligible for the survey and the total sample size for the Cumulative Data File was 55,674. (See the Appendix for additional methodological information.) While this dataset only consistently measures one dimension of group consciousness over time (Polar Affect), it has the advantage of: 1) being able to capture public opinion both before and after President Obama ascends to national politics; and 2) featuring a significant number of Blacks when the sample years are pooled together (n = 6,509). For these analyses, the models were estimated separately for the pre-Obama years (1948–2004) and the Obama years (2008–2012).[3] Table 5.4 presents the results. During the pre-Obama years, the effect of ISID on party identification was 0.763 – 0.775 * *Polar Affect*. More recently, the effect of ideological self-identification on party identification was 1.446 – 1.611 * *Polar Affect*. Based on the relative size of these coefficients, it appears as if ideological self-identification had a larger effect on party identification during the Obama years.

Figure 5.4 helps translate these results into what this meant substantively for the Republican Party's ability to attract Black conservatives by presenting the predicted probability of identifying with the different parties at varying levels of polar affect. During the pre-Obama years, self-identified Black conservatives who preferred Blacks had a 0.01 probability of identifying with the Republican Party. Among those conservatives who preferred Whites, the probability of identifying with the Republican Party increased by 0.17. This difference, however, was not statistically significant (p < 0.10). During the Obama years, the likelihood that the Republican Party could attract Black conservatives was even greater. Among self-identified Black conservatives who preferred Blacks, the probability of identifying with the Republican Party was nearly zero. The probability of identifying with the GOP among self-identified Black

---

[3] Even though President Obama was elected to the U.S. Senate in 2004, he was still a relative unknown, particularly to the Black community, as late as February 2007 when he announced his candidacy for the presidency (Walters 2007).

TABLE 5.4 *The effect of ideological self-identification on party identification and party affect, by polar affect*

	Pre-Obama Years 1948-2004		Obama Years 2008-2012	
	Party ID	Party Affect	Party ID	Party Affect
Ideological Self-Identification	0.762 (0.51)	0.039 (0.08)	1.446* (0.80)	0.192* (0.11)
Polar Affect	−0.673 (0.48)	−0.155* (0.08)	−1.119 (0.93)	−0.288* (0.11)
Ideological Self-Identification * Polar Affect	−0.775 (0.93)	−0.012 (0.15)	−1.611 (1.42)	−0.216 (0.19)
Age	−0.007* (0.00)	−0.001* (0.00)	−0.006 (0.00)	0.000 (0.00)
Female	−0.279* (0.07)	−0.036* (0.01)	−0.410* (0.12)	−0.040* (0.02)
Income	0.027 (0.12)	−0.001 (0.02)	0.065 (0.21)	0.012 (0.03)
Education	−0.234 (0.14)	−0.003 (0.02)	0.103 (0.23)	−0.011 (0.04)
Campaign Interest	−0.470* (0.10)	−0.054* (0.01)	−0.137 (0.15)	−0.059* (0.02)
Cut1	−0.526 (0.30)		−0.207 (0.58)	
Cut2	0.726 (0.30)		1.164 (0.57)	
Constant		.496* (0.05)		.444* (0.07)
N	1,505	1,210	1,097	1,097
Pseudo R-square/R-square	0.04	0.06	0.06	0.10
Log likelihood	−1106.41		−469.32	

Note: Coefficients for Party identification are weighted ordered probit estimates. Coefficients for Party affect are weighted OLS estimates. Standard errors appear in parentheses. Party identification is coded 0 (Democrat), 0.5 (Independent), and 1 (Republican). Party affect is coded 0 (prefers the Democratic Party) to 1 (prefers the Republican Party). Ideological self-identification is coded 0 (liberal), 0.5 (moderate), and 1 (conservative). Polar affect is coded from 0 (prefers Whites) to 1 (prefers Blacks). Starred values are significant at the $p < 0.10$ level (two-tailed test).
Source: American National Election Studies Cumulative Data File, 1948–2012.

conservatives who preferred Whites was 0.34. This was a statistically significant difference ($p < 0.10$). At the same time, there was a greater erosion of Democratic Party identification during the Obama years than during the pre-Obama years among self-identified Black conservatives as

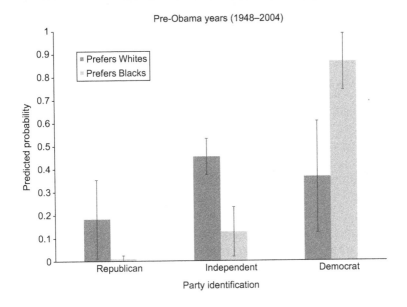

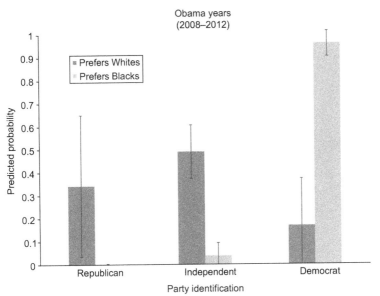

FIGURE 5.4 Party identification, by polar affect among Black conservatives, pre-Obama years and Obama years

Note: Bars represent the predicted probability of self-identifying as Democrat, Republican or Independent, with 90 percent confidence intervals. Conservatives include extremely conservative, conservative, and slightly conservative. Democrats include strong Democrats and weak Democrats. Republicans include Strong Republicans and weak Republicans. Polar affect represents respondents' preference for Whites subtracted from their preference for Blacks and is coded from 0 (prefers Whites) to 1 (prefers Blacks). Values are based on weighted ordered probit regression estimates.

Source: American National Election Studies Cumulative Date File, 1948–2012.

preferences on polar affect moved from Blacks to Whites. Specifically, the probability of Obama-era Black conservatives who preferred Blacks identifying with the Democratic Party was 0.96. Among those who preferred Whites, this probability was 0.17, a statistically significant (p < 0.10) difference of 0.78. The equivalent difference among Black conservatives during the pre-Obama years was 0.50, which was also statistically significant.

Figure 5.5 compares the mean placement of Black conservatives on the party affect scale by levels of polar affect. During the pre-Obama years, when self-identified Black conservatives preferred Whites on the polar affect measure, their mean placement on party affect was 0.43. This was just left of center, showing a slight preference for the Democratic Party. When Black conservatives had a preference for other Blacks, their mean

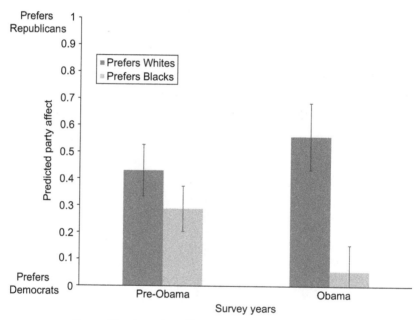

FIGURE 5.5 Party affect by polar affect among Black conservatives, pre-Obama years and Obama years

Note: Bars represent the predicted party affect of self-identified conservatives, with 90% confidence intervals. Conservatives include extremely conservative, conservative, and slightly conservative. Party affect represents respondents' preference for the Democratic Party subtracted from their preference for the Republican Party and is coded 0 (prefers the Democratic Party) to 1 (prefers the Republican Party). Polar affect represents respondents' preference for Whites subtracted from their preference for Blacks and is coded from 0 (prefers Whites) to 1 (prefers Blacks). Values are based on weighted OLS estimates.
Source: American National Election Studies Cumulative Date File, 1948–2012.

placement on party affect was 0.29, indicating a fairly strong preference for the Democratic Party. In comparison, Black conservatives during the Obama years with a preference for Whites on the polar affect measure had a mean placement of 0.56 on the party affect scale, indicating that they had a slight preference for the Republican Party. On the other hand, Obama-era Black conservatives who preferred Blacks on the polar affect scale had a very strong preference for the Democratic Party; their mean placement on party affect was 0.06. Moreover, this 50 degree difference among Obama-era Black conservatives was statistically significant at the $p < 0.10$ level.

To sum, the results provide support for the argument that group consciousness moderates the relationship between ideological self-identification and party identification. Unfortunately, the tests of the hypothesis regarding Black conservatives and Republican identification yielded insignificant results, even though the effects were in the expected direction. There were too few Black Republicans in either the 2010 or the 2012 samples to reliably predict when Blacks would ultimately deviate completely from the Democratic Party. The results, however, did allow us to examine the circumstances under which Black Democratic identification starts to break down. Among both Black liberals and conservatives, having low group consciousness loosened Black partisanship so that Blacks with low group consciousness moved from identifying as Democrats to identifying as Independents. The exception was Black conservatives in 2010, where these effects were much smaller and statistically insignificant. A similar pattern occurred when we looked at party affect. Support for the Republican Party increased among both liberals and conservatives as levels of group consciousness decreased. Again, the smallest effect was among Black conservatives in 2010, whose levels of support for the Republican Party also increased as their group consciousness decreased; the differences, nevertheless, were not statistically significant. Lastly, the analysis of the ANES further clarifies the circumstances under which Black conservatives will support the Republican Party. Using polar affect as a representation of Blacks' level of group consciousness, we were able to examine whether the Obama presidency had any bearing on the Republican Party's ability to attract Black conservatives. These results provided the strongest support for the argument that Black conservatives with low group consciousness are the group most likely to identify with the Republican Party, particularly compared to their high group-consciousness counterparts. During both the pre-Obama and Obama years, the differences between Blacks with low and high group consciousness were statistically significant (p < 0.10). Furthermore, these effects were more pronounced during the Obama years, suggesting that Obama's tenure in office was *not* anchoring Black conservatives with low group consciousness to the Democratic Party.

The qualitative interviews help to further tease out the relationship among ideology, group consciousness, and party identification. An interesting finding that emerged from the analysis of the interviews was a tension that Black Republicans revealed when asked who they would vote for in 2008. For example, Respondent 76 is a retired teacher from Indiana and a self-identified Republican. When asked about her presidential vote choice in 2008, she indicated that a sense of racial pride led her to vote for Barack Obama, even though she usually voted Republican in every other election. Respondent 49 felt a similar tension. At the time of her interview, she was torn between voting for Obama and McCain. On the one hand, she believed Obama was far more liberal than she was on most issues. On the other hand, she appreciated Obama's outreach to a more diverse population of voters and could relate to him on a personal level more than she could McCain.

This tension extended beyond electoral politics. For instance, one 36-year-old Black male respondent from Georgia explained his choice to eventually leave the Republican Party:

I originally registered as a Republican because I always felt Black people were pimped by Democrats every four years for a vote. However, after George W. Bush's first term in office, I changed to an Independent. Maybe it was the treatment of one of my heroes, Gen. Colin Powell (why I registered Republican in the first place), for the most part. But I think I just didn't identify with the Republican Party as a coming-of-age Black man anymore (Respondent 80).

These tensions lessened as levels of group consciousness decreased. When discussing his partisanship, Respondent 51, an 80-year-old Black male from New York, responded, "I resent people thinking or assuming that I've got to be a Democrat because I'm Black or look Black or whatever." In his case, he did not think it was appropriate to use race as a determinant of his partisanship or his vote choice in the 2008 presidential election. Similarly, in a discussion about her connection to other Blacks, a Black female Republican from Florida responded, "Contrary to the assertions of race-baiting Democrats, there are no barriers to success for Black people in this country. If racism were a barrier to success, then I would not have been able to achieve success in my life." With respect to ideology and partisanship, she went on to explain:

Since Blacks do not share the values of liberals, they should not support the liberals in the Democratic Party. Black people should be true to their values and support their fellow conservatives in the Republican Party. Until Blacks start leveraging their votes, as other groups do, there will be no changes in the deplorable conditions in Black communities. Blacks have been complaining about the same problems for the past 40 years, but continue voting for the Democrats whose socialist policies have created those deplorable conditions. It's time for Blacks to seize control over their own destiny and hold politicians accountable for the content of their policies, not the label of their party (Respondent 79).

For her, race was not a salient part of her identity and had no bearing on her choice of political party. She entered politics as a volunteer for Richard Nixon's 1960 presidential campaign and had consistently voted Republican ever since.

EXPLORING THE ALTERNATIVES

An alternative explanation for these results is that Black conservatives are mislabeling themselves and, therefore, it should be no surprise that their party identification does not align with their ideological self-identification. As discussed in Chapter 1, political sophistication is highly correlated with the ability to think along ideological lines (Converse 1964; Knight 1985; Jacoby 1991). Therefore, inasmuch as Blacks have on average lower levels of political knowledge than Whites (Delli Carpini and Keeter 1996), this would account for the low correlation between ideological self-identification and party identification.

More recently, Ellis and Stimson (2012) provide another explanation that may account for the findings presented in this study. In their book, *Ideology in America*, they explore why so many Americans simultaneously embrace a conservative identity and a liberal policy agenda. They argue that the root of ideological inconsistency lies in the difference between individuals' operational versus symbolic ideologies. Symbolic ideology represents the labels people assign themselves, given the psychological attachment they have developed to ideological symbols. Operational ideology, on the other hand, is citizens' ideas about the proper role of government. Further, they demonstrate that Americans often have a discrepancy between their operational and symbolic ideologies, due to a symbolic attachment to the term "conservative" and an affinity for liberal public policies. From this standpoint, Black conservatives are actually policy liberals who have labeled themselves "conservative" for symbolic reasons.

To test these alternatives, the policy positions of self-identified Black liberals and conservatives are examined to see if there are discernable differences between the two. In the PMES, respondents were asked their opinions on four issues – gays in the military, federal healthcare mandates, U.S. troops remaining in Iraq, and profiling of suspected illegal immigrants. (See Appendix for exact question wording.) Responses represented Blacks' position on a five-point Likert scale, ranging from strongly favoring the issue to strongly opposing the issue. Table 5.4 presents the percent of respondents either strongly favoring or somewhat favoring each issue. The results presented in Table 5.4 provide supporting evidence that this was not simply a matter of Black conservatives mislabeling themselves. On all four of the issues, Black conservatives were significantly more conservative than Black liberals. Specifically, Black conservatives were more likely than Black liberals to favor a federal law that prohibits openly gay men and women from serving in the military, U.S. troops remaining in Iraq, and allowing local police to stop and verify the status of suspected illegal immigrants. In contrast, Black liberals were significantly more likely to favor a federal law requiring all individuals to purchase health care insurance.

As a comparison, the issue positions of White liberals and White conservatives were also examined. As Table 5.4 indicates, Black liberals and White liberals were quite similar. The difference in the percent of Black liberals and White liberals favoring the four issues was substantively small and statistically insignificant. White conservatives, in contrast, were significantly more conservative than Black conservatives on three issues. Specifically, White conservatives more strongly favored U.S. troops remaining in Iraq and the profiling of suspected illegal immigration. White conservatives were also less likely than Black conservatives to favor mandating the purchase of health care insurance. As a result, the differences on issue positions between White liberals and White conservatives were larger than they were between Black liberals and conservatives. Nevertheless, the differences between Blacks and Whites were modest – ranging from 9.5 to 15.6 percentage points. Thus, mislabeling appears to have been minimal among Blacks and it was unlikely that the alternative hypotheses could account for the findings presented earlier. Table 5.4 also suggests that Blacks are using ideological labels to compare themselves to each other whereas Whites label themselves relative to the extremes of the liberal–conservative spectrum.

TABLE 5.5 *Mean issue positions, by ideological self-identification and race*

	Blacks			Whites		
	Liberals	Conservatives	Difference	Liberals	Conservatives	Difference
Federal law that currently prohibits openly gay men and women from serving in the military	18.4 (0.39) N=89	37.9 (0.49) N=75	19.5*	10.8 (0.31) N=100	44.2 (0.50) N=146	33.4*
Federal law that requires all individuals to purchase health care insurance or face a penalty if they don't	29.6 (0.46) N=88	16.0 (0.37) N=75	13.6*	36.3 (0.48) N=100	7.1 (0.26) N=146	29.2*
U.S. troops remaining in Iraq to advise and assist the Iraqi authorities	15.9 (0.37) N=88	**26.8** (0.45) N=75	10.9*	18.1 (0.39) N=100	**42.4** (0.50) N=147	24.3*
Legislation that authorizes local police to stop and verify the immigration status of anyone they suspect of being an illegal immigrant	29.6 (0.46) N=89	**53.3** (0.50) N=74	23.7*	39.7 (0.49) N=100	**72.9** (0.45) N=147	33.2*

Note: Values are weighted means. Standard deviations appear in parentheses. Statistical significance was calculated using t-tests for independent samples. Percent favor include those who strongly favor and somewhat favor each issue. Liberals include extremely liberal, liberal, and slightly liberal. Conservatives include extremely conservative, conservative, and slightly conservative. Starred values indicate differences between liberals and conservatives of the same race are statistically significant at the p < 0.10 level (two-tailed test). Bolded values indicate differences between Blacks and Whites of the same ideological group are statistically significant at the p < 0.10 level (two-tailed test).
Source: 2010 Midterm Election Study.

CONCLUSION

A growing number of Blacks are calling themselves conservative because they are in fact conservative relative to their liberal counterparts. While self-identified Black conservatives may not be as conservative on public policies as White conservatives, they do place themselves right of center on issues such as gays in the military, federal healthcare mandates, and the profiling of suspected illegal immigrants. Furthermore, Black conservatives are significantly more conservative than Black liberals on these three issues. Based on this, one would expect a greater proportion of Black Republicans in the American electorate. Yet, this has not been the case. African Americans continue to identify with the Democratic Party despite the increased heterogeneity in their ideological self-identification.

Previous research on Black partisanship has offered racial considerations as an explanation as to why Blacks continue to support the Democratic Party. Much of this work has modeled African-American party identification without accounting for the effect of ideological self-identification and none of this research has considered the joint relationship between racial group consciousness and ideological self-identification. This omission, I believe, fails to capture the complexity in African-American partisanship. Once we account for the moderating effect group consciousness has on ideological self-identification, we can see why there is not more variance in Black partisanship. Specifically, the results suggest that group consciousness supplants the expression of Blacks' ideological self-identification, thereby homogenizing party identification.

The combination of data sources used in this chapter helped to determine when the homogeneity in African-American partisanship began to breakdown. Using the two smaller survey samples from 2010 and 2012, we were able to observe that lower levels of racial consciousness led to an increased likelihood of identifying as Independent and a decreased likelihood of identifying as Democratic. The larger ANES pooled samples demonstrated that Black conservatives with low group consciousness were most likely to identify with the Republican Party. Taken together, the evidence suggests that there is a very small segment of the African-American electorate that could be open to the Republican Party and its appeals. It is more likely, however, that this cadre of Blacks will identify as Independents before they completely convert from Democrats to Republicans.

So far, exploring the moderating effect of group consciousness on ideological self-identification among Blacks has been confined solely to the examination of Black partisanship. Before we can make a conclusive statement about the future of African Americans and the Republican Party, it is worth discovering how other evaluations and behaviors are similarly affected. Therefore, Chapter 6 explores whether Black conservatives' voting behavior and evaluations of public figures is also conditioned by a sense of group consciousness.

6

Filling in the Blanks

Group Consciousness and Ideology beyond Partisanship

I don't necessarily like his policies; I don't like much that he advocates, but for the first time in my life, history thrusts me to really seriously think about it.

– Armstrong Williams

Part of the central thesis of this book has been that the applicability of Blacks' ideological self-identification to their party identification is contingent on levels of group consciousness. As levels of group consciousness diminish, the correlation between Blacks' party identification and ideological self-identification strengthens. So far, this theoretical proposition has been tested by examining African Americans' party identification and party affect. Chapter 5 demonstrated that identification with the Democratic Party began to break down as levels of group consciousness waned, particularly among self-identified conservatives with no group consciousness. But how do Black conservatives negotiate between their ideology and racial group consciousness, beyond partisanship? Are there other areas in which racial consciousness moderates ideological ideals? As we see in the opening quote, Armstrong Williams – businessman, talk show host, and noted Black conservative – is expressing the tension he felt between his conservative ideals and the opportunity to vote for the man who would eventually become the nation's first Black president. Williams, who followed this statement with, "I can honestly say I have no idea who I'm going to pull that lever for in November. And to me, that's incredible" (Frommer 2008), was not alone in his ambivalence. Gen. Colin Powell, former Secretary of State under Republican President George W. Bush, has articulated this tension through his disappointment in the Republican Party's reputation on race:

I think what the Republican Party needs to do now is take a very hard look at itself and understand that the country has changed. The country is changing demographically. And if the Republican Party does not change along with that demographic, they're going to be in trouble. And so, when we see that in one more generation, the minorities of America, African-Americans, Hispanic Americans, and Asian Americans will be the majority of the country, you can't go around saying we don't want to have a solid immigration policy. We're going to dismiss the 47 percent. We are going to make it hard for these minorities to vote as they did in the last election. What did that produce? The court struck most of that down and most importantly, it caused people to turn out and stand in line because these Republicans were trying to keep us from voting. There's also ... a dark vein of intolerance in some parts of the Party ... When I see a former governor say that the president is shuckin' and jivin', that's a racial era slave term. When I see another former governor after the president's first debate where he didn't do very well, [say] that the president was lazy. He didn't say he was slow, he was tired, he didn't do well, he said he was lazy. Now, it may not mean anything to most Americans but to those of us who are African-Americans, the second word is shiftless ... Why do senior Republican leaders tolerate this kind of discussion within the Party? I think the Party has to take a look at itself (Powell 2013).

General Powell goes on to explain that he voted for Barack Obama in both the 2008 and 2012 presidential elections, even though he voted for Republican candidates in the seven presidential elections prior to 2008. And although he endorsed President Obama in the two most recent elections, General Powell still declared his loyalty to the Republican Party (Powell 2012). In these two instances, a sense of racial solidarity was in direct odds with each man's conservative issue positions and previous party loyalties. And yet, they were at least willing to consider straying from their traditional voting pattern in favor of voting for a candidate who was at a minimum a symbolic representation of what was best for the race. This example suggests that group consciousness not only moderates the relationship between ideology and party identification, but it might also affect the relationship between ideology and other political evaluations and behaviors. Thus, this chapter explores how varying levels group consciousness affects Black conservatives' political evaluations as well as their political behavior.

The political behavior and evaluations of Black conservatives with high group consciousness will be of particular interest, given their unique position at the intersection of race and ideology. Black conservatives with high group consciousness, also known as Afrocentric conservatives (Lewis 2013), Black nationalist conservatives (Simpson 1998), or Afrocentric nationalists (Austin 2006), are different than other conservatives, even other Black conservatives. In her book, *Conservatism in the Black*

Community: To the Right and Misunderstood, Professor Angela Lewis describes Afrocentric conservatives as follows:

> While other camps of black conservatives focus their belief system on the appropriate role of the government, Afrocentric conservatives base their views on self-reliance and are antigovernment, but not in the same sense as other conservatives or even the American conservative tradition. They are antigovernment because they understand that American society has utilized the government to enslave Blacks (Lewis 2013, 57).

Similar to conservatives in general, Afrocentric conservatives place importance on religion and morality. At the same time, they also exhibit high levels of Black pride and support Black self-determination (Lewis 2013). Thus, Afrocentric conservatives are distinct from other conservatives in that they are "committed to the notion that race is an important factor in the lives of African Americans" (Simpson 1998, 32). Because of this, Afrocentric conservatives may be caught between a rock and a hard place when it comes to politics. Often, their conservative ideals conflict with policies and candidates that are deemed best for African Americans.

  Therefore, Chapter 6 examines Afrocentric conservatives' reaction to Obama's candidacy and presidency. The election of Barack Obama as the U.S.'s first African-American president and the evaluation of his tenure provide the perfect backdrop against which to explore how Black conservatives with high racial consciousness navigate the political world. Initially, Obama's Blackness was contested and his authenticity as a Black leader was questioned. Unlike leaders such as Al Sharpton and Jesse Jackson, whose familiarity comes as a result of their grassroots work with the Black community and connection to the Civil Rights Movement, Obama was introduced to most Black Americans at the 2004 Democratic National Convention, a non-indigenous institution (Walters 2007). Further:

> He appeared to be of African descent, but the cultural markers to which traditional American Blacks were exposed presented him as someone born of a White American mother and a Kenyan father and raised in Hawaii. Also, the fact that he had lived for a while in Indonesia complicated the matter further. In short, his identity omitted many of the cultural markers with which Blacks are more familiar to the extent that it has promoted a curiosity of "cultural fit" that in turn has become an issue of political trust (Walters 2007, 13).

  The inability to validate his identity also gave many Black voters pause when it came to trusting whether Obama supported issues most relevant to the Black agenda. Although the National Association for the Advancement of Colored People gave Obama 100 percent on his voting record on issues of interest to the Black community while he was in the U.S. Senate, Obama shied away from labeling any of these issues "Black issues." Instead, Obama often framed his support for liberal policies in universal terms by emphasizing that there was not anything race-specific about wanting to improve Americans' access to quality education, jobs, and healthcare (Walters 2007). He also strategically deemphasized race during his presidential bid in order to build an interracial electoral coalition that rivaled the diversity of Franklin Roosevelt's New Deal Coalition (Walton and Smith 2014; Winant 2009).

Despite his attempts to neutralize his campaign, Barack Obama came to embody Blackness (Kinder and Dale-Riddle 2012).

Ultimately, the idea of Obama – a talented, handsome, and charismatic young black man – becoming president captivated the entire black community, and support for him became a marker of one's blackness and loyalty to the black community. After hundreds of years of slavery, lynching, and Jim Crow segregation, Obama's candidacy came to embody Dr. King's dream (Walton and Smith 2014, 163).

Given that Obama is a Black Democrat with liberal to moderate policy positions, how did Afrocentric conservatives react to his candidacy and presidency? Were Afrocentric conservatives inspired by a shared racial ancestry or repelled by incongruent ideological leanings? The rest of this chapter is devoted to answering these questions.

TURNOUT AND THE 2008 AND 2012 ELECTIONS

The historic election of Barack H. Obama in 2008 as the U.S.'s first African-American president could largely be attributed to the increased voter turnout among Blacks (Philpot et al. 2009). According to the U.S. Census, 2 million more Blacks cast ballots in 2008 than they did in 2004. As seen in Figure 6.1, Black voter turnout reached an unprecedented 65 percent, the highest it had been in any presidential election since 1996, when the U.S. Census Bureau began keeping this time series (File and Crissey 2012).

Obama's margin of victory afforded by the increase in Black voter turnout was spurred by the mobilization efforts of the Democratic Party and the Obama campaign which did not want to take for granted that his

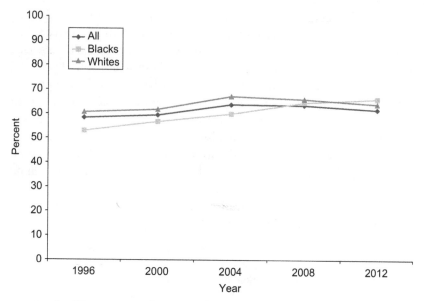

FIGURE 6.1 Voter turnout, by race and year
Source: U.S. Census Bureau.

"natural" constituency would simply show up on Election Day (Philpot et al. 2009). For instance, dozens of Black churches in cities like Des Moines and Waterloo were heavily targeted during the Iowa Democratic Caucus, even though Blacks constituted less than 2 percent of the Caucus's participants (Zeleny 2008). Obama strategists also expended considerable resources in making sure registered Black voters who had not voted in previous elections actually cast ballots in the November 2008 election (Wallsten 2008).

The Obama campaign also benefited from mobilization efforts from Black institutions, such as the Black church and the Black media. In 2008, for example, the Tom Joyner Morning Show and the National Association for the Advancement of Colored People (NAACP), with funding from the Teamsters Union, established a hotline where people could register to vote and report instances of voting irregularities to attorneys. It was estimated that the hotline "received more than 300,000 phone calls in 2008, registered nearly 100,000 voters, and protected black voter access in primaries and on November 4 in dozens of states, providing enormous benefit to Obama's and other Democrats' candidacies, efforts" (Leonardo 2012, 666).

In order to examine whether Black conservatives[1] were similarly ener-gized to vote during the 2008 election, I rely on survey data from the 2010 Post-Midterm Election Study, which was previously described in detail in Chapter 3. As part of the 2010 PMES, respondents were asked if they voted in the 2008 elections. (See the Appendix for exact question wording.) In general, 71.4 percent of the sample reported turning out for the 2008 election. Black liberals also reported voting at substan-tially higher rates than Black conservatives (80.9 percent, compared to 68.4 percent).

In order to test whether racial group consciousness had a moderating effect on the expression of Blacks' ideological self-identification, a logistic regression model was used to estimate the effect of ideological self-identification on self-reported voter turnout, given varying levels of group consciousness[2]. Because these are non-linear, interactive models, the dif-ferences in the predicted probability of not voting among Black conserva-tives at various levels of group consciousness were calculated for the ease of interpretation. These results are presented in Figure 6.2, along with their respective 90 percent confidence intervals.[3] Among Afrocentric Black conservatives, the probability of not voting was 0.07. As Figure 6.2 indicates, the probability of not voting increased to 0.38 among those Black conservatives with low group consciousness. The results provide evidence to suggest that the observed difference between liberals and conservatives was due to the presence of a cadre of Black conservatives with low group consciousness. Note, however, that these differences are suggestive but not statistically significant ($p < 0.10$).

Figure 6.2 also examines self-reported voter turnout in 2012. In 2012, President Obama ran for reelection. Observers of the 2008 presidential election predicted that Black voter turnout would return to its pre-2008 levels "partly because it was thought unlikely that Obama's reelection would generate the kind of enthusiasm as the first election of a black president" (Walton and Smith 2014, 188). In 2012, however, the level of voter turnout among Blacks exceeded that of Whites. As Figure 6.1

---

[1] In this chapter, ideological self-identification is a three-category variable, ranging from liberal – which includes those who are slightly liberal, liberal and extremely liberal (0) – to conservative (1) – which includes those who are slightly conservative, conservative, and extremely conservative.

[2] The results of this estimate are presented in Table A6.1 in the Appendix.

[3] All of the predicted probabilities in this section were calculated using the margins com-mand in Stata 13 by holding categorical and continuous variables constant at their means and dichotomous variables constant at their modes.

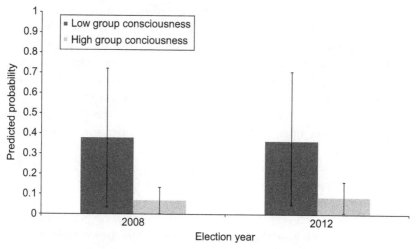

FIGURE 6.2 Probability of not voting among Black conservatives in the 2008 and 2012 elections

Note: Bars represent the predicted probability of not voting, with 90 percent confidence intervals. Values are based on weighted logistic regression estimates (see Table A6.1 in the Appendix). Voter turnout is coded 1 if respondent reported voting in November general election and 0 if respondent did not. Group consciousness is coded from 0 (low group consciousness) to 1 (high group consciousness). Conservatives include those who are slightly conservative, conservative, and extremely conservative.

Source: 2010 Post-Midterm Election Study and 2012 American National Election Study.

indicates, Black voter turnout in 2012 was 66.2 percent, compared to 64.1 percent among Whites. Hence, not only had African-American voter turnout been at its highest level in any recent history, for the first time ever, it had exceeded White voter turnout.

Walton and Smith (2014) attribute the continued high level of voter turnout among Blacks to a number of factors. First, they note the widespread effort to suppress the Black vote:

In 2012, in several states with Republican governors and state legislatures – Florida, Ohio, Texas, Pennsylvania, South Carolina, and Tennessee – new restrictions and voting requirements were enacted. Among other things, there requirements included limits on the abilities of churches and community groups to register voters, proof of citizenship, government issued photo identifications, reductions in early voting, and new restrictions (in Iowa and Florida) on felony voting. The photo identification laws were believed to be particularly onerous since 25 percent of blacks compared to 8 percent of whites lacked government-issued photo identifications. Some of these restrictive laws were blocked by courts, and the Obama campaign deployed resources to cope with them. Nevertheless, they were widely publicized and attacked by civil rights leaders as a "war on the black vote" and a new form of Jim Crow (Walton and Smith 2014, 188).

The attempts at suppressing the Black vote might have had the unintended consequences of incensing Blacks and spurring them to mobilize. In response to voter suppression efforts, the NAACP launched its "This Is My Vote!" campaign in 2012. This nation-wide campaign registered approximately 375,000 new voters and mobilized over 1.2 million voters for the 2012 election (NAACP 2013).

Second, the Obama campaign took a more aggressive approach to mobilizing its base of supporters in 2012 than it did in 2008. In February 2012, President Obama launched "African-Americans for Obama" as part of his targeted outreach to individual voting blocs (Liasson 2012). Featured on the African-Americans for Obama website was the President's proposed plan for lifting Blacks out of poverty, financially supporting minority-owned businesses, and providing tax credits for African-American families. The campaign also focused on volunteer recruitment, voter registration, and voter turnout by targeting historically Black institutions such as HBCUs and Black civic organizations (Dwyer 2012). This microtargeting of Black voters was particularly successful in battleground states. In Ohio, where the Black vote was crucial, the share of the Black vote increased from 11 to 15 percent between 2008 and 2012 (Walton and Smith 2014).

Finally, Blacks may have been motivated by a "rally around the brother" sentiment in response to unrelenting attacks from Congressional Republicans (Walton and Smith 2014). As Skocpol and Jacobs (2012) explain, "At the elite level, Republican congressional leaders attuned to a dispirited, heavily white-southern voter base – and goosed on by flamboyant right-wing media commentators – decided from the start of Obama's presidency on all-out opposition" (13). Republican legislators in both houses of Congress employed every delaying and obstructionist tactic possible to prevent the President's policy agenda from progressing, with hopes of ensuring Obama would only be a one-term president (Skocpol and Jacobs 2012). The attacks against the incumbent president were not limited to members of Congress. In 2011, perennial Republican presidential nominee hopeful, Donald Trump, questioned President Obama's American citizenship and demanded that the President publicly release his certification of live birth, as well as his long form birth certificate. Once the documents were released, Trump questioned their authenticity until their validity could be tested. In November 2012,

Trump once again attacked President Obama, this time questioning his academic integrity and demanding the release of his undergraduate and law school transcripts (Hughey and Parks 2014).

To examine how this affected voter turnout among Black conservatives in 2012, the American National Election Studies 2012 Time Series Study (ANES) was employed. The 2012 ANES featured both face-to-face and internet samples. The total sample size was 5,914 (2,054 face-to-face and 3,860 online), including 1,016 Blacks (ANES 2012). For these analyses, only the Black respondents were used. As in the 2010 PMES, respondents were asked if they recalled voting in the November general elections. (See the Appendix for exact question wording and methodological details of the 2012 ANES.) In the 2012 ANES sample, 82.9 percent of Black respondents report voting in the November election. When looking at voter turnout by ideological self-identification, we see once again that Black liberals were more likely to vote than Black conservatives. This difference between the two, however, was not as big in 2012 as it was in 2008. Among Black liberals, self-reported voter turnout was 86.4 percent; among Black conservatives, turnout was 79.1 percent.

Once again, a logistic regression model was run in order to test whether racial group consciousness had a moderating effect on the expression of Blacks' ideological self-identification.[4] Figure 6.2 presents the differences in the predicted probability of not voting among Black conservatives at various levels of group consciousness, along with their respective 90 percent confidence intervals. Substantively, there was a considerable difference between Afrocentric conservatives and Black conservatives with low group consciousness. Among Afrocentric conservatives, the probability of not voting in 2012 was 0.08. For Black conservatives with low racial consciousness, the probability of not voting in the same election was 0.36. Although these differences were not statistically significant, they are identical to those found in the 2010 sample. In both presidential elections, it appears as if Black conservatives with low group consciousness were less motivated to vote.

To sum, Blacks responded to mobilization efforts in 2008 and 2012 by turning out in record numbers to vote for the nation's first African-American president. Taken together, however, the results from the 2010 PMES and 2012 ANES suggest that not all Blacks were equally motivated to cast ballots. Conservatives with low group consciousness,

---

[4] The results of this estimate are presented in Table A6.1 in the Appendix.

who neither shared a common ideology with Obama nor an affinity for the race, were less likely to vote. In contrast, Afrocentric conservatives may not have shared Obama's policy positions but were nevertheless inspired by seeing a co-ethnic on the ballot. These results should be interpreted with caution as neither of the effects in the two election years were statistically significant.

PRESIDENTIAL JOB APPROVAL

Another area worth examining is Barack Obama's presidential approval ratings. Presidential approval ratings are a widely accepted means of gauging the public's evaluation of the presidency:

For the office of president, they outline the parameters for governing-the institutional constraints affecting all presidents and the areas of discretion within which they can work. At the level of practical advice, they recommend to presidents the kind of activity most likely to bring public support (Brace and Hinckley 1991, 994).

Figure 6.3 presents President Obama's approval ratings by race for his first term in office. One of the most defining characteristics of President Obama's presidential approval has been the stark differences between Black and White evaluations of his performance. Since President Obama took office in January 2009, the average difference between Black and White presidential approval during his first term was 48 percentage points. At its lowest, this gap was 23 percentage points during his first month in office. As illustrated in Figure 6.3, Obama benefited from 63 percent approval among Whites and 86 percent among Blacks during this time. While Black approval would average 88.7 percent over the first half of his administration, Obama's approval among Whites would never again reach the heights experienced during the honeymoon phase of his presidency. To be sure, Obama's average approval ratings among Whites between 2009 and 2012 were 40.6 percent. At their lowest, Obama's approval ratings among Whites dipped to 31 percent several times between 2009 and 2012. The lowest Blacks' approval ratings reached during the same period was in late 2011 and again in early 2012 when Obama's Black approval was 79 percent. His highest approval among Blacks was during 2009, when they reached 96 percent.

Even when compared to approval ratings of other Democratic presidents, the gap between Blacks and Whites is incredibly large. Abrajano and Burnett (2012) compared the racial gap in Clinton and Obama's

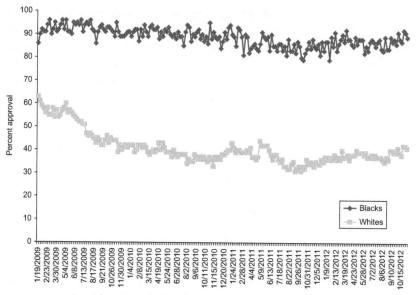

FIGURE 6.3 President Barack H. Obama's weekly job approval ratings, by race
Source: Gallup Presidential Job Approval.

approval ratings during both presidents' first 29 months in office. They found that, on average, Black approval was 21.9 percentage points higher than White approval for President Clinton. For President Obama, the difference between Blacks and Whites was 39.7 percentage points. A closer examination of each president's approval ratings revealed that the observed difference was due to Blacks' higher approval of Obama. Among Whites, Clinton received an average approval rating of 42.9 percent, while Obama's approval rating was 44.3 percent. In contrast, Obama benefited from an average approval rating of 92.7 percent among Blacks, compared to Clinton, whose average approval rating among Blacks was 68.3 percent (Abrajano and Burnett 2012).

By using the 2010 PMES and the 2012 ANES, we are able to take a more in-depth look at presidential approval among Blacks. In both sample years, respondents were asked whether they approved or disapproved of the way President Obama was handling his job as president. (See the Appendix for exact question wording.) Respondents in 2010 were given five response options, ranging from strongly disapprove (0) to strongly approve (1); in 2012, there were four response options ranging from strongly disapprove (0) to approve (1). In the 2010 sample, 72.3 percent of Blacks approved[5] of Obama's handling of his job. If we further delineate this by ideological self-identification, we see that presidential approval was 10 percentage points lower among Black conservatives. Indeed, 80.9 percent of Black liberals approved of Obama, compared to 70.7 of Black conservatives.

Based on OLS estimates, which estimated the joint effect of ideological self-identification and group consciousness on presidential approval, Figure 6.4 presents predicted presidential approval among Black conservatives.[6] Specifically, Figure 6.4 examines whether group consciousness could explain Black conservatives' lower approval of President Obama's job performance. Among Afrocentric conservatives, Obama's job approval was 77 percent. His approval among those Black conservatives with low group consciousness was 68 percent. This 9 percentage point difference was not statistically significant ($p < 0.10$), suggesting that, at least in 2010, group consciousness did not provide a dividing line between Afrocentric conservatives and other conservatives.

As a point of comparison, Obama's approval ratings in 2012 among Black conservatives were also examined. The first notable difference between 2010 and 2012 was that Obama's overall approval ratings among Blacks were much higher in 2012 during his reelection bid than they were during the midterm (92.9, compared to 72.3). Among Black liberals in the 2012 sample, Obama's presidential approval was an astounding 96.9 percent. His approval among Black conservatives was 88.7, 8 percentage points lower.

Using an OLS model, the joint effect of ideological self-identification and group consciousness on presidential approval.[7] Based on these estimates, Figure 6.4 presents predicted presidential approval among Black conservatives. The results suggest that group consciousness played a more important role in determining Obama's presidential approval in 2012 than it did in 2010. When Black conservatives had high levels of racial consciousness, their predicted approval of Obama's job performance was 94.5 percent. As Figure 6.4 indicates, Obama's presidential approval dropped to 80.0 among Black conservatives with low group consciousness, a statistically insignificant difference of 15.4 percentage

[5] Included in this group are those respondents who indicated that they either approved or strongly approved of President Obama's handling of his job.

[6] All of the predicted values in this section were calculated using the margins command in Stata by holding categorical and continuous variables constant at their means and dichotomous variables constant at their modes.

[7] The results of this estimate are presented in Table A6.2 in the Appendix.

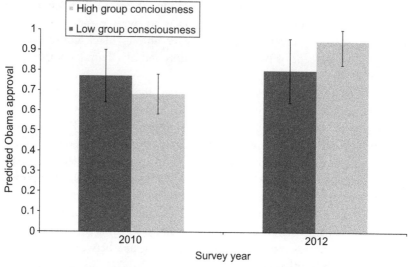

FIGURE 6.4 Predicted Obama approval ratings among Black conservatives
Note: Bars represent the predicted point estimates of Obama's approval ratings, with 90 percent confidence intervals. Values are based on weighted OLS estimates (see Table 6.2 in the Appendix). Presidential approval is coded from 0 (strongly disapprove) to 1 (strongly approve). Group consciousness is coded from 0 (low group consciousness) to 1 (high group consciousness). Conservatives include those who are slightly conservative, conservative, and extremely conservative.
Source: 2010 Post-Midterm Election Study and 2012 American National Election Study.

points, however. Although not presented, it is also important to note that a similar moderating effect did not occur among Black liberals. President Obama's predicted presidential approval was equally as high among Black liberals with low and high levels of group consciousness (0.97 and 0.94, respectively) and the difference between the two groups was not statistically significant.

Why was there such a difference between 2010 and 2012? President Obama's approval ratings throughout his presidency have remained high among African Americans, especially compared to his approval ratings among Whites. During the mid-term elections in 2010, when Obama experienced an overall downward trend nationally in his approval rating, however, Black conservatives were also less likely to approve of Obama's job performance. Regardless of levels of group consciousness, Black conservatives were more likely than Black liberals to disapprove of how President Obama was handling his job as president. In the 2010 PMES sample, 5.6 percent of Black liberals disapproved of Obama, compared to

14.7 percent among Black conservatives. If Obama's support among Blacks is partly driven by a "rally around the brother" effect, then it makes sense that his support would wane during a period when he was not up for re-election and the threat against him was comparatively lower. During this time, group consciousness would not be activated, and the division between Afrocentric conservatives and those conservatives with low group consciousness would be minimal.

During the 2012 election, when President Obama was in direct competition with his electoral opponents, group consciousness became salient to political evaluations. Here is where we see clear differences between high and low group consciousness Black conservatives. While Black conservatives gave President Obama the lowest approval ratings he experienced among Blacks, Afrocentric conservatives' evaluations of him were on par with that of Black liberals.

EVALUATIONS OF THE OPPOSITION

Finally, the evaluations of those figures that serve as the antithesis of Obama were examined. An interesting finding in contemporary politics has been a "spillover of racialization" effect caused by the presence of the nation's first Black president. Not only has President Obama, as a figure, become racialized, but so have ostensibly non-racial policies that are seen to be connected to him (Tesler 2012). Further, the spillover of racialization carries over to people. For instance, in response to Obama's candidacy in 2008, Tessler and Sears found that, "public responses to people and policies strongly associated with Obama, whether situated in opposition or accordance with him, were also more polarized by racial attitudes than they had been before the election year" (Tesler and Sears 2010, 7).

To examine whether a spillover of racialization occurred among Black conservatives, the evaluations of three Republican figures were analyzed. The first of these was 2008 Republican Vice-Presidential nominee Sarah Palin. Sarah Palin, then Governor of Alaska, became the first female Republican vice-presidential candidate when her name was placed on the ticket in 2008. In contrast to Obama, Palin was a social conservative.

Furthermore, Palin's own small-town roots may also have served as a means to connect the GOP ticket to those voters who may have felt slighted by the comments made by Obama in the Democratic primaries when he referred to small-town Americans as "bitter" people who cling to their guns and religion (Knuckey 2012, 276).

Palin was arguably one of the most notable (and perhaps most polarizing) vice-presidential candidates in recent history; Knuckey (2012) found that 34 percent of respondents in the 2008 ANES felt cold toward Palin on a feeling thermometer, which was much higher than the median level for all other vice-presidential candidates. Only two other vice-presidential candidates – Dan Quayle and Dick Cheney – had received such cold evaluations. Furthermore, Knuckey also found that evaluations of Sarah Palin in 2008 had a larger effect on vote choice than any other vice-presidential candidate had on their respective elections since 1980.

Using the 2010 PMES, we can examine Palin's evaluations among Blacks. On a feeling thermometer scaled from zero to one, where zero represents coldest feelings and one represents warmest feelings (see the Appendix for exact question wording), Blacks place Palin at 0.25. Breaking this down further by ideology, we see that Black conservatives had slightly warmer evaluations of Palin. Their placement of her on a feeling thermometer was 0.34, compared to Black liberals who placed her at 0.22.

In order to examine feelings towards Sarah Palin as a function of the joint relationship between ideology and group consciousness, an OLS model was run.[8] Based on these estimates, Figure 6.5 presents Sarah Palin's predicted feeling thermometer scores among Black conservatives.[9] As with Black liberals, Palin's predicted feeling thermometer placement among Afrocentric conservatives is 0.23. Those Black conservatives with low racial consciousness place Sarah Palin higher on the feeling thermometer measure at 0.46, which is almost at the neutral mark. The difference between high and low group consciousness Black conservatives fails to meet conventional levels of statistical significance ($p < 0.10$).

The second Republican figure examined was George W. Bush. As the two-term incumbent president in 2008, President Bush was not in direct political competition with Obama. Nevertheless, Bush evaluations had an impact on the 2008 election because a "sitting president is his party's most prominent public face, and his performance in office inevitably colors popular attitudes toward the party, affecting its image and attractiveness as an object of individual identification" (Jacobson 2009, 7).

---

[8] The results of this estimate are presented in Table A6.3 in the Appendix.

[9] All of the predicted values in this section were calculated using the margins command in Stata by holding categorical and continuous variables constant at their means and dichotomous variables constant at their modes.

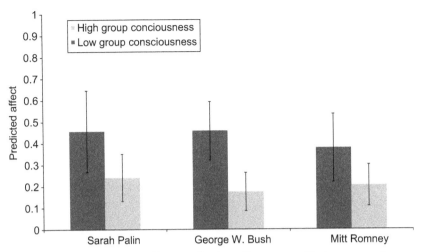

FIGURE 6.5 Predicted Republican politician affect among Black conservatives
Note: Bars represent the predicted point estimates of Republican politician's feeling thermometer scores, with 90 percent confidence intervals. Values are based on weighted OLS estimates (see Table 6.3 in the Appendix). Affect is coded from 0 (very cold) to 1 (very warm). Group consciousness is coded from 0 (low group consciousness) to 1 (high group consciousness). Conservatives include those who are slightly conservative, conservative, and extremely conservative.
Source: 2010 Post-Midterm Election Study and 2012 American National Election Study.

Thus, President Obama's candidacy represented change, whereas George W. Bush represented more of the same.

By the time the 2008 election rolled around, more of the same was not a good thing. In November 2008, President Bush's presidential approval was 28 percent. At year's end, Bush's job approval was averaging around 29 percent, with 34 percent of Whites approving of his job performance and just 7 percent of Blacks giving him job approval (Jones 2009).

Four years later, the 2012 ANES allows us to examine Bush evaluations among Blacks as measured by a feeling thermometer. On a scale from zero to one, Blacks place Bush at 0.25, indicating very cold feelings towards the former president. At first glance, there does not seem to be much difference between Black liberals and Black conservatives. Black liberals' mean placement of President Bush on a feeling thermometer was 0.22, while Black conservatives placed him at 0.29.

A more interesting difference emerges when we examine Bush's evaluations by ideology and group consciousness. Based on an OLS model that examined feelings towards George W. Bush as a function of the joint relationship between ideology and group consciousness[10], Figure 6.5 presents predicted feeling thermometer scores among Black conservatives. As we can see in Figure 6.5, Black conservatives with high group consciousness were as cool towards Bush as their liberal counterparts. Their predicted placement of President Bush on the feeling thermometer measure was 0.17. In contrast, Black conservatives with low group conscious placed Bush at 0.46. Further, this 29 percentage point difference was statistically significant at the $p < 0.10$ level.

Lastly, evaluations of Mitt Romney – President Obama's opponent during his bid for reelection in 2012 – are examined. As Sabato (2013) explains, although Romney had been a relative moderate while Governor of Massachusetts, he was forced to take a strong, conservative stance on issues like immigration and abortion during the Republican primaries and caucuses in order to win the Party's nomination. Once Romney secured his party's nomination, his advisors had planned to reshape his image back into the pro-choice moderate he had been during the 1990s. This did not happen, however, because of pushback from the more conservative Republican Party leadership (Sabato 2013).

Although Romney made an effort to reach out to them, the push to the far right put off many minority voters. During his speech delivered at the NAACP's national convention in Houston, TX in 2012, Romney asked Black voters to give him a chance. He highlighted his family's civil rights legacy and suggested that his policies were better for families of color than President Obama's. When Romney voiced his criticism of Obamacare and stated that President Obama's policies were doing nothing to create jobs, however, he received a round of loud boos and hisses from the audience (Rucker 2012). According to one source, Romney's speech at the NAACP's convention "received the most hostile reaction from any campaign audience" during that year (Rucker 2012). On Election Day, Mitt Romney received just 6 percent of the Black vote (Sabato 2013). This is only slightly more than the 4 percent of the Black vote that McCain received in 2008, but still lower than the roughly 10 percent of the Black vote that Republican presidential candidates had garnered in previous elections (Walton and Smith 2014). Undoubtedly, the increased Democratic share of the African-American vote is a consequence of a Black presidential candidate.

To get a sense of how Blacks evaluated Mitt Romney beyond their electoral choices, I again used the 2012 ANES. On average, Blacks placed

---

[10] The results of this estimate are presented in Table A6.3 in the Appendix.

Romney at 0.27 on a feeling thermometer. As was the case with Bush's evaluations, there was not much difference between Black liberals and Black conservatives in terms of where they placed Romney on the feeling thermometer scale. Both groups felt particularly cool towards Romney, with Black liberals placing him at 0.25 and Black conservatives placing him at 0.29.

Figure 6.5 presents Mitt Romney's predicted feeling thermometer scores among Black conservatives. These values were derived by estimating the joint relationship between ideology and group consciousness, using an OLS model.[11] As Figure 6.5 indicates, there was a stark contrast between Afrocentric conservatives and Black conservatives with low group consciousness. The predicted feeling thermometer score for Mitt Romney among Afrocentric conservatives was 0.20. Among low group consciousness Black conservatives, his predicted placement on the feeling thermometer was 0.38. This difference of 18 percentage points, however, was not statistically significant ($p < 0.10$).

In summary, the magnitude of the effects across all three politicians is the same, even though not all of the effects reach conventional levels of statistical significance. Based on the consistency of these findings, it would appear that group consciousness moderates the relationship between ideological self-identification and public figures. When it came to GOP figures, Black support for the three Republican politicians examined never reaches beyond 0.50, which is the neutral point on the feeling thermometer. These results do illustrate, however, under what circumstances Blacks start to "warm up" to Republicans running for national office. Sharing a common ideology is not enough to move Black conservatives towards Republican politicians. It is only when African Americans lack a sense of racial group oneness that GOP candidates and elected officials become more appealing.

CONCLUSION

The results presented in Chapter 6 demonstrate that racial considerations mitigate the expression of ideological self-identification beyond party identification. To be sure, group consciousness moderates ideology's effect on voting behavior, presidential approval, and political evaluations.

---

[11] The results of this estimate are presented in Table A6.3 in the Appendix.

For instance, high group consciousness helps explains why some Black conservatives were equally as excited about a Democratic presidential candidate as Black liberals. Self-reported voter turnout was as high among Afrocentric Black conservatives as it was among Black liberals. In contrast, Black conservatives with low group consciousness had a higher likelihood of staying home on Election Day.

Furthermore, throughout his tenure in office, President Obama received unparalleled presidential approval from African Americans. This was true regardless of how Blacks identified themselves on the liberal-conservative continuum. The exception was Black conservatives with low group consciousness. Although low group consciousness Black conservatives' evaluations of the Obama presidency were never as low as that of Whites, there was a considerable difference between them and other Blacks. Not even liberals with low levels of group consciousness deviated from the group when it came to evaluations of President Obama.

With respect to public figures, the results suggested that Afrocentric Black conservatives had similar preferences as liberals. Overall, Blacks do not have favorable evaluations of Republican politicians. On average, Blacks placed the three figures examined – Sarah Palin, George W. Bush, and Mitt Romney – about quarter of the way up on a scale that ran from zero to one. Black conservatives with low group consciousness, however, had slightly more neutral evaluations of these politicians.

What does this mean for the future of African Americans and the Republican Party? The findings in Chapter 6 certainly would allow the GOP to be more hopeful than if we only looked at partisanship as our dependent variable. Using a multitude of measures, we can see that there is quite a bit of heterogeneity among Blacks' reactions to the political environment, even when a co-ethnic presides in the Oval Office. This suggests that Black support for one party over another is not completely and permanently fixed in contemporary American politics. Specifically, Black conservatives who lack group consciousness are those who will be most open to Republican candidates and GOP political appeals. Nevertheless, there are two important points that the Republican Party needs to consider when developing a strategy to attract African American voters. First, there are only a small number of Black conservatives with low levels of group consciousness. Appealing solely to this group will only bring about limited headway into the African-American electorate. Second, as General Colin Powell cautions in the introduction to this chapter, without modifying its reputation on race, the GOP risks alienating Black conservatives with moderate to high levels of group consciousness who had once identified with the Party. There are a number of Black Republicans who have grown disenchanted with the Party over recent years precisely because of its position on race (see Weiner 2015). The prevalence of group consciousness among Blacks, including Black conservatives, does not appear to be declining. Unless the GOP can adjust to the shifting demographics in the American electorate, it is unlikely that the Democratic Black voting bloc will break up any time soon.

7

African Americans, Ideology, and Consequences for the Two-Party System

> We seldom study the condition of the Negro to-day honestly and carefully.
> It is so much easier to assume that we know it all. Or perhaps, having
> already reached conclusions in our own minds, we are loth to have them
> disturbed by facts.
>
> – W.E.B. DuBois

One of the basic tenets of representative democracy rests on the premise that citizens are presented with choices when selecting political leaders. As Ranney explains, "popular control over government which is the essence of democracy can best be established by the popular choice between and control over alternate responsible parties; for only such parties can provide coherent, unified sets of rulers who will assume collective responsibility to the people for the manner in which government is carried on" (Ranney 1962, 12). In the United States, voters are usually offered a dichotomous choice between the Democratic and Republican Parties. Although some scholars and political elites argue that the two-party system in which we function is less than democratic (e.g., Guinier 1994), few would disagree that some choice is better than none at all.

Yet, throughout history, African Americans have essentially operated in a one-party system (Gurin et al., 1989; Walton and Smith 2003; Frymer 1999).

A review of the history of party politics from the perspectives of black leaders and the black electorate finds that parties have always treated blacks as pawns in their bids for electoral power. As such, blacks have been used tactically, and their interests often were sacrificed. Indeed, even their status as pawns has been tenuous. At any time, only one party ... has come even close to representing their interests, and that party often shunned them. More often than not, the opposing party attempted to remove blacks from the game completely, through disenfran-chisement. Black leaders have persistently searched for strategies to use in their attempts to gain greater influence in party politics; they have worried about dependency on a single party; and they have advocated independence when they believed it would enhance the group's political effectiveness (Gurin et al., 1989, 4).

Early in the dawn of our republic, African-Americans' political loyal-ties rested exclusively with the Republican Party, while the Democratic Party was the party of White supremacy, disenfranchisement, and forced segregation (Walton and Smith 2014). For a brief period between 1936 and 1964, Blacks operated in a two-party system. At the national level, Blacks voted for Democratic President Franklin D. Roosevelt and became part of his New Deal Coalition. Black partisanship, however, lagged behind Black presidential voting behavior as many Blacks split their ticket by voting for Roosevelt in the 1936 election but voted for Republican mayoral, senatorial, and gubernatorial candidates between 1937 and 1939 (Weiss 1983). African Americans would then suspended support for Democratic presidential candidates when they voted for Dwight Eisenhower, who along with a Republican-led Supreme Court, enforced school desegregation (Philpot 2007). Nevertheless, by 1964 the New Deal Coalition would collapse as southern segregationists left the Democratic Party in support of Republican presidential candidate Barry Goldwater's advocacy of states' rights – a thinly veiled euphemism for continued segregation (Aistrup 1996). With the Republican Party no longer a realistic alternative as a result of these shifts in alliances, Blacks have all but exclusively backed the Democratic Party and its candidates (see Chapter 1 for empirical evidence to support this claim).

Blacks' confinement to a one-party system becomes even more prob-lematic once their ideological self-identification is taken into account. As was illustrated in the introduction to this book, a growing number of African Americans have been self-identifying as conservative. Further-more, the correlation between Blacks' party identification and ideological self-identification is lower than that of other racial groups. This is par-ticularly noteworthy in a time when the overall American electorate's party identification and ideology has become increasingly more aligned. This suggests that at least part of the Black electorate is captured by a party that is not representative of their ideological ideals.

Blacks constitute a significant and distinctive subgroup of the Ameri-can electorate, in terms of both size and behavior. No other group in the United States votes as cohesively during presidential elections as African Americans. Yet, the variance in Blacks' education levels, income, geographic location, and political attitudes continues to increase. Why does a group facing greater heterogeneity along a number of dimensions still vote as a Democratic bloc when their socioeconomic characteristics suggest that a larger proportion of them should be voting Republican? I believe the answer to this question lies in the complexity and distinctiveness in Black opinion that are often concealed, particularly since on Election Day public opinion effectively gets reduced to a series of dichotomous choices. The basis of these choices is rarely dissected. When we take a closer look at Black ideology, however, we find considerable variance. Kilson argues that "while conservatism has made major in-roads among White ethnic voter blocs since the 1972 presidential election – Italians, Jews, Poles – its success among Black American voters has been distinctly limited" (Kilson 1993, 4). I respectfully disagree with Kilson's argument. While the number of Black conservatives as we traditionally think of them remains limited, conservative thinking permeates multiple domains of Black ideology. The difference is that conservatism among Blacks does not necessarily translate into Republican identification.

Because of the lack of variance in African-American partisanship, American politics scholars have largely ignored the heterogeneity in the policy attitudes or ideological preferences of African Americans. Models of Black partisanship and voting behavior assume race is all that is needed to explain Blacks' attachment to political parties. Rarely considered is whether there is congruence between Blacks' partisanship and their ideological ideals. Consequently, the extent to which Blacks are truly underrepresented in the American political system is underestimated.

Conservative but Not Republican has sought to fill this void by examining the factors that influence both the predictors of Black ideology and the applicability of ideology to Blacks' partisan evaluations. The central argument guiding this endeavor is that the correlation between Black party identification and Black ideology is a function of two phenomena. First, Blacks have developed a multidimensional and hierarchical conceptualization of the liberal–conservative continuum, which has grown out of their distinct position in American society. Blacks' conceptualization of the liberal–conservative continuum does not neatly overlap with that of the general electorate, causing a weaker correlation between Blacks' party identification and ideological self-identification than observed among other racial groups. Second, the expression of Blacks' ideology is conditional on their level of group consciousness – the lower Blacks' levels of group consciousness, the more likely they are to deviate from their Democratic Party identification.

Conservative but Not Republican explores the ways citizens make sense of ideological labels. I argue that we cannot fully understand the relationship between Blacks' ideology and party identification unless we take into account the mix of considerations – including Blacks' attitudes about religious, social welfare, racial, military, and moral issues – used to determine whether African Americans will ultimately label themselves as liberal or conservative. Furthermore, we must also consider how racial considerations can often supplant the expression Blacks' ideology when it comes to choosing with which political party to identify. Recognizing the unique conceptualization and conditional applicability of the liberal–conservative continuum offers a more comprehensive understanding of the structure and function of ideology in American public opinion.

A highlight of this book has been its use of a bevy of different data sources to test its thesis. The evidence presented in *Conservative but Not Republican* came from quantitative analysis of the American National Election Studies, as well as two original surveys – the 2010 Post-Midterm Election Study (PMES) and the 2012 Religious Worldview Study (RWS). Both the PMES and the RWS featured sizable representative national samples of both Blacks and Whites, which allowed for interracial comparisons when necessary. To augment the quantitative analyses, this book also featured original qualitative data collected from over 80 semi-structured in-depth interviews, which were designed to provide a more detailed illustration of the nature of individuals' descriptions of ideological labels. Finally, a content analysis was conducted of 1,600 *New York Times* articles over a 150-year period and 679 *New York Amsterdam News* articles over an 80-year period in order to examine how ideological labels have been used in elite discourse.

These data have revealed a number of key empirical findings consistent with the book's thesis. First, the use of ideological labels has become more specialized over time, with the use of the terms *liberal* and *conservative* in elite discourse growing increasingly more policy-specific. In addition to using ideological labels to describe the general nature of government and politics, these labels are often being used to describe politics in particular issue areas. Blacks are especially likely to associate ideological labels with social welfare, religious, and moral issues.

Second, by operationalizing these policy-specific ideological domains, we can see that Blacks are not uniformly liberal. While Blacks are significantly more liberal than Whites when it comes to racial, social welfare, and military issues, there are no meaningful differences (statistically or substantively) between the two racial groups on moral issues.

Furthermore, Blacks' mean placement on military and moral issues indicated that they are fairly moderate in these areas. Finally, Blacks were significantly more conservative than Whites on religious issues.

Another key finding revealed by this investigative inquiry is that not all policy-specific ideological domains are applicable to Blacks' conceptualization of their ideological self-identification. Salient to Blacks' ideological self-identification are the religious and social welfare issue areas. As Blacks become more conservative on religious and social welfare issues, they become more likely to self-identify as conservative. To a lesser extent, the military dimension was also a predictor of Black ideological self-identification. As Blacks become more conservative on military issues, however, they become *less* likely to identify as conservative, a finding seemingly counterintuitive unless one considers the historic relationship between Blacks and the military (see Chapter 2). Note two important follow-up points to these findings. First, accounting for political sophistication does not alter the results. That is, political sophisticates use mostly the same constructs as non-political sophisticates when determining their ideological self-identification.[1] Second, a parallel analysis of Whites indicates that Blacks have a unique conceptualization of their ideological self-identification which is not explained by levels of political sophistication and may account for the idiosyncratic relationship between Black ideology and party identification.

Adding to the observed idiosyncratic relationship between Blacks' ideology and party identification is the role group consciousness plays in mitigating the expression of ideological self-identification. When group consciousness is high, Blacks' identification with the Democratic Party is nearly unanimous, regardless of ideological self-identification. Blacks with low group consciousness are more likely to show less support for the Democratic Party and are more likely to identify as Independent. Support for the Republican Party remains tenuous, even among Black conservatives with low group consciousness.

By building upon extant theories spanning across several fields – including political psychology, public opinion, and voting behavior – in order to develop a theoretical framework for understanding why and to what extent African Americans conceptualize the liberal–conservative continuum differently, *Conservative but Not Republican* has implications

---

[1] The one exception is that political sophisticates are significantly more likely to use the moral dimension in determining their ideological self-identification.

that extend beyond Black Politics. Indeed, the debate over whether individuals have enough information to adequately participate in politics is on-going (Lupia and McCubbins 1998; Jackson and Marcus 1975; Delli Carpini and Keeter 1996; Luskin 1990; Hayes and Guardino 2011; Kam 2005; Berelson 1952). And at the heart of this debate lies the question of how widespread is the capacity to think along ideological lines (Federico and Hunt 2013; Converse 1964; Sullivan, Piereson, and Marcus 1978; Ansolabehere et al., 2008).

As the behavioral revolution in political science ushered in new ways of understanding the relationship between citizens and the political environment, the democratic competency of the American voter was almost immediately called into question. In particular, it was argued that ideological constraint demonstrated ones capacity for understanding political phenomena.

The proper functioning of a democratic system presupposes that members of the polity can act in a rational self-interested manner. For this reason, the concept of ideological constraint can play an important part in most theories on democratic behavior. Here, the concept of ideological constraint refers to the existence of psychological and logical pressures upon an individual to react consistently to political decision-making situations responding to political stimuli in a way consistent with his perceived interest (Jackson and Marcus 1975, 93).

Only a tiny fraction of Americans, however, met the qualifications needed to be characterized as ideologues. Moreover, citizens' reliance on alternative constructs (e.g., group interests, nature of the times, etc.) to make political decisions were thought to somehow undermine democracy and, therefore, thought to be cause for concern (Converse 1964).

Since this initial bleak outlook on America's democratic prospects, scholars have reevaluated the extent to which citizens are prepared to make political decisions, concluding that the fate of U.S. democracy was not nearly as grim. For one thing, there is evidence to suggest that levels of ideological constraint are not as low as originally thought. For instance, Nie and Anderson (1974) argue that Converse's findings, which relied on data from the 1950s, were time-bound because the political upheavals of the 1960s and 70s changed the way Americans fundamentally interpreted politics. Looking at a number of domestic and foreign policy issues featured repeatedly on surveys between 1956 and 1972, they confirmed the lack of internal attitudinal consistency in 1956 but also demonstrated an increase in issue constraint in the 16 years following. Likewise, in an examination of candidate preference, Radcliff (1993) found that a sizable majority of respondents in the 1972 to 1984 American National

Election Studies structured their presidential candidate preferences along a left-right ideological dimension.

Aside from exploring whether citizens possessed the necessary levels of ideological constraint required to adequately participate in politics, scholars have also questioned whether being an ideologue was even essential for properly functioning in democracy:

> To appreciate the tenuous linkage between adroit decisionmaking and democratic survival, imagine the worst-case election scenario. That is, hapless voters tossed coins, sold their votes, or otherwise decided in ways contravening any known reasonableness criteria. The upshot might then be such "calamities" as popular referenda being accidentally defeated, out-of-touch candidates put in office, and, assuredly, postelection bewilderment among TV network commentators. These inept choices resulted in inferior, disliked policies. But, and this is absolutely critical, would these elections be inherently undemocratic? Assuredly not. In fact, if postelection survey probes into voter skill were never executed, this ineptitude would pass entirely unnoticed. Surely we cannot stipulate that poll's postmortem necessarily certifies "democracy." Would these elections be more democratic if everyone voted brilliantly but, as is commonplace elsewhere, violence marred the balloting and disgruntled losers pursued armed insurrection instead (Weissberg 2001, 264)?

In an examination of public support for ballot referenda, Lupia (1994) finds evidence to support this argument. Specifically, Lupia found that relatively uninformed voters were able to glean enough information from information shortcuts to emulate the political decisions of their more informed counterparts. In thinking about ideological constraint, Lupia's study suggests that – even in the absence of the ability to articulate issue constraint– people are still able to make decisions that serve in their best interest.

Conservative but Not Republican offers additional considerations for the discussion of citizens' readiness to function in democracy. First, this book argues for an expanded notion of what is meant by "ideological constraint." By the strictest definition, ideological constraint denotes an individual's ability to exhibit internal consistency across all issue positions, which ultimately signifies an underlying belief system (Converse 1964). Since the advent of micro level studies of ideology, the ideal nature, structure, and content of belief systems have been informed by the dominant culture and superimposed by the researcher. Not only has there been little room for the possibility of belief structures that have developed organically out of subcultures in American society (Dawson 2001; Harris-Lacewell 2004), left unexplored has been how the content of mainstream belief structures, such as the liberal–conservative continuum, varies across systematically across subcultures.

The current project speaks to the latter omission. As discussed in Chapter 2, the prevailing assumption is that a small group of elites have pre-packaged various issues and disseminated them to the masses as a cohesive belief system. As researchers, we often examine the extent to which public opinion reflects these pre-packaged ideas. In the absence of cohesive elements, as so determined by this small group of elites, researchers conclude that public opinion lacks a cohesive belief system.

What this project demonstrates, however, is that there exists alternative packaging of these elements. Whether the packaging comes from indigenous elites or grassroots discussions, there are subgroups among the American populace that otherwise arrange these constructs into alternative constrained ideologies that are historically relevant to that group. From the dominant gaze, individuals belonging to these subgroups lack the cohesion exemplified by the general electorate. To be sure, without a grounded understanding of the relationship between these groups and the political system, unconventional patterns of ideological constraint among subgroups are unobservable. Alternatively, *Conservative but Not Republican* has examined how racial groups can have nuanced understandings of the liberal–conservative continuum, which serve as the basis of their belief systems. These nuanced interpretations of *liberal* and *conservative* are entirely predictable given the interaction between that racial group and the U.S. government. Further, these intricacies have been overlooked by research that does not examine minority groups separately or that omits minority groups altogether.

Second, the observation that ideological self-identification does not correlate across the board with self-placement on political issues has led social scientists to conclude that citizens are either politically unsophisticated, less ideologically constrained, or just plain confused about the meaning of *liberal* and *conservative*. As a result, it has been questioned whether the average man or woman is competent enough to make decisions regarding the governance of this country (Berelson, Lazarsfeld, and McPhee 1954). *Conservative but Not Republican* presents another possibility – ideology is not just a summary judgment, but a rank ordering of all ideological referents. From this standpoint, people understand the liberal-conservative continuum and aptly identify themselves based on which dimensions are most important to them. Conceptualizing ideology as both multidimensional *and* hierarchical helps to explain some of the apparent internal inconsistency in the political ideology of the American electorate.

Finally, the theoretical framework presented in this book not only provides a template for predicting which constructs citizens will utilize when defining the liberal–conservative continuum, but also how race moderates the use of the liberal–conservative continuum for Blacks. Race continues to play an important role in the political calculus of Black Americans because of persistent political, social, and economic inequalities. Therefore, as the results presented in this book demonstrate, in addition to racial considerations by themselves affecting support for political parties, racial considerations also operate *in conjunction* with other factors such as ideology. As a consequence, Blacks vote for the Democratic Party, even when their ideology suggests that they would do otherwise.

By exploring the relationship between ideology and Black group consciousness in determining party identification, we gain a better understanding of why there are not more ideologues in the American electorate. For decades, scholars have commented on the use of group-centered considerations rather than ideological ones in the political expressions of the American public (Lane 1962; Converse 1964; Campbell et al. 1960; Lazarsfeld, Berelson, and Gaudet 1948; Berelson et al. 1954). These scholars concluded that this demonstrated a deficit in the political understanding of citizens, which undermined representative democracy. While studies have explored the use of group-based considerations at the expense of ideological considerations (Abramowitz and Saunders 2006; Green, Palmquist, and Schickler 2002), none have explored the interaction between the two. Failure to do so, I believe, has minimized the observable role of ideology in political evaluations. This project reveals that individuals are able to think along ideological lines but that group considerations restrict the expression of ideology when making political decisions. Further, the use of group-based considerations is no less rational or beneficial than the use of ideological ones given societal distinctions that continue to endure.

IMPLICATIONS FOR CONTEMPORARY BLACK POLITICS

Voter Suppression in the Twenty-First Century

In a five-to-four decision, the Supreme Court ruled in *Shelby County* v. *Holder* (2013) that Section 4 of the 1965 Voting Rights Act (VRA) was unconstitutional. Section 4 of the VRA established the formula for "preclearance" requirements detailed in Section 5, which requires states with a history of racial discrimination to "apply to the U.S. Justice Department or the U.S. District Court in Washington before making any change in their election laws or procedures" (Walton and Smith 2014, 208). Under Section 4, (1) states that had previously used tests or devices as a condition of registering or voting or (2) states with low voter registration and turnout (less than 50 percent) were subject to preclearance. The majority opinion was that this formula was unconstitutional since it was based on practices that had been eradicated decades ago. In her dissenting opinion, Justice Ruth Bader Ginsberg wrote that while the preclearance southern states "accounted for only 25 percent of the population, since 1982 56 percent of the successful race discrimination cases in voting (under Section 2 of the VRA) were from the South, nearly four times more than noncovered northern states" (Walton and Smith 2014, 264). In other words, while based on eradicated practices, this formula was still a strong predictor of where acts of voting discrimination were more likely to occur.

In the wake of *Shelby County v. Holder*, many southern states once restricted by Section 5 of the VRA began changing their voting laws almost immediately. For instance, within 24 hours of the Supreme Court's decision, five states that had previously been under preclearance – South Carolina, Texas, Mississippi, Virginia, and Alabama – moved forward with their voter identification laws, which had previously passed in their respective Republican-led state legislatures. Prior to the Supreme Court's decision, these laws were unenforceable because the states were awaiting federal approval or the laws had been blocked in federal court (Childress 2013). Texas's voter ID law, in particular, had previously been blocked by a federal court because it disproportionately affected minority voters (Cooper 2013). Since the *Shelby County v. Holder* decision, however, 41 states have introduced restrictive voting legislation, with 18 of those bills passed into law (Childress 2013).

Advocacy groups, particularly minority organizations, likened the states' actions to modern-day vote suppression.[2] The Advancement Project, which challenged North Carolina's voting restrictions on behalf of the North Carolina NAACP State Conference, issued a 2013 press release in which they stated that North Carolina's law was reminiscent of the state's "sordid Jim Crow past" (Farmer 2013). The president and director-counsel of the NAACP's Legal Defense Fund, John Payton, believed that the states' voting restriction laws were "a carefully targeted

---

[2] Three Republican leaders have admitted on record that voter ID laws were targeted attempts to prevent Blacks from casting ballots (Tobin 2012; Farmer 2013).

response to the remarkable growth of the minority electorate, and threaten[ed] to disproportionally diminish the voting strength of African-Americans and Latinos" (Nichols 2013). In 2011, when South Carolina initially passed its voter ID law, NAACP president Benjamin Todd Jealous referred to the law as "little more than a 21st Century poll tax ... While some may quibble over the intent, there is no doubt the effect of this law would disproportionately block Black South Carolinians from voting" (Lowe 2011).

In addition to the changes in voting laws being framed as attempts to suppress the Black vote, Black elites also made sure that Black voters understood that the proposed changes were directives of the Republican Party. In an article titled, "How Voter Suppression Backfired on the GOP," featured in *The Grio* (a news website primarily targeted towards African Americans), Reverend Al Sharpton — talk show host and president of the National Action Network – stated the following with respect to voter turnout in the 2012 election: "From the tours we did in 22 states, it became clear to us that many Blacks that were apathetic and indifferent became outraged and energized when they realized that [Republicans] were changing the rules in the middle of the game, in terms of voter ID laws, ending 'souls to the polls' ... So what was just another election, even though it dealt with the re-election of the first Black president, took on a new dimension when they realized that [Republicans] were implementing the disenfranchisement of Black voters" (Reid 2012). Representative John Lewis (D-GA), who has become a heroic symbol in the struggle for Black voting rights, penned an essay in 2015 entitled "The Unfinished Work of Selma." In it, he wrote, "in 2013, the Supreme Court gutted key aspects of the law. In the weeks that followed, Republicans in statehouses across the country quickly passed laws making it harder to vote ... Couched in language about 'protecting the ballot box', Republicans have pushed voter ID laws that disproportionately impact certain blocks of voters – African-Americans, women, Latinos, the poor and young people – who tend to vote against them" (Lewis 2015). Indeed, the messaging was clear: the efforts to curtail Black voting were led by Republican-controlled state legislatures in states more likely than not ran by a Republican governor.

The timing of the Republican-led voting reforms could not be more deleterious for the relationship between the GOP and Black voters. In 2015, the United States celebrated the 50th anniversary of the passage of the 1965 Voting Rights Act. Part of the celebration included commemorating the 50th anniversary of "Bloody Sunday" – the day when over

500 African-American demonstrators were met with violence from local police officials while trying to cross the Edmund Pettus Bridge on their way from Selma to Montgomery, Alabama. Attending the commemoration of "Bloody Sunday" were President Obama, Attorney General Eric Holder, and Representative John Lewis, who had been severely beaten during the demonstration 50 years ago (Basu, Shelbayah, and Brumfield 2015). The weekend of events, which included a series of speeches from notable Black leaders (including President Obama) and a recreation of the march across the Edmund Pettus Bridge, served as a reminder to African Americans that the franchise was (and still is) the cornerstone of the struggle for Black civil rights.

Also heightening the salience of the Black struggle for voting rights was the release of Ava DuVernay's (2015) *Selma*, a critically acclaimed cinematic chronicling of the march from Selma to Montgomery. In order to widen *Selma*'s audience, a movement known as "Selma for Students" provided over 275,000 free tickets to middle school-aged children to view the film in cities across the U.S. (Tuttle 2015). This effort allowed future generations of Black voters to connect with the past (albeit a Hollywood version) and gain an understanding of the importance of voting and the struggle that went with attaining suffrage rights.

The GOP-proposed franchise restrictions juxtaposed against the commemoration of the 1965 VRA likely distanced Black voters further from the Republican Party. The results presented in this book suggest that the Republican Party is most likely to attract Black conservatives for whom race is less salient. Currently, the GOP has a difficult time appealing to Black voters because there are very few for whom race is not salient. That is not to say that race is chronically salient for Blacks (see White 2007), but the Republican Party certainly does itself no favors by attacking what is arguably the greatest symbol of equality and citizenship for African Americans. In the current political climate, voting rights and race are intimately intertwined. The Republican Party's pursuit of voting restriction laws will: (1) result in Blacks associating the Party with disenfranchisement and (2) heighten the salience of race among Blacks. As a consequence, African Americans who would otherwise support the Republican Party due to shared ideological ideals will be more concerned with maintaining their fundamental right to participate in the political system. Therefore, when they are making political decisions, it is unlikely that the liberal–conservative continuum will supersede racial considerations, particularly when evaluating political parties.

Run, Ben, Run!: The GOP's Hope for the Future?

On May 4, 2015, Ben Carson announced the launching of his presidential bid in front of a cheering audience at the Music Hall Center for the Performing Arts in Detroit, Michigan. As a retired neurosurgeon, he is a Washington outsider who campaigned on an anti-politician platform. With the campaign slogan, "Heal Inspire Revive," Dr. Carson delivered a message in Detroit that was rooted in individualism and small government. He proposed reforming government to more closely mirror that envisioned by the framers of the Constitution. At the same time, Dr. Carson announced the convening of an exploratory committee that would transform government into "something that looks more like a well-run business than a behemoth of inefficiency" (Carson 2015).

While he was never the top contender for the Republican nomination, poll results from around the time he formally announced his candidacy placed Dr. Carson among the top tier of Republican candidates, averaging roughly 10 percent support among national samples of voters (Booker 2014; Jackson 2015). Furthermore, the National Draft Ben Carson Committee, a super PAC formed by John Philip Sousa IV to support Dr. Carson's candidacy, raised $13.5 million in 2014. As a point of comparison, a similar super PAC formed for Hillary Clinton's campaign raised $12.9 million in 2014 (Newman 2015). Thus, during the pre-primary season, Ben Carson was considered to be as viable of a candidate as anyone else in the race.

As the only African-American GOP presidential primary candidate, Ben Carson's nomination would have uniquely positioned him as potentially the only Republican candidate that could have competed with Hillary Clinton for the Black vote. Ben Carson has been described as the "embodiment of Black achievement," rising from an impoverished single-mother household in Detroit to become the youngest and first Black director of pediatric neurosurgery at Johns Hopkins Hospital (Samuels 2015). Dr. Carson's 1990 autobiography, *Gifted Hands: The Ben Carson Story*, has become required reading in the Black community, particularly among Black religious leaders and educators, who use the book to teach about spirituality, social mobility, and achievement (Samuels 2015). He is not only well respected in the Black community for his accomplishments, but also for his philanthropy – distributing close to $700,000 in scholarships and raising money to refurbish nearly 150 school libraries in low-income areas (Samuels 2015). And while it is unrealistic that his candidacy would be enough to draw the majority of

Black voters to the Republican Party, it is estimated that garnering just 17 percent of the Black vote would prevent any Democratic presidential candidate from winning the general election (Moody 2014).

The problem is that, in recent years, Ben Carson has taken a sharp turn to the right. To be sure, conservative ideals were present in Dr. Carson's earlier writings and speeches. Raised a Seventh-day Adventist, he is deeply religious. He is also a proponent of hard work and self-reliance. *Gifted Hands*, for instance, has religious undertones and an emphasis on individualism. But Dr. Carson garnered significant media attention in the months leading up to his run for the Republican presidential nomination for his far-right and controversial views on homosexuality and for being a vocal critic of President Obama's policies, particularly on health care and immigration (Rutenberg 2015). For example, during his speech at the Voter Values Summit in 2013, Dr. Carson criticized Obamacare for being "the worst thing that has happened in this nation since slavery" (Sullivan 2013). In a 2014 interview with conservative news outlet Breitbart, he went as far as to compare the Obama Administration to Nazi Germany in response to the Internal Revenue Service's scrutiny of conservative political organizations (Bobic 2014). Dr. Carson has been critical of the U.S. welfare system and has proposed paring it back, although not eliminating it entirely. He also indicated, in an interview on CNN, that he believed that homosexuality was a choice because some people "go into prison straight – and when they come out, they're gay" (Rutenberg 2015).

While Dr. Carson's religious and moral views have him ideologically aligned with most Blacks, he is an outlier with respect to his views on social welfare issues (see Chapter 3). Had he been the Republican presidential nominee, this could have potentially served as an obstacle to him winning Black votes, since the social welfare policy dimension is more salient in determining Blacks' ideological self-identification than the other two dimensions. In other words, despite the overlap between Dr. Carson and Black voters on religious and moral issues, there is considerable distance between them on the issues that matter most to Black political decision-making.

Furthermore, Ben Carson's attacks on President Obama have undermined his authenticity as a Black leader. As discussed in Chapter 6, President Obama has become the best-known symbolic representation of African-American success. His presidential approval among Blacks is relatively high, even among Black conservatives with low group consciousness. Thus, an attack on President Obama during his time as president is arguably the equivalent of attacking Blackness itself.

Moreover, Dr. Carson's attacks on President Obama likely activated Black voters' group consciousness, creating a "rally-around-the-brother" effect towards President Obama. At the same time, Dr. Carson became vilified for these criticisms among African Americans. As evidence, those who had previously idolized him, have expressed a lack of trust in him and have now labeled Dr. Carson a "sellout" (Timm 2015). Some Black clergy have stopped recommending *Gifted Hands* to their congregants and members of minority medical organizations have described Dr. Carson as an "embarrassment" (Samuels 2015). All of this suggests that Ben Carson would probably fall short of the 17 percent of the Black vote needed to defeat a Democratic opponent in a general presidential election, should he ever become the Republican nominee.

Federalism and the Protection of Civil Rights

As discussed in Chapters 2 and 3, the racial policy dimension was less salient among Blacks than other constructs, such as social welfare and religion. It was speculated that since the passage of the 1960s civil rights legislation, securing basic civil rights has been less of a concern among African Americans. Instead, Blacks' policy priorities have shifted to issues such as unemployment, education, and health care. While not race-specific, these areas still experience large racial disparities. Recently, however, the salience of race among Blacks has significantly increased. In December 2014, the Gallup Organization reported that 13 percent of Americans indicated that race relations and racism were the most important problems facing the country today. Not since the Los Angeles riots in 1992 that resulted from the acquittal of three of the policemen captured on videotape violently assaulting Rodney King have Americans viewed race to be this big of a problem (Berman 2014). More telling are the importance of race relations and racism by the race of respondent – 31 percent of Blacks, compared to just 8 percent of Whites believed race relations and racism to be the most important problem facing the nation (Gallup).

The heightened importance of race comes, in part, as a consequence of a series of unpunished violent killings of African Americans. Among these were the deaths of Eric Garner and Michael Brown, two unarmed Black men who each died at the hands of the police. In Eric Garner's case, a bystander captured on video Garner being put in a chokehold (which has been banned by the New York Police Department for over two decades) and wrestled to the ground by the police. The video depicts Garner uttering the words "I can't breathe" eleven times, as several police officers piled on top of him and held him down (Baker, Goodman, and Mueller 2015). Garner died as a result of that encounter, with the medical examiner ruling his death a homicide due to neck and chest compressions (Calabresi 2014). Garner's death, by itself, was enough to cause outrage; his alleged crime was selling untaxed cigarettes – a crime not fitting his punishment. Protests erupted across the country, however, when a New York grand jury decided not to indict the police officer who held Garner in a chokehold, thereby causing his death. A week earlier, a grand jury in Missouri had also failed to indict the police officer who fatally shot Michael Brown, which also spurred protests. But the video of Eric Garner's violent demise was viewed by millions of people around the world. Yet it proved to be insufficient evidence. For many African Americans, this was not only a miscarriage of justice, but a signal that there was no system of justice at all for Blacks in the United States (see e.g., Love 2014). In a poll taken shortly after the New York grand jury's decision, only 10 percent of Blacks (compared to about half of Whites) believed that African Americans and other minorities are treated equally by the criminal justice system. Similarly, 20 percent of Blacks and 60 percent of Whites were confident that police treat Blacks and Whites equally, regardless of whether they commit a crime (Balz and Clement 2014).

To the extent that any justice has been served, it has been through federal government intervention. The federal government's ability to investigate cases of racial injustice committed by state actors is authorized by Section 1983 of Title 42 of the Unites States Code, which is the codification of a section of the Civil Rights Act of 1871 (also known as the Ku Klux Klan Act) (Shapot 1965). Passed during Reconstruction, the Ku Klux Klan Act brings crimes such as murder, arson, and assault (crimes typically tried on the state and local level) under federal jurisdiction when two or more people are racially motivated to conspire to deprive anyone "equal protection of the laws" or "equal privileges and immunities under the laws" (Smith 2003, 130). With respect to those acting under the "color of the law," Section 1983 stipulates:

Every person who, under color of any statute, ordinance, regulation, custom, or usage, of any State or Territory or the District of Columbia, subjects, or causes to be subjected, any citizen of the United States or other person within the jurisdiction thereof to the deprivation of any rights, privileges, or immunities secured by the Constitution and laws, shall be liable to the party injured in an action at law, suit in equity, or other proper proceedings for redress, except that in any action brought against a judicial officer for an act or omission taken in such officer's judicial capacity, injunctive relief shall not be granted unless a declaratory decree was violated or declaratory relief was unavailable. For the purposes of this section, any Act of Congress applicable exclusively to the District of Columbia shall be considered to be a statute of the District of Columbia (Nahmod 2013, 1020).

For most of its lifespan, Section 1983 laid mostly dormant.[3] In 1961, however, the Supreme Court ruled in *Monroe v. Pape*[4] that the federal government could "override certain state laws and to provide a remedy where state laws were inadequate" (Nahmod 2013, 1055). Further, the Supreme Court ruled that the federal government could "provide a remedy where state law remedies were unavailable in practice, even if not in theory" (Nahmod 2013, 1055). As a consequence of the *Monroe v. Pape* decision, individuals could seek remedy in federal court for any violation of their Constitutional rights at the hands of state actors, regardless of whether redress had been previously sought at the state level (Friedman and Delaney 2011).

Using this statute, federal investigations were launched to examine the deaths of both Michael Brown and Eric Garner. With respect to Michael Brown, the U.S. Department of Justice launched two investigations, which ran concurrently with St. Louis County's investigation. One investigation examined the general practices of the Ferguson Police Department; the second investigation specifically examined whether Ferguson Police Officer Darren Wilson's shooting of Michael Brown violated his civil rights. Similar to the St. Louis County grand jury, the Justice Department did not find sufficient evidence to support bringing federal civil rights charges against Officer Wilson. The Justice Department did, however, find that the Ferguson Police Department engaged in "a pattern or practice of conduct that violates the First, Fourth, and Fourteen

---

[3] It is not clear why the Civil Rights Act of 1871 had gone underused. Gressman (1952) suggests that parts of the Civil Rights Act of 1871 had either been repealed by the Democrats who had subsequently taken control of Congress and the Presidency or struck down by the Supreme Court by the end of Reconstruction (but see Weinberg 1991).

[4] In 1958, 13 Chicago police officers broke into the family home of James Monroe and ordered him and his wife to stand naked in the living room as they searched every room, without a search or an arrest warrant. The Monroe's young children were present as the officers leveled racial epithets at the couple. Mr. Monroe was detained and interrogated for 10 hours. He was not allowed to contact his family or an attorney and he was never taken before a magistrate. Mr. Monroe was eventually released and no charges were brought against him (Nahmod 2013).

Amendments of the Constitution" (DOJ 2015).[5] While the Department of Justice's investigation did little to bring closure to Michael Brown's family, it did highlight the pattern of police brutality and abuse of authority that had plagued the Ferguson community – a (very) small victory that otherwise would not have been won without federal intervention.

Amidst the racial upheavals that have sprung up throughout the U.S., the Republican Party has remained noticeably silent. None of the Party's leadership or those who sought the Party's presidential nomination in 2016 made statements regarding the pattern of unjustifiable force used by police in cities across the nation. While Representative Justin Amash (R-MI) and Senator Rand Paul (R-KY), who both are libertarian-leaning Republicans, have commented on the militarization of the nation's police forces, there has been little discussion of the racial implications of the use of excessive force by the police (Sullivan 2014).

Thus, the increased saliency of the racial policy dimension will likely mean that Blacks will continue to support the Democratic Party. African Americans are significantly more liberal than Whites on this dimension. To be sure, Blacks are much more likely to favor government intervention in ensuring civil rights than their White counterparts. Over the past five decades, Blacks have perceived the Democratic Party to be the stronger of the two major parties on race (Philpot 2007). Further, President Obama (a Democrat) and his administration have been responsible for interjecting when the states and localities have failed to bring about a just solution to civil rights infractions. Since the Republican Party has not sought a bipartisan or even an alternative solution to the systemic racism experienced by African Americans, Black party identification will likely remain solidly Democratic.

BEYOND BLACK POLITICS: A GUIDE FOR FUTURE RESEARCH

Conservative but Not Republican has presented a general theoretical framework for understanding how groups can develop individualized conceptualizations of the liberal–conservative continuum that is based

---

[5] The Department of Justice came to similar conclusions upon completing its investigation of the Cleveland Police Department. Most recently, the Cleveland Police Department has come under scrutiny when an officer fatally shot Tamir Race, a 12-year-old African-American boy who was playing with a toy gun in a neighborhood park (Liebelson and Reilly 2014).

on that group's interaction with the political world. To test this theory, this book has juxtaposed Blacks' historic relationship with government and politics with Blacks' contemporary posture towards various policy domains. Using multiple policy domains allowed us to discern whether definitions of ideological self-identification varied systematically by group. The evidence presented in earlier chapters suggested that Blacks' definition of ideological self-identification was predictable given the political environment in which they have had to maneuver in order to attain their political goals.

The natural extension of the current study is to examine how this theoretical framework applies to other groups, particularly other racial and ethnic groups. Certainly, one of the most important lessons of the 2012 Presidential Election was the growing significance of minority voting blocs.[6] Thus, it is a worthwhile enterprise to compare how other minority groups in American politics make sense of the liberal-conservative continuum and how these conceptualizations affect their partisanship and voting behavior.

As the fastest growing minority group, the roots of Latino ideological self-identification should be of particular interest. The majority of Latinos identify as Democrats, although not to the extent that African Americans do. A notable exception is Cubans in Florida, who mostly identify as Republican. Ideologically, Latinos are more liberal on both racial and non-racial issues than non-Latino Whites (Segura 2012). Yet, despite a general propensity to be liberal on a host of issues, there is evidence to suggest that Latinos are conservative on moral and social issues (Ellison, Acevedo, and Ramos-Wada 2011). Thus, there is a complexity to Latinos' ideology when multiple policy domains are taken into consideration.

Adding to this complexity is the significant heterogeneity within the Latino electorate, which would impact the study of Latino ideology. Among these factors are national origin, nativity and generation, religion, acculturation, and group identity (Segura 2012; Kaufmann 2003; Ellison et al. 2011). For instance, opposition to abortion is significantly higher among Protestant (compared to Catholic) Latinos (Bartkowski, Ramos-Wada, Ellison, and Acevedo 2012), who now constitute about 25 percent

---

[6] Latinos turned out in record numbers during the 2012 election, lifting their vote share from 6 percent in 2008 to 10 percent in 2012. Moreover, 71 percent of Latinos voted for President Obama, which was a 4 percentage point increase from 2008 (Preston and Santos 2012). Turnout among Asian Americans in 2012 was also higher than it had ever been. Furthermore, like Latinos, 73 percent of Asian Americans voted for President Obama in 2012 (Taylor 2012).

of the Latino population (Ellison et al. 2011). Opposition to abortion also varies by national origin; Cuban Americans are significantly more conservative on this issue than Mexican Americans and Puerto Ricans (Bolks, Evans, Polinard, and Wrinkle 2000). With respect to ideological self-identification, the liberal–conservative continuum strongly correlates with Latino party identification, but the strength of this correlation varies by national origin (Hero, Garcia, Garcia, and Pachon 2000).

Therefore, exploring Latino ideology would provide rich and fertile ground upon which to test the boundaries of the theoretical framework presented in this book. But extending this research should not be a matter of simply substituting one group for another. Being able to predict how Latinos conceptualize the liberal–conservative continuum and whether and how their ideology will correlate with their party identification requires understanding the unique journey Latinos have travelled as they have struggled to achieve political equality in the United States. While both groups are racial minorities, Latinos have not had the same history with the two major parties as have Blacks. Party outreach to Latino voters is a fairly recent phenomenon (Hero et al. 2000). Furthermore, the political experiences of Latinos vary by the factors discussed earlier, including national origin, generation, etc. Thus, any attempt at exploring how the theoretical framework presented in *Conservative but Not Republican* applies to other groups – racial, ethnic, religious, or otherwise – must consider how that group has traversed the American political landscape.

The theoretical framework presented in this book is not restricted to racial and ethnic minorities. Public opinion scholars can extend this work to understanding any cross-pressured group that experiences dissonance between their ideological self-identification and their party identification. For instance, Hillygus and Shields (2008) found that ideology played a much larger role than party identification in the political decision making of southern voters in the 2000 election. As a result, a conservative Democrat in the South was significantly more likely to support Bush, while a conservative Democrat in the non-South was more likely to support Gore (Hillygus and Shields 2008). By extension, conceptualizing the ideological self-identification of southern voters as multidimensional and hierarchical may help explain their political distinctiveness.

Campaign scholars can also extend this research by exploring whether it is effective to tailor campaign appeals based on the saliency of an issue domain to voters' ideological self-identification. Already scholars (Carroll 1999; Elder and Greene 2007) have examined whether microtargeting "soccer moms" or "NASCAR dads" has been a successful campaign strategy. These studies have found that such campaign appeals have been ineffective because they are based on media-fabricated delineations of subpopulations of the electorate. Further, using these artificial distinctions leads political elites to take positions on issues that are not important to them, which undercuts elite attempts at recruiting these voters. By understanding the actual hierarchical ordering of issue preferences among voters, political elites can make better campaigning decisions and scholars can better predict when such appeals will be successful.

FINAL THOUGHTS

As the African-American electorate grows more heterogeneous, the nature of Black Politics will continue to grow more complex. Even with the growing body of knowledge on the subject, what scholars have been able to reveal about how and why African Americans interact with the political system has barely scratched the surface. This is evident as new data has become available and the breadth of methodologies used to study Black Politics continues to expand (Philpot and Walton 2014). To keep up with these changes, we must think beyond generalized theories that use race as a blanket explanation to account for all of Black decision-making. We must create more nuanced models of how Blacks think about politics (see White 2007 for strong support for this argument).

Furthermore, the lessons learned from the study of Black Politics and other marginalized groups need to be incorporated into theories of mainstream political participation and public opinion. To be sure, the seminal work on political participation neglected to account for African-American political participation (see Philpot and Walton 2014 for a review of this literature). And yet, Blacks' fight for political incorporation has spurred significant realignments throughout the history of the Republic (Philpot 2007; Weiss 1983; Gurin et al. 1989). Given the importance of race, particularly to the two-party system, theories that have failed to include African Americans and their agency on the American political system are incomplete. In order to fully comprehend citizens' ideological orientations and how they affect their partisan preferences, we must explain rather than omit the exceptions to the existing rules. The evidence presented in *Conservative but Not Republican* suggests that without doing so, we miss key features and failures of the American democratic system.

Appendix

A Methodology for Content Analysis of *The New York Times*

New York Times articles were retrieved using ProQuest Historical Newspapers electronic database. This database covers the period from 1851 (the founding of the newspaper) to 2012. Our sample frame, however, begins with 1857, the first time the newspaper is published under the title *The New York Times*, rather than its original name the *New-York Daily Times*. To make the data collection manageable, sampling was done by decade instead of year, with the sample frame ending in 2007. For each year included in the sample frame, articles were retrieved using the search terms *liberal* and *conservative*. Articles were eligible if these search terms appeared anywhere in the title or text of the article. A random sample of 100 articles (50 featuring liberal and 50 featuring conservative) was included for each sample year. This sampling method produced 1,599 articles. Of the 1,599, 467 were excluded from the analysis due to non-relevant uses of the search terms, such as "Liberal Arts College" or "a conservative estimate." Each article was systematically coded for its discussion of *liberal* and *conservative* in conjunction with laissez-faire, racial, military, social welfare, religious, and moral.

Laissez-faire (n = 576)
The article describes liberal/conservative ideals related to non-specified federal government intervention and spending and general sentiments about the size of government.

Racial (n = 105)

The article describes the liberal/conservative side of a debate related to racial issues, racial groups, or race relations. Examples of racial issues include immigration, affirmative action, school desegregation, and coalition building.

Military (n = 124)

The article describes a liberal/conservative use of military force, the liberal/conservative sides of a military conflict, or the liberal/conservative approach to military spending.

Social Welfare (n = 200)

The article describes a liberal/conservative side of a debate about a social welfare issues such as the redistribution of wealth, aid to disadvantaged groups, public education, health care, social security, etc.

Religious (n = 67)

The article describes liberal/conservative aspects of religion, including religious beliefs and practices.

Moral (n = 60)

The article describes the use of moral or ethical appeals, i.e., statements about objective standards of what is right and wrong, in conjunction with liberal/conservative sides of a policy debate.

B Methodology for Content Analysis of *New York Amsterdam News*

New York Amsterdam News articles were retrieved using ProQuest Historical Newspapers electronic database. This database covers the period from 1922 to present. To correspond with the *New York Times* analyses, our sample frame begins with 1927. To make the data collection manageable, sampling was done by decade instead of year, with the sample frame ending in 2007. For each year included in the sample frame, articles were retrieved using the search terms *liberal* and *conservative*. Articles were eligible if these search terms appeared anywhere in the title or text of the article. A random sample of 100 articles (50 featuring liberal and 50 featuring conservative) was included for each sample year. Exceptions were in those years in which less than 50 articles were available. Those years were 1927, 1937 (conservative), 1947 (conservative), 1957 (conservative), 1967 (conservative), 1987, 1997, and 2007. This sampling method produced 679 articles. Of the 679, 109 were excluded from the analysis due to non-relevant uses of the search terms, such as "Liberal Arts College" or "a conservative estimate." Each article was systematically coded for its discussion of *liberal* and *conservative* in conjunction with laissez-faire, racial, military, social welfare, religious, and moral. Values below exceed 570 because some articles fell into more than one category.

Laissez-faire (n = 66)
The article describes liberal/conservative ideals related to non-specified federal government intervention and spending and general sentiments about the size of government.

Racial (n = 233)
The article describes the liberal/conservative side of a debate related to racial issues, racial groups, or race relations. Examples of racial issues include immigration, affirmative action, school desegregation, and coalition building.

Military (n = 28)
The article describes a liberal/conservative use of military force, the liberal/conservative sides of a military conflict, or the liberal/conservative approach to military spending.

Social Welfare (n = 172)
The article describes a liberal/conservative side of a debate about a social welfare issues such as the redistribution of wealth, aid to disadvantaged groups, public education, health care, social security, etc.

Religious (n = 45)
The article describes liberal/conservative aspects of religion, including religious beliefs and practices.

Moral (n = 55)

The article describes the use of moral or ethical appeals, i.e. statements about objective standards of what is right and wrong, in conjunction with liberal/conservative sides of a policy debate.

C Methodology for Coding Open-Ended Survey Responses

In survey years 1978, 1980, 1984, 1988, and 1992, respondents were asked the following set of questions:

- People have different things in mind when they say that someone's political views are liberal or conservative. We'd like to know more about this. Let's start with liberal. What sorts of things do you have in mind when you say someone's political views are liberal?
- And what do you have in mind when you say that someone's political views are conservative?

Each respondent was given the chance to offer up to three responses for both liberal and conservative. Responses were categorized by one of six ideological dimensions – laissez-faire, racial, military, social welfare, religious, and moral.

Laissez-faire

Responses were related to non-specified federal government intervention and spending and general sentiments about the size of government. Examples include describing liberals or conservatives as favoring or opposing "tight economic policy" or "government control over the economy."

Racial

Responses were related to racial issues, racial groups, or race relations. Examples include describing liberals or conservatives as favoring or opposing "Blacks," "civil rights, "busing," "forced integration," etc.

Military

Responses were related to military conflict or military spending. Examples include describing liberals or conservatives as favoring or opposing "war" or "isolationism."

Social Welfare

Responses were related to social welfare issues such as the redistribution of wealth or aid to disadvantaged groups. Examples include describing liberals or conservatives as interested/not interested in social problems or supporting/opposing "the little people," "unions," "minimum wage legislation," "social security," "socialized medicine," etc.

Religious

Responses were related to aspects of religion, including religious beliefs and practices. Examples include describing liberals or conservatives as favoring or opposing "prayer in schools," "Christians," or "strong religious beliefs."

Moral

Reponses were related to questions of deviant behavior or control over life and death (see Scheepers and Slik 1998). Examples include describing liberals or conservatives as favoring or opposing "legalization of pot," "abortion," "birth control," etc.

General Use (Not Presented but Included in Analyses)

Responses were non-policy related. Examples include describing liberals or conservatives as "moderate," "extreme," "consistent," etc.

D Methodology for Semi-Structured Interviews

Between 2006 and 2010, 81 semi-structured qualitative interviews were conducted in Texas, New Jersey, Washington DC, Michigan, New York, and California. Respondents were primarily recruited through an ad placed on Craigslist.org. In order to solicit enough African-American participation, subjects were also recruited from Black civic and fraternal organizations, religious institutions, and beauty and barber shops. The interviews ranged in length from 15 to 104 minutes and each participant received $20 for his or her participation. Just over half (50.6 percent) of the respondents were Black, while 43.2 percent were White. Fifty-three percent of the respondents were female and the mean age of all respondents was 43.18. Approximately two-thirds of respondents were

Democrats and 20.3 percent were Republicans, while 48.2 percent identified as liberal and 18.5 percent identified as conservative. Geographic-
ally, the majority of respondents (53.1 percent) lived on the East Coast,
19.8 lived in the Midwest, 14.8 lived in the South, and 12.4 lived on the
West Coast. Finally, 65.4 percent of respondents had earned a college
degree at the time their interview had been conducted.

For the purposes of Chapter 1 , respondents were asked the following
set of questions:

1. What does it mean to be conservative/liberal?
2. What issues, candidates, and groups do you associate with being
   conservative/liberal?

Each respondent was given the chance to offer up as many responses as he
or she could think of for both liberal and conservative. Coding was done
using Atlas.ti, a computer program used primarily for qualitative data
analysis. Responses were categorized by one of six ideological dimensions: laissez-faire, racial, military, social welfare, religious, and moral.
Once the coding was complete, a query was conducted to see the number
of times an ideological dimension occurred in a respondent's definition of
either the meaning of liberal or the meaning of conservative. Atlas.ti
simultaneously calculated a c-coefficient for each dimension, which stand-
ardizes the co-occurrences by making them a function of the total number
of occurrences of the ideological dimension throughout the interview
and all attempts to define liberal and conservative. The formula for the
c-coefficient is as follows:

$$\frac{n_{12}}{(n_1 + n_2) - n_{12}}$$

Laissez-faire

Responses were related to non-specified federal government intervention
and spending and general sentiments about the size of government.
Examples include describing liberals or conservatives as favoring or opposing "tight economic policy" or "government control over the economy."

Racial

Responses were related to racial issues, racial groups, or race relations.
Examples include describing liberals or conservatives as favoring or
opposing "Blacks," "civil rights, "busing," "forced integration," etc.

Military
Responses were related to military conflict or military spending. Examples include describing liberals or conservatives as "anti-war" or "against military spending."

Social Welfare
Responses were related to social welfare issues such as the redistribution of wealth or aid to disadvantaged groups. Examples include describing liberals or conservatives as," "unions," "minimum wage legislation," "social security," "socialized medicine," etc.

Religious
Responses were related to aspects of religion, including religious beliefs and practices. Examples include describing liberals or conservatives as favoring or opposing "prayer in schools," "Christians," or "strong religious beliefs."

Moral
Reponses were related to questions of deviant behavior or control over life and death (see Scheepers and Slik 1998). Examples include describing liberals or conservatives as favoring or opposing "legalization of pot," "abortion," "birth control," etc.

General Use (Not Presented but Included in Analyses)
Responses were non-policy related. Examples include describing liberals or conservatives as "moderate," "extreme," "consistent," etc.

CHAPTER 3

A Methodology for Quantitative Analyses in Chapter 3

The 2010 Post-Midterm Election Study was conducted by Knowledge Networks. Knowledge Networks is based on a representative probability sample of the whole United States. Unlike other online panels that rely on opt-in recruitment efforts, Knowledge Networks is the only online panel that relies on probability-based recruitment. The primary shortcoming of other opt-in panels is that prospective respondents must have internet access in order to be initially chosen for the panel. To overcome this shortcoming, Knowledge Networks uses "address-based sampling" to select panelists and then provides each panelist with internet access. This selection method allows Knowledge Networks to achieve greater representation among populations that are difficult to survey, including cell phone users and minority groups.

The primary focus of the 2010 Post-Midterm Election Study was citizens' ideological orientations and their correlates. Thus, the PMES included 18 items, which tapped into the military, social, moral, religious, laissez-faire and racial dimensions of ideology. The items were selected based on their ability to capture ideological ideals without referencing specific public policies or figures. Rather, these items asked respondents to indicate what they thought the proper relationship between individuals, society, and government ought to be. Responses were coded on a five-point Likert scale, ranging from strongly agree to strongly disagree. For the sake of consistency, all items were recoded so that the most conservative response was coded 1 and the most liberal response was coded 0, with all other values falling somewhere in between. The three items for each ideological domain were then added together into an additive index ranging from 0 (most liberal) to 1 (most conservative). Table A3.1 presents the exact question wording for each item, along with the item's mean by race.

Additionally, the following variables were included in the analyses:

Ideological Self-Identification

"In general, do you think of yourself as Extremely liberal, Liberal, Slightly liberal, Moderate/middle of the road, Slightly conservative, Conservative, Extremely conservative?" Unless otherwise noted, collapsed into a three-category variable, 0 = Extremely liberal, Liberal, Slightly liberal, 0.5 = Moderate/middle of the road, 1 = Slightly conservative, Conservative, Extremely conservative.

(mean = 0.48, standard deviation = 0.36)

Age

Age in years.

(mean = 43.72, standard deviation = 15.38)

TABLE A3.1 *Mean placement on ideological referents, by race*

	Blacks	Whites	Difference
Military (α = 0.65)	0.55	0.63	−0.08*
Every able male should willingly serve for a period of time in his country's military service.	0.45	0.52	−0.07*
A man who is ready to die for his country deserves the highest honor.	0.74	0.82	−0.08*
If called upon to do so, a citizen should be willing to sacrifice his life for his country.	0.44	0.54	−0.10*
Social (α = 0.75)	0.36	0.52	−0.16*
The government should guarantee every citizen enough to eat.	0.28	0.44	−0.16*
It is the responsibility of the government to take care of people who can't take care of themselves.	0.37	0.51	−0.14*
If the government must go deeper in debt to help people, it should do so.	0.43	0.61	−0.18*
Religious (α = 0.81)	0.63	0.50	0.13*
Children should receive religious instruction.	0.70	0.54	0.16*
This country would be better off if religion had a greater influence in daily life.	0.68	0.59	0.09*
It should be against the law to do anything which the Bible says is wrong.	0.52	0.36	0.16*
Laissez-faire (α = 0.64)	0.52	0.67	−0.15*
The strength of this country today is largely a product of the free enterprise system.	0.61	0.70	−0.09*
Regulation of business by government usually does more harm than good.	0.48	0.62	−0.14*
When something is run by government, it is apt to be inefficient and wasteful.	0.49	0.68	−0.19*
Moral (α = 0.55)	0.45	0.43	0.02
Abortion should be a private matter between a woman and her doctor.	0.33	0.34	−0.01
Homosexuals should be able to do what they want to so long as they don't hurt other people.	0.41	0.32	0.09*
There are too many shows on television that make fun of traditional family values.	0.61	0.61	0.00
Racial (α = 0.60)	0.35	0.57	−0.22*
It is the government's responsibility to ensure racial equality.	0.33	0.49	−0.16*

(*continued*)

Table A3.1 (*continued*)

	Blacks	Whites	Difference
There has been so much progress over the past several years that special programs for Blacks are no longer needed.	0.34	0.63	−0.29*
Black people depend too much on government programs.	0.38	0.58	−0.20*

Note: Entries are the weighted means. Respondents used a five-point Likert scale, ranging from strongly agree to strongly disagree, to respond to each statement. All measures are coded from zero (most liberal) to one (most conservative). Starred values are statistically significant at the $p < 0.10$ level (two-tailed test).
Source: 2010 Post-Midterm Election Study.

Campaign Interest
"Some people don't pay much attention to political campaigns. How about you? Would you say that you were very much interested, somewhat interested or not much interested in the political campaigns this year?" Three-category Likert scale where $0 =$ not much interested, $0.5 =$ somewhat interested, and $1 =$ very much interested.
    (mean $= 0.53$, standard deviation $= 0.36$)

Education
Highest grade completed or degree received imputed from Knowledge Networks panelist profile. Fourteen-category variable, ranging from $0 =$ no formal education to $1 =$ professional or doctorate degree.
    (mean $= 0.66$, standard deviation $= 0.15$)

Political Sophistication
Dichotomous variable based on the *Education* and *Campaign Interest* variables. $1 =$ college degree or higher and very much interested in campaigns, $0 =$ some college or less and somewhat or not much interested in campaigns.
    (mean $= 0.10$, standard deviation $= 0.30$)

Income

Household income imputed from Knowledge Networks panelist profile. Nineteen-category variable ranging from o = less than $5,000 to 1 = $175,000 or more.

(mean = 0.38, standard deviation = 0.24)

Female

Respondent's sex imputed from Knowledge Networks panelist profile, o = male, 1 = female.

(mean = 0.56, standard deviation = 0.50)

Note that the mean and the standard deviation listed for each variable describe the Black sample only.

B Interview Protocol for Qualitative Analyses in Chapter 3

- Do you consider yourself liberal or conservative? Why?
- Do you consider yourself to be liberal or conservative when it comes to religious issues? Why?
- What do you believe is the proper role of religion in society?
- Do you think religion and politics should mix? Why or why not?
- Do you consider yourself to be liberal or conservative when it comes to moral issues? Why?
- What do you believe is the proper role of morality in society?
- Do you think morality and politics should mix? Why or why not?
- Do you consider yourself to be liberal or conservative when it comes to racial issues? Why?
- What is the proper role of race in American society?
- Should government ensure racial equality? Why or why not?
- Do you consider yourself to be liberal or conservative when it comes to military/defense issues? Why?
- Are there circumstances in which the U.S. should get involved in military matters?
- Are there circumstances in which the U.S. should never get involved in military matters?
- Do you consider yourself to be liberal or conservative when it comes to social issues? Why?
- What role should government play in providing social programs to Americans?

- How much of a role should government play in the lives of Americans? Why?
- Are there things that only the government should handle?
- Are there things where government should never be involved?

CHAPTER 4

A Methodology for Quantitative Analyses in Chapter 4

The 2010 Post-Midterm Election Study was described in detail in the Appendix to Chapter 3. The 2012 Religious Worldviews Study (RWS) was also conducted by Knowledge Networks. The primary focus of the 2012 Religious Worldviews Study was citizens' religious outlooks and their correlates. Additionally, the RWS included measures of the multiple dimensions of group coconsciousness, allowing us to compare across survey years. The following variables were included in the analyses:

Group Identity

2010: "Do you think that what happens generally to Blacks in this country will have something to do with what happens in your life?" Four-category variable, $0 =$ not at all, $0.33 =$ not very much, $0.67 =$ some, $1 =$ a lot.

2012: "How much do you believe what happens to the following groups has something to do with what happens in your life?" This question was asked for "Blacks." Four-category variable, $0 =$ nothing at all, $0.33 =$ very little, $0.67 =$ some, $1 =$ a lot.

(2010: mean $= 0.63$, standard deviation $= 0.31$)
(2012: mean $= 0.64$, standard deviation $= 0.32$)

Polar Affect

2010: "I'd like to get your feelings toward some of our political leaders and other people who are in the news these days. I'd like you to rate that person or group using something we call a feeling thermometer. 100 means that you feel extremely warm towards this person or group, while 0 means you feel extremely cold towards them. A rating of 50 means that you don't feel particularly warm or cold toward the person or group. Keeping this in mind, how would you rate your feelings towards..."

2012: "We'd like to get your feelings toward some of our political leaders and other people who are in the news these days. We'll show the name of a person and we'd like you to rate that person using something we call the feeling thermometer. Ratings between 50 degrees and 100 degrees mean that you feel favorable and warm toward the person. Ratings between 0 degrees and 50 degrees mean that you don't feel favorable toward the person and that you don't care too much for that person. You would rate the person at the 50 degree mark if you don't feel particularly warm or cold toward the person. If we come to a person whose name you don't recognize, you don't need to rate that person."

Continuous variable, running from 0 to 100. This question was asked for "Blacks" and "Whites." Polar affect was calculated by subtracting the feeling thermometer scores for "Whites" from the "Blacks" feeling thermometer. This variable was then scaled from 0 (Blacks prefer for Whites) to 1 (Blacks prefer Blacks).

(2010: mean = 0.58, standard deviation = 0.13)
(2012: mean = 0.57, standard deviation = 0.14)

Polar Power
2010: "Some people think that certain groups have too much influence in American life and politics, while other people feel that certain groups don't have as much influence as they deserve. Do you think [Blacks/Whites] have too much influence, the right amount of influence, or too little influence?" Three-category variable, 0 = too little influence, 0.5 = the right amount of influence, 1 = too much influence. Responses to the Black influence question were subtracted from the White influence question to determine the perceived relative position of each group. Polar power was scaled from zero to one, where zero indicated Blacks were believed to have greater influence than Whites and one indicated that respondents believed that Whites have more influence than Blacks.

2012: "Some people think that certain groups have too much influence in American life and politics, while other people feel that certain groups don't have as much influence as they deserve. Please indicate whether or not the following groups have too much influence, the right amount of influence, or too little influence." This question was asked for "Blacks" and "Whites." Three-category variable, 0 = too little influence, 0.5 = the right amount of influence, 1 = too much influence. Responses to the Black influence question were subtracted from the White influence question to determine the perceived relative position of each group. Polar power was scaled from zero to one, where zero indicated Blacks were believed to have greater influence than Whites and one indicated that respondents believed that Whites have more influence than Blacks.

(2010: mean = 0.83, standard deviation = 0.23)
(2012: mean = 0.83, standard deviation = 0.22)

Individual vs. System Blame

2010: "Which of these two statements do you agree with: (a) It's lack of skill and abilities that keep many Black people from getting a job. It's not just because they're Black. When a Black person is trained to do something, he is able to get a job; or (b) Many qualified Black people can't get a good job. White people with the same skills wouldn't have any trouble." Two-category variable, 0 = (a), 1 = (b)

2012: "Below are series of statements people have made about issues in America. Some people are at point 1 while others are at point 7. Still other people take positions in between points 1 and 7. Please indicate where you would place yourself in regards to these statements." This question was asked for the following two statements: "(a) It's lack of skill and abilities that keep many Black people from getting a job. It's not just because they're Black. When a Black person is trained to do something, he is able to get a job; or (b) Many qualified Black people can't get a good job. White people with the same skills wouldn't have any trouble." Seven-category variable scaled from zero (individual blame) to one (system blame).

(2010: mean = 0.62, standard deviation = 0.49)
(2012: mean = 0.63, standard deviation = 0.30)

Group Consciousness

An additive index composed of group identity, polar affect, polar power, and individual vs. system blame. The group consciousness index was rescaled from zero (low group consciousness) to one (high group consciousness).

(2010: mean = 0.66, standard deviation = 0.21)
(2012: mean = 0.67, standard deviation = 0.14)

Married

Marital status imputed from Knowledge Networks panelist profile, 0 = widowed, divorced, separated, never married, living with partner; 1 = married.

(2010: mean = 0.26, standard deviation = 0.44)
(2012: mean = 0.37, standard deviation = 0.48)

Age

Age in years.

(2010: mean = 43.72, standard deviation = 15.38)
(2012: mean = 45.54, standard deviation = 15.82)

Education

Highest grade completed or degree received imputed from Knowledge Networks panelist profile. Fourteen-category variable, ranging from 0 = no formal education to 1 = professional or doctorate degree.

(2010: mean = 0.66, standard deviation = 0.15)
(2012: mean = 0.69, standard deviation = 0.14)

Income

Household income imputed from Knowledge Networks panelist profile. Nineteen-category variable ranging from 0 = less than $5,000 to 1 = $175,000 or more.

(2010: mean = 0.38, standard deviation = 0.24)
(2012: mean = 0.52, standard deviation = 0.25)

Female

Respondent's sex imputed from Knowledge Networks panelist profile, 0 = male, 1 = female.

(2010: mean = 0.56, standard deviation = 0.50)
(2012: mean = 0.57, standard deviation = 0.50)

South

Based on state residence, 0 = not living in a Confederate state, 1 = living in one of the eleven states of the Confederacy.

(2010: mean = 0.51, standard deviation = 0.50)
(2012: mean = 0.48, standard deviation = 0.50)

Living in Large City

"Which of the following areas do you currently live?" Dichotomous variable coded 0 = rural area, small town, small city, or suburb of a large city and 1 = large city.

(2012: mean = 0.26, standard deviation = 0.44)

Home Owners

Imputed from ownership status of living quarter featured in Knowledge Networks panelist profile, 0 = rented for cash or occupied without payment of cash rent, 1 = owned or being bought by you or someone in your household.

(2010: mean = 0.45, standard deviation = 0.50)
(2012: mean = 0.52, standard deviation = 0.50)

Employed

Imputed from current employment status featured in Knowledge Networks panelist profile, 0 = not working because of temporary layoff from job, currently looking for work, retired, disabled or other, 1 = working as a paid employee or self-employed.

(2010: mean = 0.46, standard deviation = 0.50)
(2012: mean = 0.53, standard deviation = 0.50)

Church Attendance

"How often do you attend religious services?" Six-category variable, 0 = never, 0.20 = once a year or less, 0.40 = a few times a year, 0.60 = once or twice a month, 0.80 = once a week, 1 = more than once a week.

(2010: mean = 0.65, standard deviation = 0.32)
(2012: mean = 0.62, standard deviation = 0.30)

Black Church Attendance
"At your best guess, what percentage of your congregation is of your race?" Dichotomous variable coded one (51 percent or higher) and zero (50 percent or lower).

(2012: mean = 0.70, standard deviation = 0.46)

HBCU Attendance
"Did you attend a Historically Black College or University?" Dichotomous variable coded 0 = no, 1 = yes.

(2012: mean = 0.11, standard deviation = 0.31)

Black Organization Membership
"Are you a member of any organization working to improve the status of Black Americans?" Dichotomous variable coded 0 = no, 1 = yes.

(2012: mean = 0.13, standard deviation = 0.34)

Note that the mean and the standard deviation listed for each variable describe the Black sample only.

B Interview Protocol for Qualitative Analyses in Chapter 4

- Do you think that what happens generally to the Black people in this country will have something to do with what happens in your life?
- Do you think that Black women and Black men have different political views from non-Black women and men?
- What does it mean to be a Black woman/Black man?
- Do you think that Black women should identify themselves first as women or Blacks? Why?
- Do you think that Black women face more/different discrimination than Black/White men or White women?

CHAPTER 5

A Methodology for Quantitative Analyses in Chapter 5

The 2010 Post-Midterm Election Study and the 2012 Religious World-views Study were described in further detail in the Appendices to Chapters 3 and 4, respectively. The American National Election Study Time Series Cumulative Data File merges cross-section cases from the ANES Time Series studies from 1948 to 2012. Included in the dataset are questions that have been asked in at least three survey years. Although it has varied over the last 65 years, the most common study design of the ANES has been a cross-section, equal probability, sample ("Time Series Cumulative Data File" 2015). The sample sizes of the ANES cross-sections have also varied across sample years: 1948: N = 662; 1952: N = 1899; 1954: N = 1139; 1956: N = 1762; 1958: N = 1822; N = 1450; 1960: N = 1181; 1962: N = 1297; 1964: N = 1571; 1966: N = 1291; 1968: N = 1557; 1970: N = 1507; 1972: N = 2705; 1974: N = 1575; 1976: N = 2248; 1978: N = 2304; 1980: N = 1614; 1982: N = 1418; 1984: N = 2257; 1986: N = 2176; 1988: N = 2040; 1990: N = 1980; 1992: N = 2485; 1994: N = 1795; 1996: N = 1714; 1998: N = 1281; 2000: N = 1807; 2002: N = 1511; 2004: N = 1212; 2008: N = 2322; 2012: N = 5914. Data for the ANES were collected through face-to-face interviews; however, the 2012 study also includes an internet sample (American National Election Studies and Stanford University 2015). Below are descriptions of the variables included in the analyses for Chapter 5. Note that the mean and the standard deviation listed for each variable describe the Black sample only.

Party Identification

2010 and 2012: "Generally speaking, do you think of yourself as a Republican, Democrat, Independent, Another party, No preference?"

ANES: "Generally speaking, do you usually think of yourself as a Republican, a Democrat, an Independent, or what?"

Three-category variable, 0 = Democrat, 0.5 = Independent/Another party/No preference, 1 = Republican.

(2010: mean = 0.19, standard deviation = 0.27)
(2012: mean = 0.14, standard deviation = 0.24)
(ANES: mean = 0.18, standard deviation = 0.29)

Ideological Self-Identification

2010 and 2012: "In general, do you think of yourself as Extremely liberal, Liberal, Slightly liberal, Moderate/middle of the road, Slightly conservative, Conservative, Extremely conservative?"

ANES: "We hear a lot of talk these days about liberals and conservatives. When it comes to politics, do you usually think of yourself as extremely liberal, liberal, slightly liberal, moderate or middle of the road, slightly conservative, extremely conservative, or haven't you thought much about this?

Unless otherwise noted, collapsed into a three-category variable, 0 = Extremely liberal, Liberal, Slightly liberal, 0.5 = Moderate/middle of the road, 1 = Slightly conservative, Conservative, Extremely conservative.

(2010: mean = 0.48, standard deviation = 0.36)
(2012: mean = 0.40, standard deviation = 0.37)
(ANES: mean = 0.40, standard deviation = 0.39)

Group Identity

2010: "Do you think that what happens generally to Blacks in this country will have something to do with what happens in your life?" Four-category variable, 0 = not at all, 0.33 = not very much, 0.67 = some, 1 = a lot.

2012: "How much do you believe what happens to the following groups has something to do with what happens in your life?" This question was asked for "Blacks." Four-category variable, 0 = nothing at all, 0.33 = very little, 0.67 = some, 1 = a lot.

(2010: mean = 0.63, standard deviation = 0.31)
(2012: mean = 0.64, standard deviation = 0.32)

Polar Affect

2010: "I'd like to get your feelings toward some of our political leaders and other people who are in the news these days. I'd like you to rate that person or group using something we call a feeling thermometer. 100 means that you feel extremely warm towards this person or group, while 0 means you feel extremely cold towards them. A rating of 50 means that you don't feel particularly warm or cold toward the person or group. Keeping this in mind, how would you rate your feelings towards"

2012: "We'd like to get your feelings toward some of our political leaders and other people who are in the news these days. We'll show the name of a person and we'd like you to rate that person using something we call the feeling thermometer. Ratings between 50 degrees and 100 degrees mean that you feel favorable and warm toward the person. Ratings between 0 degrees and 50 degrees mean that you don't feel favorable toward the person and that you don't care too much for that person. You would rate the person at the 50 degree mark if you don't feel particularly warm or cold toward the person. If we come to a person whose name you don't recognize, you don't need to rate that person."

ANES: "We'd also like to get your feelings about some groups in American society. When I read the name of a group, we'd like you to rate it with what we call a feeling thermometer. Ratings between 50 degrees to 100 degrees mean that you feel favorably and warm toward the group; ratings between 0 and 50 degrees mean that you don't feel favorably towards the group and that you don't care too much for that group. If you don't feel particularly warm or cold toward a group you would rate them at 50 degrees. If we come to a group you don't know much about, just tell me and we'll move on to the next one.

Continuous variable, running from 0 to 100. This question was asked for "Blacks" and "Whites." Polar affect was calculated by subtracting the feeling thermometer scores for "Whites" from the "Blacks" feeling thermometer. This variable was then scaled from 0 (Blacks prefer for Whites) to 1 (Blacks prefer Blacks).

(2010: mean $= 0.58$, standard deviation $= 0.13$)
(2012: mean $= 0.57$, standard deviation $= 0.14$)
(ANES: mean $= 0.56$, standard deviation $= 0.10$)

Polar Power

2010: "Some people think that certain groups have too much influence in American life and politics, while other people feel that certain groups don't have as much influence as they deserve. Do you think [Blacks/Whites] have too much influence, the right amount of influence, or too little influence?" Three-category variable, $0 =$ too little influence, $0.5 =$ the right amount of influence, $1 =$ too much influence. Responses to the Black influence question were subtracted from the White influence question to determine the perceived relative position of each group. Polar power was scaled from zero to one, where zero indicated Blacks were believed to have greater influence than Whites and one indicated that respondents believed that Whites have more influence than Blacks.

2012: "Some people think that certain groups have too much influence in American life and politics, while other people feel that certain groups don't have as much influence as they deserve. Please indicate whether or not the following groups have too much influence, the right amount of influence, or too little influence." This question was asked for "Blacks" and "Whites." Three-category variable, $0 =$ too little influence, $0.5 =$ the right amount of influence, $1 =$ too much influence. Responses to the Black influence question were subtracted from the White influence question to determine the perceived relative position of each group. Polar power was scaled from zero to one, where zero indicated Blacks were believed to have greater influence than Whites and one indicated that respondents believed that Whites have more influence than Blacks.

(2010: mean $= 0.83$, standard deviation $= 0.23$)
(2012: mean $= 0.83$, standard deviation $= 0.22$)

Individual vs. System Blame

2010: "Which of these two statements do you agree with: (a) It's lack of skill and abilities that keep many Black people from getting a job. It's not just because they're Black. When a Black person is trained to do something, he is able to get a job; or (b) Many qualified Black people can't get a good job. White people with the same skills wouldn't have any trouble." Two-category variable, $0 = (a)$, $1 = (b)$

2012: "Below are series of statements people have made about issues in America. Some people are at point 1 while others are at point 7. Still other people take positions in between points 1 and 7. Please indicate where you would place yourself in regards to these statements." This question was asked for the following two statements: "(a) It's lack of skill and abilities that keep many Black people from getting a job. It's not just because they're Black. When a Black person is trained to do something, he is able to get a job; or (b) Many qualified Black people can't get a good job. White people with the same skills wouldn't have any trouble." Seven-category variable scaled from zero (individual blame) to one (system blame).

(2010: mean $= 0.62$, standard deviation $= 0.49$)
(2012: mean $= 0.63$, standard deviation $= 0.30$)

Group Consciousness

An additive index composed of group identity, polar affect, polar power, and individual vs. system blame. The group consciousness index was rescaled from zero (low group consciousness) to one (high group consciousness).

(2010: mean = 0.66, standard deviation = 0.21)
(2012: mean = 0.67, standard deviation = 0.14)

Party Affect

2010: "I'd like to get your feelings toward some of our political leaders and other people who are in the news these days. I'd like you to rate that person or group using something we call a feeling thermometer. 100 means that you feel extremely warm towards this person or group, while 0 means you feel extremely cold towards them. A rating of 50 means that you don't feel particularly warm or cold toward the person or group. Keeping this in mind, how would you rate your feelings towards"

2012: "We'd like to get your feelings toward some of our political leaders and other people who are in the news these days. We'll show the name of a person and we'd like you to rate that person using something we call the feeling thermometer. Ratings between 50 degrees and 100 degrees mean that you feel favorable and warm toward the person. Ratings between 0 degrees and 50 degrees mean that you don't feel favorable toward the person and that you don't care too much for that person. You would rate the person at the 50 degree mark if you don't feel particularly warm or cold toward the person. If we come to a person whose name you don't recognize, you don't need to rate that person."

ANES: "We'd also like to get your feelings about some groups in American society. When I read the name of a group, we'd like you to rate it with what we call a feeling thermometer. Ratings between 50 degrees to 100 degrees mean that you feel favorably and warm toward the group; ratings between 0 and 50 degrees mean that you don't feel favorably towards the group and that you don't care too much for that group. If you don't feel particularly warm or cold toward a group you would rate them at 50 degrees. If we come to a group you don't know much about, just tell me and we'll move on to the next one.

Continuous variable, running from 0 to 100. This question was asked for "The Democratic Party" and "The Republican Party." Party affect was calculated by subtracting the feeling thermometer scores for "The Democratic Party" from the "The Republican Party" feeling thermometer. This variable was then scaled from 0 (Blacks prefer for the Democratic Party) to 1 (Blacks prefer the Republican Party).

(2010: mean = 0.30, standard deviation = 0.19)
(2012: mean = 0.24, standard deviation = 0.20)
(ANES: mean = 0.33, standard deviation = 0.18)

Age
Age in years.

(2010: mean = 43.72, standard deviation = 15.38)
(2012: mean = 45.54, standard deviation = 15.82)
(ANES: mean = 43.36, standard deviation = 16.81)

Education
2010 and 2012: Highest grade completed or degree received imputed from Knowledge Networks panelist profile. Fourteen-category variable, ranging from 0 = no formal education to 1 = professional or doctorate degree.

ANES: Seven-category variable, ranging from 0 = 8 grade or less to 1 = advance degree

(2010: mean = 0.66, standard deviation = 0.15)
(2012: mean = 0.69, standard deviation = 0.14)
(ANES: mean = 0.37, standard deviation = 0.29)

Campaign Interest
"Some people don't pay much attention to political campaigns. How about you? Would you say that you were very much interested, somewhat interested or not much interested in the political campaigns this year?" Three-category Likert scale where 0 = not much interested, 0.5 = somewhat interested, and 1 = very much interested.

(2010: mean = 0.53, standard deviation = 0.36)
(ANES: mean = 0.53, standard deviation = 0.39)

Political Interest

"In general, how interested are you in politics and public affairs?" Four-category Likert scale where 0 = not at all interested, 0.33 = slightly interested, 0.67 = somewhat interested, and 1 = very interested.

(2012: mean = 0.55, standard deviation = 0.32

Income

2010 and 2012: Household income imputed from Knowledge Networks panelist profile. Nineteen-category variable ranging from 0 = less than $5,000 to 1 = $175,000 or more.

ANES: Respondents' family income computed in percentiles. Five-category variable ranging from 0 = 0 to 16 percentile to 1 = 96 to 100 percentile.

(2010: mean = 0.38, standard deviation = 0.24)
(2012: mean = 0.52, standard deviation = 0.25)
(ANES: mean = 0.26, standard deviation = 0.31)

Female

2010 and 2012: Respondent's sex imputed from Knowledge Networks panelist profile.

ANES: Interviewer coded sex.

Dichotomous variable, 0 = male, 1 = female.
(2010: mean = 0.56, standard deviation = 0.50)
(2012: mean = 0.57, standard deviation = 0.50)
(ANES: mean = 0.60, standard deviation = 0.49)

Issue Positions

- "Do you favor or oppose the federal law that currently prohibits openly gay men and women from serving in the military?" Response categories were: Strongly favor, Somewhat favor, Neither favor nor oppose, Somewhat oppose, Strongly oppose.
  (mean = 0.44, standard deviation = 0.31)
- "Do you favor or oppose the federal law that requires all individuals to purchase health care insurance or face a penalty if they don't?" Response categories were: Strongly favor, Somewhat favor, Neither favor nor oppose, Somewhat oppose, Strongly oppose.
  (mean = 0.59, standard deviation = 0.30)

- "Do you favor or oppose U.S. troops remaining in Iraq to advise and assist the Iraqi authorities?" Response categories were: Strongly favor, Somewhat favor, Neither favor nor oppose, Somewhat oppose, Strongly oppose.
  (mean = 0.37, standard deviation = 0.28)
- "Do you favor or oppose legislation that authorizes local police to stop and verify the immigration status of anyone they suspect of being an illegal immigrant?" Response categories were: Strongly favor, Somewhat favor, Neither favor nor oppose, Somewhat oppose, Strongly oppose.
  (mean = 0.50, standard deviation = 0.33)

Each item was recoded into a five-category variable, ranging from 0 = most liberal position, 1 = most conservative position.

B Interview Protocol for Qualitative Analysis in Chapter 5

- Do you think that what happens generally to the Black people in this country will have something to do with what happens in your life?
- Generally speaking, which of the two parties do you vote for when it comes to deciding who will become president?
- Who did you vote for in the 2004 presidential election? If you didn't vote in the 2004 presidential election, which candidate was more appealing to you? Why?
- Who will/did you vote for in the 2008 presidential election? Why?
- Are there circumstances in which you would vote for the other candidate? What are they?
- Do you identify more with the Democratic or Republican Party? Why?
- In general, do you think Blacks are liberal or conservative? Why? What should they be?

CHAPTER 6

A Methodology for Quantitative Analyses in Chapter 6

The 2010 Post Midterm Election Study was previously described in Chapter Three. The 2012 ANES Time Series Study (ANES 2012) featured both face-to-face and internet samples. The target populations for both the face-to-face and internet samples were U.S. citizens age 18 or older.

The face-to-face interviews were conducted using an address-based, stratified, multi-stage cluster sample. The internet sample was administered by GfK (formally Knowledge Networks). The sample is based on a representative probability sample of the whole United States. GfK uses address-based sampling to select panelists and then provides each panelist with internet access, if they do not already have it. The pre-election, face-to-face interviews were conducted between September 8 and November 5, 2012. The post-election, face-to-face interviews occurred November 7, 2012 to January 13, 2013. Pre-election, internet interviews were conducted October 11, 2012 to November 6, 2012 and the post-election, internet interviews were conducted November 29, 2012 to January 24, 2013. The total sample size was 5, 914 (2,054 face-to-face and 3,860 online), including 1,016 Blacks. The median length of the internet pre-election interview was 83 minutes and the median length of the post-election interview was 94 minutes. Likewise, the median length of the face-to-face pre-election interview was 95 minutes and the average length of the post-election interview was 96 minutes. The response rate for the face-to-face sample was 38 percent and the internet sample's response rate was 2 percent.[1]. Below are descriptions of the variables included in the analyses for Chapter 6. Note that the mean and the standard deviation listed for each variable describe the Black sample only.

Voter Turnout

2010: "Did you happen to vote in the 2008 presidential election?" 1 = yes, 0 = no.

2012: PREPOST Summary: Did R vote in November general election? 1 = yes, 0 = no.

(2010: mean = 0.73, standard deviation = 0.45)

(2012: mean = 0.83, standard deviation = 0.38)

Presidential Approval

"Do you approve or disapprove of the way Barack Obama is handling his job as President?" In 2010: Five category variable, 0 = Strongly disapprove, 0.25 = Disapprove, 0.5 = Neither approve nor disapprove,

---

[1] The completion rate was calculated using AAPOR RR1.

0.75 = approve, 1 = Strongly approve. In 2012: Four category variable, 0 = Strongly disapprove, 0.33 = Disapprove, 0.67 = approve, 1 = Strongly approve.

(2010: mean = 0.74, standard deviation = 0.23)
(2012: mean = 0.89, standard deviation = 0.23)

Affect for Republican Politicians

"I'd like to get your feelings toward some of our political leaders and other people who are in the news these days. I'll read the name of a person and I'd like you to rate that person using something we call the feeling thermometer. Ratings between 50 degrees and 100 degrees mean that you feel favorable and warm toward the group. Ratings between 0 degrees and 50 degrees mean that you don't feel favorable toward the group and that you don't care too much for that group. You would rate the group at the 50 degree mark if you don't feel particularly warm or cold toward the group." Continuous variable, running from 0 to 100. This variable was then scaled from 0 (cool feelings towards figure) to 1 (warm feelings towards figure). This question was asked for "Sarah Palin," "George W. Bush," and "Mitt Romney."

(Sarah Palin 2010: mean = 0.25, standard deviation = 0.27)
(George W. Bush 2012: mean = 0.25, standard deviation = 0.26)
(Mitt Romney 2012: mean = 0.27, standard deviation = 0.24)

Ideological Self-Identification

2010: "In general, do you think of yourself as Extremely liberal, Liberal, Slightly liberal, Moderate/middle of the road, Slightly conservative, Conservative, Extremely conservative?" Unless otherwise noted, collapsed into a three-category variable, 0 = Extremely liberal, Liberal, Slightly liberal, 0.5 = Moderate/middle of the road, 1 = Slightly conservative, Conservative, Extremely conservative.

2012: "We hear a lot of talk these days about liberals and conservatives. Here is a seven-point scale on which the political views that people might hold are arranged from extremely liberal to extremely conservative. Where would you place yourself on this scale, or haven't you thought much about this?" Unless otherwise noted, collapsed into a three-category variable, 0 = Extremely liberal, Liberal, Slightly liberal,

0.5 = Moderate/middle of the road, 1 = Slightly conservative, Conservative, Extremely conservative.

(2010: mean = 0.48, standard deviation = 0.36)
(2012: mean = 0.44, standard deviation = 0.43)

Group Identity

2010: "Do you think that what happens generally to Blacks in this country will have something to do with what happens in your life?" Four-category variable, 0 = not at all, 0.33 = not very much, 0.67 = some, 1 = a lot.

2012: "Do you think that what happens generally to Black people in this country will have something to do with what happens in your life?" If yes, "Will it affect you a lot, some, or not very much?" Four-category variable, 0 = not at all, 0.33 = not very much, 0.67 = some, 1 = a lot.

(2010: mean = 0.63, standard deviation = 0.31)
(2012: mean = 0.49, standard deviation = 0.40)

Polar Affect: "I'd like to get your feelings toward some of our political leaders and other people who are in the news these days. I'll read the name of a person and I'd like you to rate that person using something we call the feeling thermometer. Ratings between 50 degrees and 100 degrees mean that you feel favorable and warm toward the group. Ratings between 0 degrees and 50 degrees mean that you don't feel favorable toward the group and that you don't care too much for that group. You would rate the group at the 50 degree mark if you don't feel particularly warm or cold toward the group." Continuous variable, running from 0 to 100. This question was asked for "Blacks" and "Whites." Polar affect was calculated by subtracting the feeling thermometer scores for "Whites" from the "Blacks" feeling thermometer. This variable was then scaled from 0 (Blacks prefer for Whites) to 1 (Blacks prefer Blacks).

(2010: mean = 0.58, standard deviation = 0.13)
(2012: mean = 0.57, standard deviation = 0.11)

Polar Power

2010: "Some people think that certain groups have too much influence in American life and politics, while other people feel that certain groups don't have as much influence as they deserve. Do you think [Blacks/ Whites] have too much influence, the right amount of influence, or too little influence?" Three-category variable, $0 =$ too little influence, $0.5 =$ the right amount of influence, $1 =$ too much influence.

2012: "How much influence do [Blacks/Whites] have in U.S. politics?" Three-category variable, $0 =$ too little influence, $0.5 =$ the right amount of influence, $1 =$ too much influence.

Responses to the Black influence question were subtracted from the White influence question to determine the perceived relative position of each group. Polar power was scaled from zero to one, where zero indicated Blacks were believed to have greater influence than Whites and one indicated that respondents believed that Whites have more influence than Blacks.

(2010: mean $= 0.83$, standard deviation $= 0.23$)
(2012: mean $= 0.82$, standard deviation $= 0.23$)

Individual vs. System Blame

2010: "Which of these two statements do you agree with: (a) It's lack of skill and abilities that keep many Black people from getting a job. It's not just because they're Black. When a Black person is trained to do something, he is able to get a job; or (b) Many qualified Black people can't get a good job. White people with the same skills wouldn't have any trouble." Two-category variable, $0 = $ (a), $1 = $ (b)

2012: Respondents level of agreement to two statements: (1) "Irish, Italians, Jewish and many other minorities overcame prejudice and worked their way up. Blacks should do the same without any special favor," representing an individual explanation for racial inequality and (2) "Generations of slavery and discrimination have created conditions that make it difficult for Blacks to work their way out of the lower class," representing an systemic explanation for racial inequality. Responses to statement (1) were subtracted from statement (2) to assess the relative agreement with these statements. Responses were coded from zero (indicating strongest agreement with an individual explanation for racial inequality) to one (indicating strongest agreement with a systemic explanation for racial inequality).

(2010: mean $= 0.62$, standard deviation $= 0.49$)
(2012: mean $= 0.58$, standard deviation $= 0.25$)

Group Consciousness: An additive index composed of group identity, polar affect, polar power, and individual vs. system blame. The group consciousness index was rescaled from zero (low group consciousness) to one (high group consciousness).

(2010: mean = 0.66, standard deviation = 0.21)
(2012: mean = 0.61, standard deviation = 0.17)

Campaign Interest

"Some people don't pay much attention to political campaigns. How about you? Would you say that you have been very much interested, somewhat interested or not much interested in the political campaigns so far this year?" Three-category Likert scale where 0 = not much interested, 0.5 = somewhat interested, and 1 = very much interested.

(2010: mean = 0.53, standard deviation = 0.36)
(2012: mean = 0.71, standard deviation = 0.31)

Age
Age in years.

(2010: mean = 43.72, standard deviation = 15.38)
(2012: mean = 43.94, standard deviation = 16.63)

Education
Highest grade completed or degree received. 2010: Fourteen-category variable, ranging from 0 = no formal education to 1 = professional or doctorate degree. 2012: Sixteen-category variable, ranging from 0 = no formal education to 1 = professional or doctorate degree.

(2010: mean = 0.66, standard deviation = 0.15)
(2012: mean = 0.60, standard deviation = 0.14)

Income
Household income. 2010: Nineteen-category variable ranging from 0 = less than $5,000 to 1 = $175,000 or more. 2012: Twenty-eight-category variable ranging from 0 = less than $5,000 to 1 = $250,000 or more.

(2010: mean = 0.38, standard deviation = 0.24)
(2012: mean = 0.36, standard deviation = 0.28)

Female
Respondent's sex, 0 = male, 1 = female.

(2010: mean = 0.56, standard deviation = 0.50)
(2012: mean = 0.54, standard deviation = 0.50)

Figures 6.2, 6.4, and 6.5 are based on the estimates presented in Tables A6.1, A6.2, and A6.3, respectively.

TABLE A6.1 *The effect of ideological self-identification on reported voter turnout, by group consciousness*

	Voted in 2008	Voted in 2012
Ideology	0.658	1.126
	(1.72)	(1.26)
Group Consciousness	1.941	3.326*
	(1.58)	(1.44)
Ideological Self-Identification * Group Consciousness	0.181 (2.46)	−2.661 (2.13)
Age	0.026*	0.030*
	(0.01)	(0.01)
Female	1.471*	0.306
	(0.37)	(0.32)
Income	2.365*	0.985*
	(0.86)	(0.59)
Education	0.721	2.972*
	(1.56)	(1.23)
Campaign Interest	2.494*	0.626
	(0.51)	(0.49)
Constant	−4.281*	−4.040*
	(1.56)	(1.22)
N	298	837
Pseudo R-square	0.24	0.12
Log likelihood	−127.05	−232.56

Note: Coefficients are weighted logit estimates. Standard errors appear in parentheses. Voter turnout is coded 1 if respondent reported voting in November general election and 0 if respondent did not. Ideological self-identification is coded 0 (liberal), 0.5 (moderate), and 1 (conservative). Group consciousness is coded from 0 (low group consciousness) to 1 (high group consciousness). Starred values are significant at the $p < 0.10$ level (two-tailed test). *Source*: 2010 Post-Midterm Election Study and 2012 American National Election Study.

TABLE A6.2 *The effect of ideological self-identification on presidential job approval, by group consciousness*

	Presidential Approval 2010	Presidential Approval 2012
Ideology	0.384*	−0.174
	(0.11)	(0.11)
Group Consciousness	0.530*	−0.029
	(0.11)	(0.08)
Ideological Self-Identification * Group Consciousness	−0.620* (0.18)	0.175 (0.19)
Age	0.002*	0.000
	(0.00)	(0.00)
Female	−0.025	0.068*
	(0.03)	(0.03)
Income	−0.157*	−0.044
	(0.07)	(0.04)
Education	−0.137	−0.055
	(0.12)	(0.11)
Campaign Interest	0.093*	0.076*
	(0.04)	(0.04)
Constant	0.449*	0.879*
	(0.11)	(0.09)
N	298	829
R-square	0.15	0.07

Note: Coefficients are weighted OLS estimates. Standard errors appear in parentheses. Presidential approval is coded from 0 (strongly disapprove) to 1 (strongly approve). Ideological self-identification is coded 0 (liberal), 0.5 (moderate), and 1 (conservative). Group consciousness is coded from 0 (low group consciousness) to 1 (high group consciousness). Starred values are significant at the $p < 0.10$ level (two-tailed test).
Source: 2010 Post-Midterm Election Study and 2012 American National Election Study.

TABLE A6.3 *The effect of ideological self-identification on Republican politician affect, by group consciousness*

	Palin Affect 2010	Bush Affect 2012	Romney Affect 2012
Ideology	0.096	0.225*	−0.007
	(0.19)	(0.11)	(0.12)
Group Consciousness	−0.194	−0.035	−0.261*
	(0.17)	(0.11)	(0.10)
Ideological Self-Identification *	−0.022	−0.248	0.088
Group Consciousness	(0.28)	(0.18)	(0.18)
Age	−0.001	0.004*	0.003*
	(0.00)	(0.00)	(0.00)
Female	0.062*	−0.016	−0.055*
	(0.03)	(0.02)	(0.02)
Income	−0.014	−0.046	−0.059
	(0.09)	(0.04)	(0.05)
Education	−0.213	0.177*	0.086
	(0.14)	(0.08)	(0.08)
Campaign Interest	0.054	0.021	−0.093*
	(0.05)	(0.04)	(0.04)
Constant	0.482*	−0.034	0.346*
	(0.15)	(0.08)	(0.09)
N	298	833	831
R-square	0.08	0.10	0.10

Note: Coefficients are weighted OLS estimates. Standard errors appear in parentheses. Affect is coded from 0 (very cold) to 1 (very warm). Ideological self-identification is coded 0 (liberal), 0.5 (moderate), and 1 (conservative). Group consciousness is coded from 0 (low group consciousness) to 1 (high group consciousness). Starred values are significant at the $p < 0.10$ level (two-tailed test).
Source: 2010 Post-Midterm Election Study and 2012 American National Election Study.

Bibliography

Abrajano, Marisa, and Craig M. Burnett. 2012. "Polls and elections: Do Blacks and Whites see Obama through race-tinted glasses? A comparison of Obama's and Clinton's approval ratings." *Presidential Studies Quarterly* 42 (2):363–75.

Abramowitz, Alan. 2010. *The Disappearing Center: Engaged Citizens, Polarization, and American Democracy.* New Haven: Yale University Press.

Abramowitz, Alan I., and Kyle L. Saunders. 1998. "Ideological realignment in the U.S. electorate." *Journal of Politics* 60 (3):634–52.

—. 2006. "Exploring the bases of partisanship in the American electorate: Social identity vs. ideology." *Political Research Quarterly* 59 (2):175–87.

Achen, Christopher H. 1975. "Mass political attitudes and the survey response." *The American Political Science Review* 69 (4):1218–31.

Adorno, Theodor W., Else Frenkel-Brunswik, Daniel J. Levinson, and R. Nevitt Sanford. 1950. *The Authoritarian Personality.* New York: Harper.

Aistrup, Joseph A. 1996. *The Southern Strategy Revisited: Republican Top-Down Advancement in the South.* Lexington: The University Press of Kentucky.

Akinyela, Makungu M. 2003. "Battling the serpent: Nat Turner, Africanized Christianity, and a Black ethos." *Journal of Black Studies* 33 (3):255–80.

Aldrich, John Herbert. 1995. *Why Parties? The Origin and Transformation of Political Parties in America.* Chicago: The University of Chicago Press.

Allen, Richard L., Michael C. Dawson, and Ronald E. Brown. 1989. "A schema-based approach to modeling an African-American racial belief system." *American Political Science Review* 83 (2):421–41.

ANES Time Series Cumulative Data File. 1948–2012. (ICPSR version) [data file and codebook]. Inter-university Consortium for Political and Social Research (ICPSR) [distributor], Ann Arbor, MI.

American National Election Study, 2008: Pre- and Post-Election Survey [Computer file] ICPSR25383-V1.

The American National Election Studies (ANES; www.electionstudies.org) The ANES 2012 Time Series Study [dataset].

Ansolabehere, Stephen, Jonathan Rodden, and James M. Snyder, Jr. 2008. "The strength of issues: Using multiple measures to gauge preference stability, ideological constraint, and issue voting." *American Political Science Review* 102 (2):215–32.

Asumah, Seth N., and Valencia C. Perkins. 2000. "Black conservatism and the social problems in Black America: Ideological cul-de-sacs." *Journal of Black Studies* 31 (1):51–73.

Austin, Algernon. 2006. *Achieving Blackness: Race, Black Nationalism, and Afrocentrism in the Twentieth Century.* New York: New York University Press.

Ayres, Jr., B. Drummond. 1967. "Democrat seeks Asia peace plank." *The New York Times*, August 3, 7.

Baker, Al, J. David Goodman, and Benjamin Mueller. 2015. "Beyond the chokehold: The path to Eric Garner's death." *The New York Times*, June 14, A1.

Balz, Dan, and Scott Clement. 2014. "On racial issues, America is divided both Black and White and red and blue." *The Washington Post*, December 27.

Banfield, Edward, and James Q. Wilson. 1963. *City Politics.* New York: Vintage Books.

Bartkowski, John P., Aida I. Ramos-Wada, Chris G. Ellison, and Gabriel A. Acevedo. 2012. "Faith, race-ethnicity, and public policy preferences: Religious schemas and abortion attitudes among U.S. Latinos." *Journal for the Scientific Study of Religion* 51 (2):343–58.

Basu, Moni, Slma Shelbayah, and Ben Brumfield. 2015. "Huge crowd walks in 'Bloody Sunday' march in Selma." *CNN*, March 8.

Bennett, Stephen Earl. 1973. "Consistency among the public's social welfare policy attitudes in the 1960s." *American Journal of Political Science* 17 (3): 544–70.

Berelson, Bernard. 1952. "Democratic theory and public opinion." *The Public Opinion Quarterly* 16 (3):313–30.

Berelson, Bernard R., Paul F. Lazarsfeld, and William N. McPhee. 1954. *Voting: A Study of Opinion Formation in a Presidential Campaign.* Chicago: University of Chicago Press.

Berman, Mark. 2014. "Americans increasingly say race is the country's most important issue." *The Washington Post*, December 19.

Bernheim, A. C. 1888. "Party organizations and their nominations to public office in New York City." *Political Science Quarterly* 3 (1):99–122.

Billig, Michael, and Henri Tajfel. 1973. "Social categorization and similarity in intergroup behaviour." *European Journal of Social Psychology* 3 (1):27–52.

"Black America today: General media fact sheet." 2008. Silver Spring, MD: Radio One.

Blake, J. Herman. 1969. "Black Nationalism." *Annals of the American Academy of Political and Social Science* 382:15–25.

Blank, Rebecca M. 1985. "An analysis of workers' choice between employment in the public and private sectors." *Industrial and Labor Relations Review* 38 (2):211–24.

Bledsoe, Timothy, Susan Welch, Lee Sigelman, and Michael Combs. 1995. "Residential context and racial solidarity among African Americans." *American Journal of Political Science* 39 (2):434–58.

Bobic, Igor. 2014. "Ben Carson stands by Nazi Germany, slavery comparisons." *The Huffington Post*, December 30. www.huffingtonpost.com.

Bolks, Sean M., Diana Evans, J. L. Polinard, and Robert D. Wrinkle. 2000. "Core beliefs and abortion attitudes: A look at Latinos." *Social Science Quarterly* 81 (1):253–60.

Bone, Hugh A. 1946. "Political parties in New York City." *The American Political Science Review* 40 (2):272–82.

Booker, Brakkton. 2014. "Now, Ben Carson leads in a Republican poll." It's All Politics, May 14. Washington, DC: NPR.

Bositis, David A. 2008. *Blacks and the 2008 Democratic Convention*. Washington, DC: Joint Center for Political and Economic Studies.

Bowers, William T., William M. Hammond, and George L. MacGarrigle. 2005. *Black Soldier, White Army: The 24th Infantry Regiment in Korea*. Honolulu: University Press of the Pacific.

Box-Steffensmeier, Janet M., and Suzanna De Boef. 2001. "Macropartisanship and macroideology in the sophisticated electorate." *Journal of Politics* 63 (1):232–48.

Brace, Paul, and Barbara Hinckley. 1991. "The structure of presidential approval: Constraints within and across presidencies." *The Journal of Politics* 53 (4):993–1017.

Branch, Taylor. 1988. *Parting the Waters: America in the King Years, 1954–1963*. New York: Simon and Schuster.

Brewer, Marilynn B. 2001. "Ingroup identification and intergroup conflict: When does ingroup love become outgroup hate?" In *Social Identity, Intergroup Conflict, and Conflict Reduction*, ed. Richard D. Ashmore, Lee Jussim and David Wilder. New York: Oxford University Press.

Brock, Nailah R. 2009. "African Americans and welfare time limits: Comparative analysis of state time limit politics under the personal responsibility and work opportunity and Reconciliation Act of 1996." *Journal of Black Studies* 39 (6):962–73.

Brown-Collier, Elba K. 1998. "Johnson's great society: Its legacy in the 1990s." *Review of Social Economy* 56 (3):259–76.

Brown, Steven R. 1970. "Consistency and the persistence of ideology: Some experimental results." *The Public Opinion Quarterly* 34 (1):60–8.

Brown, Steven R., and Richard W. Taylor. 1972. "Perspective in concept formation." *Social Science Quarterly* 52 (4):852–60.

Brown, W. O. 1931. "The nature of race consciousness." *Social Forces* 10 (1):90–7.

Browning, Harley L., Sally C. Lopreato, and Dudley L. Poston, Jr. 1973. "Income and veteran status: Variations among Mexican Americans, Blacks and Anglos." *American Sociological Review* 38 (1):74–85.

Burk, James, and Evelyn Espinoza. "Race relations within the US military." *Annual Review of Sociology* 38:401–22.

Burley, Dan. 1947. "Confidentially yours': The church takes over the NNL." *New York Amsterdam News* January 11, 1947, 10.

Burns, Nancy, Donald R. Kinder, Steven J. Rosenstone, Virginia Sapiro, and Studies National Election. 2008. "American National Election Study, 2000: Pre- and Post-Election Survey."

Calabresi, Massimo. 2014. "Why a medical examiner called Eric Garner's death a 'homicide'." *Time*, December 4.

Calhoun-Brown, Allison. 1996. "African American churches and political mobilization: The psychological impact of organizational resources." *The Journal of Politics* 58 (4):935–53.

Callegaro, Mario, and Charles DiSogra. 2008a. "Computing response metrics for online panels." *Public Opinion Quarterly* 72 (5):1008–32

—. 2008b. "Computing response metrics for online panels." *Public Opinion Quarterly* 72 (5):1008–32.

Campbell, Angus, Philip Converse, Warren Miller, and Donald Stokes. 1960. *The American Voter*. New York: Wiley.

Carmichael, Stokely, and Charles V. Hamilton. 1967. *Black Power: The Politics of Liberation in America*. New York: Vintage Books.

Carmines, Edward G., Michael J. Ensley, and Michael W. Wagner. 2012. "Who fits the left-fight divide? Partisan polarization in the American electorate." *American Behavioral Scientist* 56 (12):1631–53.

Carmines, Edward G., and Harold W. Stanley. 1992. "The transformation of the New Deal party system: Social groups, political ideology, and changing partisanship among northern Whites, 1972–1988." *Political Behavior* 14 (3): 213–37.

Carmines, Edward G., and James A. Stimson. 1981. "Issue evolution, population replacement, and normal partisan change." *The American Political Science Review* 75 (1):107–18.

—. 1989. *Issue Evolution*. Princeton: Princeton University Press.

Carroll, John B. 1961. "The nature of the data, or how to choose a correlation coefficient." *Psychometrika* 26 (4):347–72.

Carroll, Susan J. 1999. "The disempowerment of the gender gap: Soccer moms and the 1996 elections." *PS: Political Science and Politics* 32 (1):7–11.

Carson, Ben. 2015. Presidential campaign announcement, May 4, 2015, at Detroit, MI.

Chang, Pauline J. 2004. "African Methodist Episcopal Church rejects gay "marriage" blessing rights." *The Christian Post*, July 8, 2004.

"Changing attitudes on gay marriage." 2015. In *Religion and Public Life*. Washington, DC: Pew Research Center.

Childress, Sarah. 2013. "With Voting Rights Act out, states push voter ID laws." *Frontline*: PBS, June 26.

Chong, Dennis, and Reuel Rogers. 2005. "Racial solidarity and political participation." *Political Behavior* 27 (4):347–74.

Clemetson, Lynette. 2004. "Both sides court Black churches in the battle over gay marriage." *The New York Times*, March 1, 2004.

"Clergywomen." 1877. *The New York Times*, July 8, 1877, 6.

Cohen, Cathy J. 1999. *The Boundaries of Blackness: AIDS and the Breakdown of Black Politics*. Chicago: University of Chicago Press.

—. 2004. "Deviance as resistance: A new research agenda for the study of Black politics." *Du Bois Review: Social Science Research on Race* 1 (1):27–45.

Cohen, Cathy J., and Michael C. Dawson. 1993. "Neighborhood poverty and African-American politics." *American Political Science Review* 87 (2):286–302.

Collins, Patricia Hill. 2004. *Black Sexual Politics: African Americans, Gender, and the New Racism*. New York: Routledge.

Collins, Randall. 1993. "Liberals and conservatives, religious and political: A conjuncture of modern history." *Sociology of Religion* 54 (2):127–46.

Collins, Sharon M. 1983. "The making of the Black middle class." *Social Problems* 30 (4):369–82.

Collins, William J. 2000. "African-American economic mobility in the 1940s: A portrait from the Palmer Survey." *The Journal of Economic History*:756–81.

Comrey, Andrew L., and John A. Newmeyer. 1965. "Measurement of radicalism-conservatism." *Journal of Social Psychology* 67 (2):357–69.

Condie, J. Spencer, and James W. Christiansen. 1977. "An indirect technique for the measurement of changes in Black identity." *Phylon* 38 (1):46–54.

Cone, James H. 1969. *Black Theology and Black Power*. New York,: Seabury Press.

—. 1970. "Black consciousness and the Black church: A historical-theological interpretation." *Annals of the American Academy of Political and Social Science* 387:49–55.

Conover, Pamela J. 1988. "The role of social groups in political thinking." *British Journal of Political Science* 18:51–76.

Conover, Pamela Johnston, and Stanley Feldman. 1981. "The origins and meaning of liberal/conservative self-identifications." *American Journal of Political Science* 25 (4):617–45.

Converse, Philip. 1964. "The nature of belief systems in mass publics." In *Ideology and Discontent*, ed. David Ernest Apter, London: Free Press of Glencoe.

Cooper, Michael. 2013. "After ruling, states rush to enact voting laws." *The New York Times*, July 6, 2013, A9.

Coser, Lewis A. 1957. "Social conflict and the theory of social change." *The British Journal of Sociology* 8 (3):197–207.

Cross, William E. 1991. *Shades of Black: Diversity in African-American Identity*. Philadelphia: Temple University Press.

Dahl, Robert A. 1961. *Who Governs? Democracy and Power in an American City*. New Haven: Yale University Press.

Danziger, Sheldon, and Peter Gottschalk. 1995. *America Unequal*. Cambridge: Harvard University Press.

Davidson, Chandler. 1992. "The Voting Rights Act: A brief history." In *Controversies in Minority Voting: The Voting Rights Act in Perspective*, ed. Bernard Grofman, and Chandler Davidson. Washington, DC: Brookings Institution.

Dawson, Michael C. 1994. *Behind the Mule: Race and Class in African-American Politics*. Princeton, NJ: Princeton University Press.

—. 2001. *Black Visions: The Roots of Contemporary African-American Political Ideologies*. Chicago: University of Chicago Press.

Delli Carpini, Michael X., and Scott Keeter. 1996. *What Americans Know about Politics and Why It Matters*. New Haven: Yale University Press.

Demo, David H., and Michael Hughes. 1990. "Socialization and racial identity among Black Americans." *Social Psychology Quarterly* 53 (4):364–74.

Desilver, Drew. 2013. *"Black unemployment rate is consistently twice that of Whites."* Washington DC: Pew Research Center.

Dewey, John. 1935. *Liberalism and Social Action*. New York, NY: G. P. Putnam.

Doise, W., G. Csepeli, H.D. Dann, C. Gouge, K. Larsen, and A. Ostell. 1972. "An experimental investigation into the formation of intergroup representations." *European Journal of Social Psychology* 2 (2):202–4.

DOJ. 2015. "*Justice Department announces findings of two civil rights investigations in Ferguson, Missouri.*" Washington, DC: Department of Justice.

Dovidio, John F., Samuel E. Gaertner, Kerry Kawakami, and Gordon Hodson. 2002. "Why can't we just get along? Interpersonal biases and interracial distrust." *Cultural Diversity and Ethnic Minority Psychology* 8 (2):88–102.

Du Bois, W. E. B. 2007 [1899]. *The Philadelphia Negro: A Social Study*. New York, NY: Oxford University Press.

DuBois, W.E.B. 2013 [1903]. *Souls of Black Folk*. 2013 ed: Start Publishing LLC.

Dwyer, Devin. 2012. "Obama targets Black voters in new campaign." In *ABC News*, February 2.

Eisenstadt, Peter. 1999. "Introduction." In *Black Conservatism: Essays in Intellectual and Political History*, ed. Peter Eisenstadt. New York: Garland Publishing, Inc.

Elder, Laurel, and Steven Greene. 2007. "The myth of 'security moms' and 'NASCAR dads': Parenthood, political stereotypes, and the 2004 election." *Social Science Quarterly* 88 (1):1–19.

Ellis, Christopher, and James A. Stimson. 2012. *Ideology in America*. New York: Cambridge University Press.

Ellison, Christopher G., Gabriel A. Acevedo, and Aida I. Ramos-Wada. 2011. "Religion and attitudes toward same-sex marriage among U.S. Latinos." *Social Science Quarterly* 92 (1):35–56.

Erikson, Robert S., Norman R. Luttbeg, and Kent L. Tedin. 1991. *American Public Opinion: Its Origins, Content, and Impact*. 4th edn. New York: Macmillan Publishing Company.

Farmer, Jennifer. 2013. "North Carolina Republican leader admits voting law was designed to hurt Democrats, restrict African-American and student voters." Advancement Project, October 24. www.advancementproject.org

Federico, Christopher M., and Corrie V. Hunt. 2013. "Political information, political involvement, and reliance on ideology in political evaluation." *Political Behavior* 35 (1):89–112.

Feldman, Stanley. 1988. "Structure and consistency in public opinion: The role of core beliefs and values." *American Journal of Political Science* 32 (2):416–40.

Feldman, Stanley, and Christopher Johnston. 2014. "Understanding the determinants of political ideology: Implications of structural complexity." *Political Psychology* 35 (3):337–58.

Feldman, Stanley, and John Zaller. 1992. "The political culture of ambivalence: Ideological responses to the welfare state." *American Journal of Political Science* 36 (1):268–307.

Ferguson, Elizabeth A. 1938. "Race consciousness among American Negroes." *The Journal of Negro Education* 7 (1):32–40.

Field, John O., and Ronald E. Anderson. 1969. "Ideology in the public's conceptualization of the 1964 election." *Public Opinion Quarterly* 33 (3):380–98.

File, Thom, and Sarah Crissey. 2012. "Voting and registration in the election of November 2008." ed. U.S. Census Bureau.

Fiske, Susan T., and Shelley E. Taylor. 1991. *Social Cognition*. 2nd edn. Reading: Addison-Wesley Publishing Company.

"The flood in Tennessee." 1867. *The New York Times*, March 27, 1867, 2.

Foster, Kenneth, Sr. 2010. "African-Americans' activists perceptions of racism and empowerment." In *African-American Political Psychology: Identity, Opinion, and Action in the Post-Civil Rights Era*, ed. Tasha S. Philpot and Ismail K. White. New York: Palgrave Macmillan.

Franklin, John Hope, and Alfred A. Moss, Jr. 1988. *From Slavery to Freedom: A History of Negro Americans*. 6th edn. New York: Alfred A. Knopf, Inc.

Fredrickson, George M. 1981. *White Supremacy: A Comparative Study of American and South African History*. Oxford: Oxford University Press.

Friedman, Barry, and Erin F. Delaney. 2011. "Becoming supreme: The federal foundation of judicial supremacy." *Columbia Law Review* 111 (6):1137–93.

Friedrich, Robert J. 1982. "In defense of multiplicative terms in multiple regression equations." *American Journal of Political Science* 26 (4):797–833.

Frommer, Frederic J. 2008. "Black conservatives conflicted on Obama campaign." In *USA Today*, June 14.

Frymer, Paul. 1999. *Uneasy Alliances: Race and Party Competition in America*. Princeton: Princeton University Press.

Gaines, Kevin Kelly. 1996. *Uplifting the Race: Black Leadership, Politics, and Culture in the Twentieth Century*. Chapel Hill: University of North Carolina Press.

Gallup News Service Poll: Honesty and Ethical Standards in Different Fields, Dec, 2014 [dataset]. USAIPOGNS2014-15, Version 2. Gallup Organization [producer], Storrs, CT: Roper Center for Public Opinion Research, RoperExpress [distributor], accessed June 16, 2015.

Garrow, David J. 1985. "The origins of the Montgomery Bus Boycott." *Southern Changes* 7:21–7.

Gibbons, Arnold, and Dana R. Ulloth. 1982. "The role of the Amsterdam News in New York City's media environment." *Journalism Quarterly* 59 (3):451–5.

Gilens, Martin. 1999. *Why Americans Hate Welfare: Race, Media, and the Politics of Antipoverty Policy*. Chicago: University of Chicago Press.

Glass, Jennifer, and Jerry Jacobs. 2005. "Childhood religious conservatism and adult attainment among Black and White women." *Social Forces* 84 (1):555–79.

Golan, Guy. 2006. "Inter-media agenda setting and global news coverage." *Journalism Studies* 7 (2):323–33.

Goldberg, Chad Alan. 2007. *Citizens and Paupers: Relief, Rights, and Race, from the Freedmen's Bureau to Workfare*. Chicago: University of Chicago Press.

Goodstein, Laurie. 2007. "Episcopal Church rejects demand for a 2nd leadership." *The New York Times*, March 22, 2007, 16.

Gosnell, Harold. 1935. *Negro Politicians*. Chicago: University of Chicago Press.

Granger, Betty. 1957. "Conversation piece: Dateline: Divorce town: USA." *New York Amsterdam News*, February 23, 1957, 8.

Green, Donald, Bradley Palmquist, and Eric Schickler. 2002. *Partisan Hearts and Minds: Political Parties and the Social Identities of Voters*. New Haven: Yale University Press.

Greenblatt, Alan. 2003. "Race in America." *The CQ Researcher* 13 (25):595–603.

Gressman, Eugene. 1952. "The unhappy history of civil rights legislation." *Michigan Law Review* 50 (8):1323–58.

Guinier, Lani. 1994. *The Tyranny of the Majority: Fundamental Fairness in American Democracy*. New York: Free Press.

Gurin, Patricia. 1985. "Women's gender consciousness." *Public Opinion Quarterly* 49:143–63.

Gurin, Patricia, Shirley Hatchett, and James S. Jackson. 1989. *Hope and Independence: Blacks' Response to Electoral and Party Politics*. New York: Russell Sage Foundation.

Gurin, Patricia, Arthur Miller, and Gerald Gurin. 1980. "Stratum identification and consciousness." *Social Psychology Quarterly* 43 (1):30–47.

Hamilton, Charles. 1982. "Measuring Black conservatism." In *State of Black American*, ed. James D. Williams. New York: National Urban League.

Hanks, Lawrence J. 2003. "Civil Rights Organizations and Movements." In *African Americans and Political Participation: A Reference Handbook*, ed. Minion K.C. Morrison. Santa Barbara: ABC-CLIO, Inc.

Harris-Lacewell, Melissa V. 2003. "The heart of the politics of race: Centering Black people in the study of White racial attitudes." *Journal of Black Studies* 34:222–49.

—. 2004. *Barbershops, Bibles, and BET: Everyday Talk and Black Political Thought*. Princeton: Princeton University Press.

Harris, Fredrick C. 1999. *Something Within: Religion in African-American Political Activism*. New York: Oxford University Press.

Hayes, Danny, and Matt Guardino. 2011. "The influence of foreign voices on U.S. public opinion." *American Journal of Political Science* 55 (4): 831–51.

Healy, Patrick. 2008. "Hopefuls differ as they reject gay marriage." *The New York Times*, November 1, 2008, A1.

Hempel, Lynn M., and John P. Bartkowski. 2008. "Scripture, sin and salvation: Theological conservatism reconsidered." *Social Forces* 86 (4):1647–74.

Herbold, Hilary. 1994. "Never a level playing field: Blacks and the G.I. Bill." *The Journal of Blacks in Higher Education* 6:104–8.

Hero, Rodney, F. Chris Garcia, John Garcia, and Harry Pachon. 2000. "Latino participation, partisanship, and office holding." *PS: Political Science and Politics* 33 (3):529–34.

Herzon, Frederick D. 1980. "Ideology, constraint, and public opinion: The case of lawyers." *American Journal of Political Science* 24 (2):233–58.

Hewstone, Miles. 1990. "The 'ultimate attribution error'? A review of the literature on intergroup causal attribution." *European Journal of Social Psychology* 20 (4):311–35.

Higginbotham, A. Leon. 1991. "An open letter to Justice Clarence Thomas from a federal judicial colleague." *The Black Scholar* 22 (1/2):120–5.

Higginbotham, Evelyn Brooks. 1993. *Righteous Discontent: The Women's Movement in the Black Baptist Church, 1880–1920.* Cambridge: Harvard University Press.

Hillygus, D. Sunshine, and Todd Shields. 2008. "Southern discomfort? Regional differences in voter decision making in the 2000 presidential election." *Presidential Studies Quarterly* 38 (3):506–20.

Hine, Darlene Clark. 1989. "Rape and the inner lives of Black women in the Middle West." *Signs* 14 (4):912–20.

Holm, John D., and John P. Robinson. 1978. "Ideological identification and the American voter." *The Public Opinion Quarterly* 42 (2):235–46.

Huddy, Leonie. 2003. "Group identity and political cohesion." *Oxford Handbook of Political Psychology*, ed. David O. Sears, Leonie Huddy and Robert Jervis. New York: Oxford University Press.

Hughey, Matthew W., and Gregory S. Parks. 2014. *The Wrongs of the Right: Language, Race, and the Republican Party in the Age of Obama.* New York: NYU Press.

Huntington, Samuel P. 1957. "Conservatism as an ideology." *American Political Science Review* 51 (2):454–73.

Hutchings, Vincent L. 2003. *Public Opinion and Democratic Accountability: How Citizens Learn about Politics.* Princeton, NJ: Princeton University.

Izadi, Foad, and Hakimeh Saghaye-Biria. 2007. "A discourse analysis of elite American newspaper editorials: The case of Iran's nuclear program." *Journal of Communication Inquiry* 31 (2):140–65.

Jackson, Byran O. 1987. "The effects of racial group consciousness on political mobilization in American cities." *The Western Political Quarterly* 40 (4):631–46.

Jackson, David. 2015. "Poll: Five Republicans tied for first with 10 percent each." *OnPolitics.* McLean, VA: USA Today, May 31.

Jackson, Thomas H., and George E. Marcus. 1975. "Political competence and ideological constraint." *Social Science Research* 4 (2):93–111.

Jacobson, Gary C. 2009. "The 2008 presidential and congressional elections: Anti-Bush referendum and prospects for the Democratic majority." *Political Science Quarterly* 124 (1):1–30.

Jacoby, William G. 1991. "Ideological identification and issue attitudes." *American Journal of Political Science* 35 (1):178–205.

—. 2010. "Policy attitudes, ideology and voting behavior in the 2008 Election." *Electoral Studies* 29 (4):557–68.

Jennings, M. Kent. 1992. "Ideological thinking among mass publics and political elites." *The Public Opinion Quarterly* 56 (4):419–41.

Jones, Jeffey M. 2009. "Conservative Republicans still widely support Bush." *Gallup Poll: Public Opinion 2008*, ed. Alec Gallup and Frank Newport. Lanham: Rowman & Littlefield.

Joseph, Peniel E. 2003. "Dashikis and democracy: Black Studies, student activism, and the Black Power Movement." *The Journal of African American History* 88 (2):182–203.

—. 2009. "The Black Power Movement, democracy, and America in the King years." *The American Historical Review* 114 (4):1001–16.

Jost, John T. 2006. "The end of the end of ideology." *American Psychologist* 61 (7):651–70.

Jost, John T., Christopher M. Federico, and Jaime L. Napier. 2008. "Political ideology: Its structure, functions, and elective affinities." *Annual Review of Psychology* 60 (1):307–37.

Kam, Cindy D. 2005. "Who toes the party line? Cues, values, and individual differences." *Political Behavior* 27 (2):163–82.

Kam, Cindy D., and Robert J. Franzese, Jr. 2007. *Modeling and Interpreting Interactive Hypotheses in Regression Analysis.* Ann Arbor: University of Michigan Press.

Katz, Ellen, Margaret Aisenbrey, Anna Baldwin, Emma Cheuse, and Anna Weisbrodt. 2006. "Documenting discrimination in voting: Judicial findings under Section 2 of the Voting Rights Act since 1982: Final report of the Voting Rights Initiative, University of Michigan Law School." *University of Michigan Journal of Law Reform* 39 (4):643–772.

Kaufmann, Karen M. 2003. "Cracks in the rainbow: Group commonality as a basis for Latino and African-American political coalitions." *Political Research Quarterly* 56 (2):199–210.

Kerlinger, Fred N. 1967. "Social attitudes and their criterial referents: A structural theory." *Psychological Review* 74 (2):110–22.

—. 1984. *Liberalism and Conservatism: The Nature and Structure of Social Attitudes.* Hillsdale, NJ: Lawrence Erlbaum Associates, Publishers.

Kerr, Willard A. 1952. "Untangling the liberalism-conservatism continuum." *Journal of Social Psychology* 35 (1):111–25.

Kevles, Daniel J. 1997. "A culture of risk." *The New York Times*, May 25, 1997, BR8.

Killian, Lewis M. 1981. "Black power and White reactions: The revitalization of race-thinking in the United States." *Annals of the American Academy of Political and Social Science* 454:42–54.

Kilson, Martin. 1993. "Anatomy of Black conservatism." *Transition* 59:4–19.

Kinder, Donald R. 1983. "Diversity and complexity in American public opinion." In *Political Science: The State of the Discipline*, ed. Finifter, Ada W. Washington, DC: American Political Science Association.

Kinder, Donald R., and Lynn M. Sanders. 1996. *Divided by Color: Racial Politics and Democratic Ideals.* Chicago: University of Chicago Press.

Kinder, Donald R., and Nicholas Winter. 2001. "Exploring the racial divide: Blacks, Whites, and opinion on national policy." *American Journal of Political Science* 45 (2):439–53.

Kinder, Donald. R., and Allison Dale Riddle. 2012. *The End of Race?: Obama, 2008, and Racial Politics in America.* New Haven: Yale University Press.

Klinkner, Philip A., and Rogers M. Smith. 1999. *The Unsteady March: The Rise and Decline of Racial Equality in America.* Chicago: University of Chicago Press.

Knight, Kathleen. 1985. "Ideology in the 1980 election: Ideological sophistication does matter." *The Journal of Politics* 47 (3):828–53.

Knoke, David. 1979. "Stratification and the dimensions of American political orientations." *American Journal of Political Science* 23 (4):772–91.

Knuckey, Jonathan. 2012. "The "Palin Effect" in the 2008 U.S. presidential election." *Political Research Quarterly* 65 (2):275–89.

Krock, Arthur. 1937. "In Washington." *The New York Times*, August 5, 1937, 22.

Krysan, Maria, Mick P. Couper, Reynolds Farley, and Tyrone A. Forman. 2009. "Does race matter in neighborhood preferences? Results from a video experiment." *American Journal of Sociology* 115 (2):527–59.

Krysan, Maria, and Reynolds Farley. 2002. "The residential preferences of Blacks: Do they explain persistent segregation?" *Social Forces* 80 (3):937–80.

Lane, Robert. 1962. *Political Ideology: Why the American Common Man Believes What He Does*. New York: Free Press of Glencoe.

Lansing, Paul. 1976. "An historical review of the legal status of Blacks in the United States." *The Comparative and International Law Journal of Southern Africa* 9 (2):211–25.

Layman, Geoffrey C., and Thomas M. Carsey. 2002. "Party polarization and "Conflict Extension" in the American electorate." *American Journal of Political Science* 46 (4):786–802.

Lazarsfeld, Paul Felix, Bernard Berelson, and Hazel Gaudet. 1948. *The People's Choice: How the Voter Makes Up His Mind in a Presidential Campaign*. [2nd]. ed. New York: Columbia University Press.

Leonardo, Micaela Di. 2012. "Grown folks radio: U.S. election politics and a "hidden" Black counterpublic." *American Ethnologist* 39 (4):661–72.

Lerner, Gerda. 1974. "Early community work of Black club women." *The Journal of Negro History* 59 (2):158–67.

Levendusky, Matthew. 2010. *The Partisan Sort: How Liberals Became Democrats and Conservatives Became Republicans*. Chicago: University of Chicago Press.

Levenstein, Lisa. 2006. "Revisiting the roots of 1960s civil rights activism: Class and gender in 'Up South'." *The Pennsylvania Magazine of History and Biography* 130 (4):388–92.

Levitan, Sar A., and Robert Taggart. 1976. "The Great Society did succeed." *Political Science Quarterly* 91 (4):601–18.

Levitin, Teresa E., and Warren E. Miller. 1979. "Ideological interpretations of presidential elections." *American Political Science Review* 73 (3):751–71.

Lewis, Angela K. 2013. *Conservatism in the Black Community: To the Right and Misunderstood*. New York: Routledge.

Lewis, John. 2015. "The unfinished work of Selma." *Pass the Mic* 2015 (March 12, 2015).

Liasson, Mara. 2012. "Obama takes new approach to Black voters for 2012." In *NPR*: National Public Radio, February 22.

Liebelson, Dana, and Ryan J. Reilly. 2014. "Feds find shocking, systemic brutality, incompetence in Cleveland Police Department." In *Huffington Post*, December 4.

Lincoln, C. Eric, and Lawrence H. Mamiya. 1990. *The Black Church in the African-American Experience*. Durham: Duke University Press.

Logan, John R., Brian J. Stults, and Reynolds Farley. 2004. "Segregation of minorities in the metropolis: Two decades of change." *Demography* 41 (1):1–22.

Long, J. Scott, and Jeremy Freese. 2014. *Regression Models for Categorical Dependent Variables Using Stata.* 3rd ed. College Station, TX: Stata Press Publication, StataCorp LP.

Love, David A. 2014. "Eric Garner proves body cameras won't save Black men." In *The Grio,* December 3.

Lowe, Frederick H. 2011. "Justice Department blocks South Carolina's photo ID law." In *The North Star News & Analysis,* December 29.

Lupia, Arthur. 1994. "Shortcuts versus encyclopedias: Information and voting behavior in California insurance reform elections." *American Political Science Review* 88:63–76.

Lupia, Arthur, and Mathew D. McCubbins. 1998. *The Democratic Dilemma: Can Citizens Learn What They Need to Know?* New York: Cambridge University Press.

Luskin, Robert C. 1990. "Explaining political sophistication." *Political Behavior* 12:331–61.

Luttbeg, Norman R., and Michael M. Gant. 1985. "The failure of liberal/conservative ideology as a cognitive structure." *Public Opinion Quarterly* 49 (1):80–93.

Lyons, William, and John M. Scheb. 1992. "Ideology and candidate evaluation in the 1984 and 1988 presidential elections." *Journal of Politics* 54 (2):573–84.

Mack, Connie. 1987. "Freedom and an American death in Nicaragua." *The New York Times,* May 28, 1987.

Mandelbaum, Michael, and William Schneider. 1978. "The new internationalisms." *International Security* 2 (3):81–98.

Margo, Robert A. 1990. *Race and Schooling in the South, 1880–1950: An Economic History.* Chicago: University of Chicago Press.

Markus, Hazel. 1977. "Self-schemata and processing information about the self." *Journal of Personality and Social Psychology* 35 (2):63–78.

—. 1983. "Self-knowledge: An expanded view." *Journal of Personality* 51 (3): 543–65.

Massey, Douglas S., and Nancy A. Denton. 1993. *American Apartheid: Segregation and the Making of the Underclass.* Cambridge: Harvard University Press.

McAdam, Douglas. 1982. *Political Processes and the Development of Black Insurgency, 1930–1970.* Chicago: University of Chicago Press.

McClain, Paula D., Jessica D. Johnson Carew, Eugene Walton, and Candis S. Watts. 2009. "Group membership, group identity, and group consciousness: Measures of racial identity in American politics?" *Annual Review of Political Science* 12 (1):471–85.

McClain, Paula D., and Steven C. Tauber. 2010. *American Government in Black and White.* Boulder: Paradigm Publishers.

McClerking, Harwood K. 2001. *We Are In This Together: The Origins and Maintenance of Black Common Fate Perception,* Department of Political Science, University of Michigan, Ann Arbor.

McDaniel, Eric L. 2008. *Politics in the Pews: The Political Mobilization of Black Churches.* Ann Arbor: University of Michigan Press.

McDaniel, Eric L., and Christopher G. Ellison. 2008. "God's party? Race, religion, and partisanship over time." *Political Research Quarterly* 61 (2):180–91.

McGuire, William J., and Alice Padawer-Singer. 1976. "Trait salience in the spontaneous self-concept." *Journal of Personality and Social Psychology* 33 (6):743–54.

Mendelberg, Tali. 2005. "Bringing the group back into political psychology: Erik H. Erikson Early Career Award Address." *Political Psychology* 26 (4):637–50.

Miller, Arthur, Patricia Gurin, Gerald Gurin, and O. Malanchuk. 1981. "Group consciousness and political participation." *American Journal of Political Science* 25:495–511.

Modell, John, Marc Goulden, and Sigurdur Magnusson. 1989. "World War II in the lives of Black Americans: Some findings and interpretation." *The Journal of American History* 76 (3):838–48.

Moody, Chris. 2014. "Inside the push to draft Ben Carson for president." In *CNN*, December 22. www.cnn.com.

Morris, Aldon D. 1984. *The Origins of the Civil Rights Movement: Black Communities Organizing for Change*. New York: Free Press.

Morton, D. Winsberg. 1985. "Flight from the ghetto: The migration of middle class and highly educated Blacks into White urban neighborhoods." *American Journal of Economics and Sociology* 44 (4):411–21.

Moskos, Charles C., Jr. 1973. "The American Dilemma in uniform: Race in the armed forces." *Annals of the American Academy of Political and Social Science* 406:94–106.

Muller, Jerry Z., ed. 1997. *Conservatism: An Anthology of Social and Political Thought from David Hume to Present*. Princeton NJ: Princeton University Press.

Murray, Paul T. 1971. "Blacks and the draft: A history of institutional racism." *Journal of Black Studies* 2 (1):57–76.

Myrdal, Gunnar. 1944. *An American Dilemma: The Negro Problem and Modern Democracy*. New Brunswick NJ: Transaction Publishers.

NAACP. 2013. "New U.S. Census report on Black voter turnout reflects NAACP efforts."

Nahmod, Sheldon H. 2013. "Section 1983 is born: The interlocking Supreme Court stories of Tenney and Monroe " *Lewis & Clark Law Review* 17 (4): 1019–62.

Nalty, Bernard C. 1986. *Strength for the Fight: A History of Black Americans in the Military*. New York: Free Press.

NATIONAL BLACK POLITICS STUDY, 1993 [Computer file] ICPSR version. Chicago, IL: University of Chicago/Detroit, MI: Wayne State University/Ann Arbor, MI: University of Michigan [producers], 1994.

National Election Pool General Election Exit Polls, 2004. Inter-university Consortium for Political and Social Research (ICPSR) [distributor].

Newman, Rick. 2015. "Here's where Ben Carson gets his campaign money." In *Yahoo! Finance*, May 4.

"News of the week." 1967. *New York Amsterdam News*, August 12, 1967, 2.

Nichols, John. 2013. "How voter backlash against voter supression is changing our politics." In *The Nation*, April 29.

Nie, Norman H., and Kristi Andersen. 1974. "Mass belief systems revisited: Political change and attitude structure." *The Journal of Politics* 36 (3):540–91.

Nie, Norman H., Sidney Verba, and John R. Petrocik. 1979. *The Changing American Voter*. Cambridge, MA: Harvard University Press.

Nielsen, Kai. 1972. "Against moral conservativism." *Ethics* 82 (3):219–31.

O'Kelly, Charlotte G. 1982. "Black newspapers and the Black protest movement: Their historical relationship, 1827–1945." *Phylon* 43 (1):1–14.

Obama, Barack H. "Transcript: Robin Roberts ABC News interview with President Obama." *ABC News*. ABC, aired May 9, 2012. Transcript.

Onkst, David H. 1998. "'First a Negro … incidentally a veteran': Black World War Two veterans and the G. I. Bill of Rights in the Deep South, 1944–1948." *Journal of Social History* 31 (3):517–43.

Page, Clarence. 1996. *Showing My Color: Impolite Essays on Race and Identity*. New York: Harper-Collins.

Parker, Christopher S. 2009. *Fighting for Democracy: Black Veterans and the Struggle Against White Supremacy in the Postwar South*. Princeton NJ: Princeton University Press.

Pattillo, Mary E. 2007. *Black on the Block: The Politics of Race and Class in the City*. Chicago: University of Chicago Press.

Phillips, Robert L., Paul J. Andrisani, Thomas N. Daymont, and Curtis L. Gilroy. 1992. "The economic returns to military service: Race-ethnic differences." *Social Science Quarterly* 73 (2):340–59.

Philpot, Tasha S. 2007. *Race, Republicans, and the Return of the Party of Lincoln*. Ann Arbor: University of Michigan Press.

Philpot, Tasha S., Daron R. Shaw, and Ernest B. McGowen. 2009. "Winning the race: Black voter turnout in the 2008 presidential election." *Public Opinion Quarterly* 73 (5):995–1022.

Philpot, Tasha S., and Hanes Walton, Jr. 2007. "One of our own: Black female candidates and the voters who support them." *American Journal of Political Science* 51 (1):49–62.

—. 2014. "African-American political participation." In *Oxford Handbook of Racial and Ethnic Politics in the United States*, ed. David L. Leal, Taeku Lee and Mark Sawyer. Oxford: Oxford University Press.

Pierce, John C. 1970. "Party identification and the changing role of ideology in American politics." *Midwest Journal of Political Science* 14 (1):25–42.

Pitts, Steven. 2011. *"Research Brief: Black Workers and the Public Sector"*. Berkeley: University of California, Berkeley Center for Labor Research and Education.

Pohlmann, Marcus D. 1999. *Black Politics in Conservative America*. 2nd edn. New York: Longman.

Poole, Keith T., and Howard Rosenthal. 1997. *Congress: A Political-Economic History of Roll Call Voting*. New York: Oxford University Press.

Popp, Elizabeth, and Thomas J. Rudolph. 2011. "A tale of two ideologies: Explaining public support for economic interventions." *The Journal of Politics* 73 (3):808–20.

Powell, Adam Clayton, Jr. 1937a. "Soap box." *New York Amsterdam News*, November 6, 1937, 11.

—. 1937b. "Soap box." *New York Amsterdam News*, October 23, 1937, 13.

Powell, Colin. 2012. "Colin Powell endorses Barack Obama for president." *CBS This Morning*, October 25.

—. "January 13: Colin Powell, Cory Booker, Haley Barbour, Mike Murphy, Andrea Mitchell." *Meet the Press*. NBC, aired January 13, 2013. Transcript.

Preston, Julia, and Fernanda Santos. 2012. "A record Latino turnout, solidly backing Obama." *The New York Times*, November 8, 2012, P13.

Pride, Armistead Scott, and Clint C. Wilson. 1997. *A History of the Black Press*. Washington DC: Howard University Press.

Quadagno, Jill S. 1994. *The Color of Welfare: How Racism Undermined the War on Poverty*. New York: Oxford University Press.

Rabbie, Jacob M., and Murray Horowitz. 1969. "Arousal of ingroup-outgroup bias by a chance win or loss." *Journal of Personality and Social Psychology* 13 (3):269–77.

Raboteau, Albert J. 2004. *Slave Religion: The "Invisible Institution" in the Antebellum South*. Oxford: Oxford University Press, USA.

Radcliff, Benjamin. 1993. "The structure of voter preferences." *The Journal of Politics* 55 (3):714–9.

Ranney, Austin. 1962. *The Doctrine of Responsible Party Government*. Urbana: University of Illinois.

Rapoport, Ronald B. 1997. "Partisanship change in a candidate-centered era." *Journal of Politics* 59 (1):185–99.

Reese, Laura A., and Ronald E. Brown. 1995. "The effects of religious messages on racial identity and system blame among African Americans." *Journal of Politics* 57 (1):24–43.

Reid, Joy-Ann. 2012. "How voter suppression backfired on the GOP." In *The Grio*, November 9.

Reiman, Jeffrey H. 1997. *Critical Moral Liberalism: Theory and Practice*. Lanham: Rowman & Littlefield.

Robinson, John P., and John A. Fleishman. 1988. "A report: Ideological identification: Trends and interpretations of the liberal-conservative balance." *The Public Opinion Quarterly* 52 (1):134–45.

Rogers, Charles E. 1997. "In 'Butterfly' Mariah Carey spreads hip-hop like 'Honey'." *New York Amsterdam News*, December 4, 1997, 23.

Rohde, David W. 1991. *Parties and Leaders in the Postreform House*. Chicago: University Of Chicago Press.

Rosenstone, Steven J., Donald R. Kinder, Warren E. Miller, and Studies National Election. 1999. "American National Election Study, 1994: Post-Election Survey [Enhanced with 1992 and 1993 Data]."

Rosenstone, Steven J., Donald R. Kinder, Warren E. Miller, and Studies National Election Studies. University of Michigan. Center for Political. 2005. "American National Election Study, 1996: Pre- and Post-Election Survey."

Rubio, Philip F. 2010. *There's Always Work at the Post Office: African American Postal Workers and the Fight for Jobs, Justice, and Equality*. Chapel Hill: University of North Carolina Press.

Rucker, Philip. 2012. "Mitt Romney met with boos in NAACP speech." *The Washington Post*, July 11.

Rutenberg, Jim. 2015. "How do you solve a problem like Ben Carson?" *The New York Times Magazine*, March 22, 2015, MM44.

Sabato, Larry J. 2013. "The Obama encore that broke some rules." In *Barack Obama and the New America: The 2012 Election and the Changing Face of Politics*, ed. Larry J. Sabato, Lanham MD: Rowman & Littlefield.

Sahgal, Neha, and Greg Smith. 2009. "*A religious portrait of African-Americans.*" Washington, DC: The Pew Forum on Religion and Public Life.

Samuels, Robert. 2015. "As Ben Carson bashes Obama, many Blacks see a hero's legacy fade." In *Washington Post*, May 2. Washington, DC.

Sanders, Arthur. 1986. "The meaning of liberalism and conservatism." *Polity* 19 (1):123–35.

Sapiro, Virginia, Steven J. Rosenstone, and Studies National Election. 2000. "American National Election Study, 1998: Post-Election Survey."

Scheepers, Peer, and Frans Van Der Slik. 1998. "Religion and attitudes on moral issues: Effects of individual, spouse and parental characteristics." *Journal for the Scientific Study of Religion* 37 (4):678–91.

Schuman, Howard, Charlotte Steeh, Lawrence Bobo, and Maria Krysan. 1997. *Racial Attitudes in America: Trends and Interpretations*. Revised Edition ed. Cambridge: Harvard University Press.

Sears, David O., and Victoria Savalei. 2006. "The political color line in America: Many 'Peoples of Color' or Black exceptionalism?" *Political Psychology* 27 (6):895–924.

Segura, Gary M. 2012. "Latino public opinion & realigning the American electorate." *Daedalus* 141 (4):98–113.

Seltzer, Richard, and Robert C. Smith. 1985. "Race and ideology: A research note measuring liberalism and conservatism in Black America." *Phylon* 46 (2):98–105.

Shapot, Marshall S. 1965. "Constitutional tort: Monroe v. Pape, and the frontiers beyond." *Northwestern University Law Review* 60 (3):277–329.

Shaw, Stephanie J. 1991. "Black club women and the creation of the National Association of Colored Women." *Journal of Women's History* 3 (2):11–25.

Sherif, Muzafer, and Carolyn W. Sherif. 1966. *Groups in Harmony and Tension: An Integration of Studies on Intergroup Relations*. New York: Octagon Books, Inc.

Sidanius, Jim, and Felicia Pratto. 1999. *Social Dominance: An Intergroup Theory of Social Hierarchy and Oppression*. New York: Cambridge University Press.

Sigelman, Lee, Timothy Bledsoe, Susan Welch, and Michael W. Combs. 1996. "Making contact? Black-White social interaction in an urban setting." *American Journal of Sociology* 101 (5):1306–32.

Sigelman, Lee, and James S. Todd. 1992. "Clarence Thomas, Black pluralism, and civil rights policy." *Political Science Quarterly* 107 (2):231–48.

Simpson, Andrea Y. 1998. *The Tie That Binds: Identity and Political Attitudes in the Post-Civil Rights Generation*. New York: New York University Press.

Singer, L. 1962. "Ethnogenesis and Negro-Americans today." *Social Research* 29 (4):419–30.

Skocpol, Theda, and Lawrence R. Jacobs. 2012. "Accomplished and embattled: Understanding Obama's presidency." *Political Science Quarterly* 127 (1):1–24.

Smith, Catherine E. 2003. "(Un)masking race-based intracorporate conspiracies under the Ku Klux Klan Act." *Virginia Journal of Social Policy and the Law* 11 (2):129–75.

Smith, Robert C. 1981. "Black power and the transformation from protest to policies." *Political Science Quarterly* 96 (3):431–43.

Smith, Sherri. 2002. "The individual ethos: A defining characteristic of contemporary black conservatism." In *Dimensions of Black Conservatism in the United States*, ed. Gayle T. Tate, and Lewis A. Randolph. New York: Palgrave.

Stimson, James A. 1975. "Belief systems: Constraint, complexity, and the 1972 election." *American Journal of Political Science* 19 (3):393–417.

Stricker, Frank. 2007. *Why America Lost the War on Poverty–And How to Win It*. Chapel Hill: University of North Carolina Press.

Sullivan, John L., James E. Piereson, and George E. Marcus. 1978. "Ideological constraint in the mass public: A methodological critique and some new findings." *American Journal of Political Science* 22 (2):233–49.

Sullivan, Sean. 2013. "Ben Carson: Obamacare worst thing 'since slavery' " In *The Washington Post*, October 11. www.washingtonpost.com.

—. 2014. "Why Republicans aren't quite sure how to talk about Ferguson either." *The Washington Post*, April 14.

Sundstrom, William A. 1992. "Last hired, first fired? Unemployment and urban Black workers during the Great Depression." *The Journal of Economic History* 52 (2):415–29.

"Table A-2. Employment status of the civilian population by race, sex, and age." 2014. ed. Statistics, U.S. Bureau of Labor: U.S. Bureau of Labor Statistics.

Tajfel, Henri. 1970. "Experiments in intergroup discrimination." *Scientific American* 223 (5):96–102.

—. 1981. *Human Groups and Social Categories*. New York: Cambridge University Press.

Tajfel, Henri, and John C. Turner. 1979. "An integrative theory of intergroup conflict." In *The Social Psychology of Intergroup Relations*, ed. William G. Austin and Stephen Worchel. Monterey, CA: Brooks/Cole Publishing Company.

Tate, Gayle T., and Lewis A. Randolph, eds. 2002. *Dimensions of Black Conservatism in the United States: Made in America*. New York: Palgrave.

Tate, Katherine. 1993. *From Protest to Politics: The New Black Voters in American Elections*. Cambridge MA: Harvard University Press.

—. 2010. *What's Going On?: Political Incorporation and the Transformation of Black Public Opinion*. Washington, DC: Georgetown University Press.

Taylor, Paul. 2012. "*The growing electoral clout of Blacks is driven by turnout, not demographics.*" Washington, DC: Pew Research Center.

Teachman, Jay D., and Lucky Tedrow. 2008. "Divorce, race, and military service: More than equal pay and equal opportunity." *Journal of Marriage and Family* 70 (4):1030–44.

Tedin, Kent L. 1987. "Political ideology and the vote." In *Research and Micropolitics*, ed. Samuel Long, London: Jai Press, Inc.

Tesler, M., and D. O. Sears. 2010. *Obama's Race: The 2008 Election and the Dream of a Post-Racial America*. Chicago: University of Chicago Press.

Tesler, Michael. 2012. "The spillover of racialization into health care: How President Obama polarized public opinion by racial attitudes and race." *American Journal of Political Science* 56 (3):690–704.

"This week in Congress." 1897. *The New York Times*, January 18, 1897, 7.

"Time Series Cumulative Data File." *American National Election Studies.* [December 31, 2015]. http://electionstudies.org/studypages/anes_timeseries_cdf/anes_timeseries_cdf.htm.

Timm, Jane C. 2015. "From idol to 'sellout': How Ben Carson is losing his legacy." In *MSNBC*, June 8. www.msnbc.com.

Tobin, Maryann. 2012. "Ohio Republican admits voter suppression targets African Americans." In *Allvoices.com*.

Tocqueville, Alexis de. 1835. *Democracy in America*. New York: Bantam Books.

Travis, Shannon. 2013. "Cain: 'Don't call me a Republican'." In *CNN Political Ticker*, April 15. Washington, DC.

Treier, Shawn, and D. Sunshine Hillygus. 2009. "The nature of political ideology in the contemporary electorate." *The Public Opinion Quarterly* 73 (4):679–703.

Turner, Sarah, and John Bound. 2003. "Closing the gap or widening the divide: The effects of the G.I. Bill and World War II on the educational outcomes of Black Americans." *The Journal of Economic History* 63 (1):145–77.

Tuttle, Brad. 2015. "275,000+ free tickets to *Selma* available for students." In *Time*, January 16. time.com.

"U.S.Religious Landscape Survey." 2008. religions.pewforum.org: Pew Forum on Religion & Public Life.

AMERICAN NATIONAL ELECTION STUDY, 2004: PRE- AND POST-ELECTION SURVEY [Computer file] ICPSR04245-v1. Ann Arbor, MI: University of Michigan, Center for Political Studies, American National Election Study [producer], 2004.

Valocchi, Steve. 1994. "The racial basis of capitalism and the state, and the impact of the New Deal on African Americans." *Social Problems* 41 (3): 347–62.

Vandiver, Beverly J., Peony E. Fhagen-Smith, Kevin O. Cokley, and William E. Cross, Jr. 2001. "Cross's nigrescence model: From theory to scale to theory." *Journal of Multicultural Counseling and Development* 29 (3):174–200.

Vercellotti, Timothy, and Paul R. Brewer. 2006. "'To Plead Our Own Cause': Public opinion toward Black and mainstream news media among African Americans." *Journal of Black Studies* 37 (2):231–50.

Wald, Kenneth D., Dennis E. Owen, and Samuel S. Hill, Jr. 1988. "Churches as political communities." *The American Political Science Review* 82 (2):531–48.

Wallsten, Peter. 2008. "Obama bets big on Florida turnout." *Los Angeles Times*, October 17, 2008, A-1.

Walters, Ron. 2007. "Barack Obama and the politics of Blackness." *Journal of Black Studies* 38 (1):7–29.

Walton, Hanes, Jr. 1985. *Invisible Politics: Black Political Behavior*. Albany: State University of New York Press.

—. 2001. "The disenfranchisement of the African American voter in the 2000 presidential election: The silence of the winner and loser." *The Black Scholar* 31 (2):21–4.

Walton, Hanes, Jr., and Robert C. Smith. 2010. *American Politics and the African American Quest for Universal Freedom.* 5th edn. New York: Addison Wesley Longman.

Walton, Hanes, and Robert C. Smith. 2003. *American Politics and the African American Quest for Universal Freedom.* 2nd ed. New York: Longman Publishers.

—. 2014. *American Politics and the African American Quest for Universal Freedom.* 7th edn. New York: Longman.

Warren, Nagueyalti. 1990. "Pan-African cultural movements: From Baraka to Karenga." *The Journal of Negro History* 75 (1/2):16–28.

Watson, Elwood. 1998. "Guess what came to American politics?–Contemporary Black conservatism." *Journal of Black Studies* 29 (1):73–92.

"Weekly Topics." 1937. *New York Amsterdam News,* September 11, 1937, 6.

Weinberg, Louise. 1991. "The Monroe mystery solved: Beyond the "unhappy history" theory of civil rights litigation." *Brigham Young University Law Review* 1991 (2):737–65.

Weiner, Rachel. 2015. "Black Republicans lament state of the GOP." *The Washington Post,* November, 17, 2015.

Weiss, Nancy J. 1983. *Farewell to the Party of Lincoln: Black Politics in the Age of FDR.* Princeton: Princeton University Press.

Weissberg, Robert. 2001. "Democratic political competence: Clearing the underbrush and a controversial proposal." *Political Behavior* 23 (3):257–84.

West, Cornel. 1993. *Race Matters.* New York: Vintage Press.

Weston, M. Moran. 1947. "Labor forum." *New York Amsterdam News,* December 20, 1947, 10.

White, E. Frances. 2001. *Dark Continent of Our Bodies: Black Feminism and the Politics of Respectability.* Philadelphia: Temple University Press.

White, Ismail K. 2007. "When race matters and when it doesn't: Racial group differences in response to racial cues." *American Political Science Review* 101 (2):339–54.

Wilkins, Roy. 1937. "Watchtower." *New York Amsterdam News,* July 19, 1937, 13.

Williams, Richard. 2012. "Using the margins command to estimate and interpret adjusted predictions and marginal effects." *The Stata Journal* 12 (2):308–31.

Wilson, William J. 1996. *When Work Disappears: The world of the New Urban Poor.* 1st ed. New York: Knopf.

Wilson, William Julius. 2008. "The political and economic forces shaping concentrated poverty." *Political Science Quarterly* 123 (4):555–71.

Winant, Howard. 2009. "Just do it: Notes on politics and race at the dawn of the Obama presidency." *Du Bois Review: Social Science Research on Race* 6 (1):49–70.

Wolseley, Roland Edgar. 1990. *The Black Press, U.S.A.* 2nd ed. Ames: Iowa State University Press.

Woodward, C. Vann. 1955. *The Strange Career of Jim Crow.* New York: Oxford University Press.

Worrell, Frank C., William E. Cross, Jr., and Beverly J. Vandiver. 2001. "Nigrescence theory: Current status and challenges for the future." *Journal of Multicultural Counseling and Development* 29 (3):201–13.

Zaller, John. 1992. *The Nature and Origins of Mass Opinion.* Cambridge: Cambridge University Press.

Zeleny, Jeff. 2008. "Saying race is no barrier, Obama still courts Blacks." *The New York Times*, January 2, 2008.

Zschirnt, Simon. 2011. "The origins & meaning of liberal/conservative self-identifications revisited." *Political Behavior* 33 (4):685–701.

Index

CPSIA information can be obtained
at www.ICGtesting.com
Printed in the USA
LVHW112136240821
696039LV00018B/155

9 781316 615959